# Rowinataworu Luhchi Yoroni

## *Tunica Language Textbook*

By

Kuhpani Yoyani Luhchi Yoroni

*The Tunica Language Working Group*

**Authors**

Andrew Abdalian, Craig Alcantara, Patricia Anderson, John Barbry, Meg Harvey, Raina Heaton, Mary Kate Kelly, Judith M. Maxwell, Brett C. Nelson, Donna Pierite, Elisabeth Pierite, Mackenzie Walters, Nathan A. Wendte

**Collaborators**

Jarrette K. Allen, Lauren Beard, Joyce Bennett, Amelia Cairns, Shayra Burgos García, Virginia Geddie, Tom Lewis, Brenda Lintinger, Ryan Lopez, Jean-Luc Pierite, Teyanna Pierite-Simon, Dave Prine, Lisa Sprowls, David Watt, Tyler Whitaker

**Illustrators**

Lydia Barbry, Rolando Cuma Chávez, Carol Hendrickson, Jean-Luc Pierite, Gail Quick

**Proofreaders**

Adebimpe Adegbite, Sofia Benedict, Holly Clark, Drew McGowan, Dave Prine

**Recorded Voices**

Sidney Barbry, Juston Broussard, Summer LeLeux, Ryan Lopez, Elisabeth Pierite, Teyanna Pierite-Simon

This book is a publication of

Indiana University Press
Office of Scholarly Publishing
Herman B Wells Library 350
1320 East 10th Street
Bloomington, Indiana 47405 USA

iupress.org



Manufactured in the United States of America

Cataloging information is available from the Library of Congress.

ISBN 978-0-253-06632-9 (paperback)
ISBN 978-0-253-06633-6 (ebook)

# Table of Contents

# Foreword

In 1964, Tunica-Biloxi tribal Chief Joseph Alcide Pierite, Sr. sent a letter to linguist Mary Haas requesting a copy of her *Tunica Dictionary* and the recordings she made in the 1930s of the last known fluent speaker and former chief, Sesostrie Youchigant (APS MS 94, Personal and Professional Papers):

> P.O. Box 101
> Marksville, La
> October 17, 1964
>
> Dear Dr. Haas:
>
> I am the chief of the Tunica Indians living on a small reservation south of Marksville. We are a small tribe of Indians. It was understood you were here to visit our tribe in the 1930s. The chief of our tribe at this time was Sam Young, or Sesostrie Youchicant [Youchigant]. He had died a few years ago. We have had several elected chief [*sic*] since this time. Now I am the chief of the Tunica Indians. The language of my people has been lost. Actually, there are only a few of my people, including myself which know how to speak our language a little. It was understood that Dr. Swanston [Swanton] had written the language about fifty-five years ago, then, you came along in the 1930s and wrote both language and songs of our tribe. I would appreciate it very much to have you write to me and tell as to where I may get the book of our language and songs. We would like the younger ones of our tribe to learn the language and songs. Please write real soon.
>
> Yours truly,
>
> Chief Joe Pierite

Language preservation and revitalization has long been a concern for the Tunica-Biloxi Tribe of Louisiana. As seen in Chief Pierite's letter, parents and elders have often encouraged our children to learn our language and culture. Until her death in 1915, Sesostrie Youchigant's mother, Arsène Chiki, spoke to her children in Tunica, and Sesostrie Youchigant recalled the children would answer in French. Referring to Tunica, she would say, "That's not good. You better study you language" (APS MS 94, Notebook 2:81).

In line with this long tradition, we present **Rowinataworu Luhchi Yoroni** *Tunica Language Textbook* (henceforth **Rowinataworu**). This book is the first Tunica grammar of its kind. Each chapter is written in a manner that makes Tunica accessible for beginning learners, and provides a means for learners to quickly internalize and utilize Tunica in everyday contexts. Tunica dialogues and practice activities facilitate reading, writing, and speaking in the language. Upon completion of the **Rowinataworu**, learners will be able to conduct everyday conversations in Tunica with family and friends at home and around the community. **Rowinataworu** affords Tunica learners the opportunity to share family stories and continue an oral tradition that had long been interrupted. **Rowinataworu** provides the Tunica learner historical documentation of the language and culture in **Tetimili** (cultural) vignettes and at the same time illustrates modern day language use through neologisms for updated concepts and ever-changing contexts. It is our hope that **Rowinataworu** will inspire the tribal community—children and adults alike—to take interest and pride in our heritage.

# Background

## Tunica history

The first mention of the Tunica people in European records comes from El Inca Garcilaso de la Vega (né Gómez Suárez de Figueroa), chronicler for the Hernando de Soto explorations of the Southeast. Garcilaso notes that when de Soto reached the Mississippi River in 1541, the Tunica people found the large Indian settlement of Quizquiz. A southern outlier of the Mississippian cultural tradition, the town was centered around a series of mounds. While the Tunica men were out working in the cornfields, the Spanish abducted some three hundred women. The Tunica chief rallied an estimated 4,000 men to take back the women, marking the first defeat of de Soto's troops during their incursion into American lands. However, along with the Spaniards came the European plagues of measles and smallpox. The Tunica population was decimated, and over the next 150 years the Tunica people moved southward. Though the settlements were smaller, the Mississippian settlement pattern of plazas and mounds was maintained.

European records indicate that in 1699 the Tunica were living at the confluence of the Arkansas and Mississippi rivers. The Tunica Tribe dominated the salt trade along the Mississippi River and its southern tributaries before the arrival of the Spanish and French. After the European contact, we added horses and European artifacts to our trade network, bringing in horses from New Mexico. The Tunica people continued to move southward, preferentially constructing villages at or near river junctions. We built massive earthen works at Haynes Bluff, near the confluence of the Yazoo and the Mississippi, as well as smaller settlements in the region. From there we moved further south to the confluence of the Red and Mississippi Rivers, where salt could be extracted from the salt dome under the Red River. We established communities at Bloodhound and Angola Farms, and also controlled the Portage of the Cross—an important shortcut for Mississippi River trade—from 1706 to 1731 (Klopotek et al. 2017).

During early colonial occupation, wars with the Europeans and with neighboring tribes, often instigated by the French and English, embroiled the Tunica people and their neighbors. The Tunica Tribe helped the French defeat the Natchez. In 1706, the Chickasaw, abetted by the English, helped drive the Tunica people from the Yazoo confluence (Klopotek et al. 2017). At one point, while the Tunica people were living along the Red River, a delegation of the Natchez and Koroa arrived asking for asylum. The Tunica chief, Cahura Joligo, agreed to receive them if they laid down their arms. The warriors agreed, but on condition that they be allowed to carry them as they entered, so as not to be demeaned in the eyes of their people. Cahura Joligo agreed and sponsored a dance-feast to receive them. After the dance, the Natchez, Koroa, and Chickasaw allies, who had hidden in a nearby canebrake, fell upon their sleeping hosts and killed the chief. The Tunica **nakachɔha** 'war-chief', Brides les Bœufs, rallied the rest of the Tunica people and, after five days and nights of fighting, defeated their assailants.

After this disastrous encounter, the Tunica Tribe moved again, this time to the Trudeau area. Here too we prospered. Tunica households were replete with European goods, utensils, and implements, as well as Native wares. Some of this wealth is known today as the "Tunica Treasure," looted grave goods recovered by the Tunica-Biloxi tribe in 1989 after a long court battle. In 1762, as the French surrendered control of the Mississippi River Valley to Spain, Tunica communities sprang up in the Pointe Coupée area and extended their cooperation to the new Spanish regents. In 1779, the Tunica Tribe answered the call of the Spanish governor, Bernardo de Gálvez y Madrid, to help drive the English out of Baton Rouge. As a reward for their service, Gálvez ceded the Tunica lands on the Avoyelles prairie.

However, when the United States government took over administration of the Louisiana territories, they failed to recognize the Spanish land cession to the Tunica Tribe. For many years they also denied recognition to the Tunica Tribe. In 1938, the Tunica chief Eli Barbry, his sub-chief Horace Pierite, Sr. (representing the Biloxi Tribe), Sam Barbry (Tunica), Clarence Jackson (Choctaw), and Joseph Villemarrette (representing Avoyelles Parish), went to Washington, D.C., to seek official recognition for an amalgamated tribe that included the Tunica Tribe (**Tayoroniku**), the Biloxi Tribe (**Tahalayihku**), the Ofo Tribe (**Tɔshpiku**) and the Avoyel Tribe (**Tashihkaltiniku**). The tribe successfully gained recognition from the state of Louisiana in 1975, and the federal government in 1981, under the leadership of **Tachɔhaku** Earl J. Barbry, Sr.

During the 1970s, 40% of the approximately 200 citizens of the Tunica-Biloxi Tribe lived on or near the reservation and designated tribal lands.[1] As of July 1, 2015, there were 1,257 enrolled Tunica-Biloxi tribal citizens residing throughout the United States and one family in the United Kingdom.[2] The percentage of citizens living on or near tribal lands in Central Louisiana has increased to approximately 42%. The largest concentration of tribal families reside in Avoyelles and Rapides Parishes in Louisiana; the second-largest concentration resides in Harris and Brazoria Counties in Texas; the third-largest concentration resides in Cook County, Illinois.[3] Enrolled citizens are very active in tribal governance, regardless of where they physically reside, regularly returning to the Tunica-Biloxi reservation for events such as the annual Tunica-Biloxi Powwow and Tribal Council meetings.

## Taluhchi Yoroni

*The Tunica language*

**Taluhchi Yoroni**, the Tunica language, is one of the heritage languages of the Tunica-Biloxi Tribe. Sesostrie Youchigant, who was **Tachɔhaku** (Chief), between 1911 and 1921, was considered the last known fluent speaker of Tunica. His parents, Arsène Chiki and Sosthène Youchigant, were married by **Tachɔhaku** Zénon La Joie in the Tunica language. Arsène Chiki spoke to Sesostrie Youchigant in Tunica until her death in 1915. After Sesostrie Youchigant's death in 1948, **Taluhchi Yoroni** was considered dormant, though tribal traditionalists retained fragments of the language and songs up to the present day.

### Documentation

As early as 1886, representatives of the Bureau of American Ethnology created records of the Tunica language. Albert Gatschet documented William Ely Johnson's knowledge of Tunica, and between 1907 and 1910 John R. Swanton documented Tunica with the assistance

[1]United States Department of the Interior (1980). Recommendation and summary of evidence for proposed finding for Federal acknowledgment of the Tunica-Biloxi Indian Tribe of Louisiana pursuant to 25 CFR 54. Washington, DC: Office of Federal Acknowledgement. https://www.bia.gov/as-ia/ofa/001-tunbil-la
[2]Tunica-Biloxi Tribe of Louisiana Office of Tribal Enrollment (2015).
[3]Tunica-Biloxi Tribe of Louisiana Language & Culture Revitalization Program (2015).

of William Ely Johnson and Volsin Chiki. Volsin was Arsène Chiki's brother and Sesostrie Youchigant's uncle. He was **Tachɔhaku** until 1911. In the 1870s, he restored tribal ceremonies and rejuvenated **Hahka Ɔshta**, the Green Corn Ceremony, a tradition central to Tunica-Biloxi culture, and acted as **Tawakaku**, leader of the Green Corn Ceremony. Into his later years, although he was blind, he led **Lawuhara**, the night dances, which persisted until the 1920s in Marksville.

From their work with Johnson and Chiki, Gatschet and Swanton published the following articles:

Gatschet, Albert S. 1889. "Sex-Denoting Nouns in American Languages." Transactions of the American Philological Association (1869–1896) 20: 159–71.

Swanton, John R. 1919. "A Structural and Lexical Comparison of the Tunica, Chitimacha, and Atakapa Languages." Bulletin / Bureau of American Ethnography 68. Washington, D.C.: Government Printing Office.

Swanton, John R. 1921. "The Tunica Language." International Journal of American Linguistics 2 (1/2): 1–39.

These published works are based on Gatschet and Swanton's vast body of unpublished work archived at the National Anthropological Archives. These materials include fieldnotes, texts, comparative vocabulary lists, and a set of approximately 1,700 dictionary slips.

Linguist Mary Haas began to document Sesostrie Youchigant's knowledge of Tunica in 1933 for her doctoral dissertation. Haas worked with Sesostrie Youchigant during the summers of 1933 and 1938. The collaboration between Haas and Sesostrie Youchigant created a large and comprehensive corpus which has been the foundation for all subsequent work on Tunica revitalization (including this textbook). From her work with Sesostrie Youchigant, Haas published a grammar,[4] a sketch grammar,[5] a dictionary,[6] and book of texts (1950), as well as a number of comparative articles looking into possible relationships between Tunica and other languages of the area.

As with Gatschet and Swanton's materials, Haas's manuscript materials dwarf her published work. A more complete version of her grammar (665 pages) and her field notes (13 notebooks) are archived with her papers at the American Philosophical Society, and the audio recordings she made, as well as some other Tunica papers, are archived with the California Language Archive.

[4]Haas, Mary R. 1940. *Tunica*. Vol. IV. Handbook of American Indian Languages. J.J. Augustin.

[5]Haas, Mary R. 1946. "A Grammatical Sketch of Tunica." In *Linguistic Structures of Native America*, edited by Cornelius Osgood, 337–66. Viking Fund Publications in Anthropology 6. Viking Fund.

[6]Haas, Mary R. 1953. *Tunica Dictionary*. University of California Press.

Copies of these documentary materials on Tunica are also available by contacting the Tunica-Biloxi Language & Culture Revitalization Program.

## Regional interactions

Throughout its long documented history, the Tunica language was in contact with a number of Native and European languages. The Tunica people had trade relations with the Biloxi people for many years, and were also in close contact with the Ofo, Avoyel, and Choctaw people. These contacts had an influence on the Tunica language, most notably in the form of words borrowed into Tunica from these other languages. For example, the Biloxi word for black-headed buzzard *exka* is found in Tunica **ɛhka** from Gatschet-Swanton (Haas, 1953). **Chula** from Choctaw for 'fox', *chula*, is found in Tunica word **Chulahipu** 'Fox Dance'. Ofo *añgo fa tcke* (from Dorsey and Swanton, 1912) and Tunica **ɔnrɔwahka** both describe rice as 'white man's corn'. There are also a number of words in Mary Haas's *Tunica Dictionary* identified as coming from Mobilian Jargon, which was a *lingua franca* in the Southeast. For example, Sesostrie Youchigant thought that the Tunica **ɔndetishi** 'milk' came from the Mobilian word for milk, *wakatishi*.

French loan words in Tunica came about following the establishment of the French colony of Louisiana. For example, the three meals of the day in Tunica are words borrowed directly from French: **teshu** from French *déjeuner* (*le petit déjeuner*) 'to eat breakfast', **tini** from French *dîner* 'to eat dinner', and **suhpi** from French *souper* 'to eat supper'. Haas describes **sinku** 'five' in Tunica as possibly from Spanish *cinco*, and **ingrasa** from Spanish *inglés* referring to 'Englishman, Irishman, or American'. The influence of English can be seen in earlier Tunica forms through borrowed translations, such as **owita'ira** 'sweater' (lit. 'sweat-clother'), and translated idioms, such as **tetit'ɛ chu** 'take the highway' (lit. 'get the highway'), or **tahkɔra kali** 'set the table' (lit. 'place the table'). Regardless of their origin, each of these words is considered authentic Tunica, as each follows Tunica sound rules.

Multilingualism was typical for Tunica speakers; it would have been uncommon for a Tunica person to speak only Tunica. Individuals who shared the Tunica language with linguists could speak a variety of languages, including Biloxi, Mobilian, French, and English, in addition to Tunica.

## Wopira

*Revitalization*

The desire to reclaim the Tunica language among the Tunica-Biloxi community continues to this day. In 2010, Council Member Brenda Lintinger reached out to Dr. Judith Maxwell of Tulane University about a partnership with Tulane's linguistics program to revitalize the Tunica language.

Lintinger and tribal citizen John Barbry had devoted a portion of their graduate studies to tribal history, museum, archival management, and Indian education. With a goal to develop and launch a permanent language revitalization program, Barbry and Lintinger developed a structure to make Tunica language resources more accessible. This would enable tribal families to learn the Tunica language and cultural lifeways of their ancestors.

Council Member Lintinger enlisted the participation of Donna and Elisabeth Pierite, whose family had spent many years preserving and revitalizing the language and other cultural traditions. The collective effort of talented tribal and university linguists, along with other professionals assembled over several years, has culminated in this most important book. To all the authors, collaborators, editors, and artists who have worked tirelessly to bring this project to successful completion, **sarahkitiman tikahch sihkyuwahkiti** 'we show gratitude and give them thanks'.

The collaboration of Tulane University and the Tunica-Biloxi Tribe was the driving force that led the tribe to establish the Tunica-Biloxi Language & Culture Revitalization Program (LCRP) in 2014. The joint Tulane-Tunica working group, now known as **Kuhpani Yoyani Luhchi Yoroni**, combines the expertise of tribal leaders, activists, linguists, and students to promote the Tunica language. Tribal teachers work with linguists and students to offer in-person and distance learning classes in Tunica, and to hold immersion camps for tribal youth. The group has also produced children's books, songs, ethnobotanical guides, signage for tribal buildings, and a body of other materials to support Tunica language in a variety of contexts.

In July 2018, the Tunica-Biloxi Tribe received a three-year Administration for Native Americans Native Language Preservation and Maintenance grant. The grant funded fellowships enabling five young Tunica-Biloxi adult apprentices to learn to speak and teach the Tunica language under the guidance of mentors who have studied the language. In addition to their intense study of Tunica, the apprentices are active in the revitalization and preservation of traditional music, dance, folklore, history, and material culture. Apprentices, along with their mentors in the LCRP, have engaged the community through education and practice in traditional culture. These Tunica apprentices have collaborated with LCRP staff and Tulane linguists to create pedagogical tools to sustain preservation of the Tunica language, working to more fully reintegrate the language and culture into community life.

This textbook is the culmination of ten years of collaborative work to revitalize Tunica by at least 80 dedicated individuals. It is our hope that **Rowinataworu Luhchi Yoroni** will stimulate interest in Tunica and help preserve it for generations to come.

# Introduction to the textbook

This textbook provides a comprehensive introduction to all the basics of Tunica that are necessary to begin speaking and reading Tunica. Each chapter follows the same format:

1. A table of contents, giving an overview of the topics covered in the chapter.
2. A **yoluyana** (vocabulary) that introduces the new words in the section.
3. A **yanalepini** (set of dialogues) that models practical conversations that you may apply in your daily routines.
4. A **lutamashu** (grammar) section that explains the new ideas and structures being presented.
5. A **hinu** (practice) section that gives learners an opportunity to practice the new skills they just learned.
6. A **tetimili** (culture) section that teaches Tunica-Biloxi history and culture through entertaining and informative narratives.

Each chapter is composed of one or more topics, so these six elements often appear multiple times within each chapter.

This book is designed to be used on its own, by any learner who may or may not have access to a Tunica class. However, we recommend that readers make use of the other Tunica language resources that are available as a supplement to this textbook. This includes the legacy documentation described in the background section on the language (like Mary Haas's *Tunica Texts*), as well as new tribal resources like the online dictionary.

This textbook is also intended to be used as a supplement to immersion-style language teaching and learning, with a teacher/speaker modeling correct language usage. When such a learning situation is possible, the teacher or teachers (ideally these would be group language presentations, which more closely approximate real language use) present the material in seven stages. These are:

*Step One: Presentation*

Here the teacher or teachers model the forms in naturalistic settings, using full sentences with slow, clear enunciation. The students simply observe, seeing and listening.

*Step Two: Physical response*

The teacher uses simple commands for action to the student. For example, if the lesson is on learning people's names, then the action required would be "Touch the one named Elaine" or "point to the one named Charles." If the lesson is on simple verbs of action, the teacher would just say "dance," "run," "stop." The student response is simply to carry out the actions as directed.

*Step Three:* ***Hon/aha*** *– yes/no questions*

The teacher asks questions using the new vocabulary, framing the questions so that the response can be simply **hon** 'yes' or **aha** 'no'. For example, if the lesson is on names, the questions might be "Is your name Kaden?", "Is her name Elizabeth?", and "Is my name Josh?" Students simply reply with **hon** or **aha**.

*Step Four: Response with known vocabulary*

The teacher uses prompts about the new topic that can be answered using known vocabulary. So if the lesson is on people's names, and the only prior lesson was on greetings, the teacher would say something like "greet the person named Elaine," and "greet me." In response, the student would perform the spoken greeting routine with the designated person. If the lesson is on verbs, the teacher would ask "Who is dancing?" or "Who is singing?" (note that in the textbook, this step is in the second chapter, which builds upon the previous lessons). In response, the student will give the name of the person doing the action.

*Step Five: Response with the target vocabulary*

At this stage, the teacher frames questions so that the response will be the new vocabulary. To again use the naming lesson example, the teacher would ask "What's your name?", "What's his name?", "What's my name?", etc., and the students would respond "My name is Ishmael," "His name is Terrence," "Your name is Legend." If the lesson is on simple actions, the teacher asks a student to do an action, and then asks another student, "What is s/he doing?" Alternatively, the teacher may ask a student to tell another student to perform an action. To increase complexity, the teacher may ask a third student what the acting student is doing.

*Step Six: Practice in small groups*

Students split up into small groups and go over the lesson on their own. The teacher circulates, animating conversation and reinforcing language use.

*Step Seven: Game or activity*

After the lesson is presented, the group comes back together and participates in an all-group game, song, or applied activity. For example, if the lesson was on naming, everyone sits in a circle and does a clapping beat, e.g., from a hand game. One person starts with a chant in time to the beat: "My name is Connie; your name is Francis." Without missing a beat, Francis must reply: "My name is Francis; your name is Thomas." People who lose the beat or miss their speaking turn have to do a penance, some small action, like greeting someone in the circle or counting to ten. Then the game resumes. Hopefully it goes until no one is making mistakes anymore. If the lesson is on simple actions, one can play "Simon says," or in the case of Tunica, **Sesostrieku niku** 'Sesostrie says'.

Just as with the aural-oral methodology, the book presents Tunica as a living, spoken language. The exercises allow the student to practice with new words and new structures. The **Tetimili** sections activate Indigenous models of understanding. The lessons in the book are sequenced to facilitate learning, but the detailed index will allow the student to move back and forth between points of interest. Students will also want to use the digital resources available, including the dictionary app. More information can be found on the Tunica-Biloxi website or by contacting the tribe.

## Basic linguistic features of Tunica, 1880–present

In this section we provide readers with a linguistic overview of Tunica. The goal is to provide the information that a linguist might expect in a typological sketch, and also discuss some of the differences between Tunica as taught in this textbook and Tunica as it appears in the earlier documentation, ca. 1880–1950. Although we do use technical linguistic terminology in describing the language, readers will become familiar with most of these terms in the process of using this textbook, and we have provided the Tunica terms for grammatical concepts where relevant. There is also a glossary of Tunica and English grammatical terms in Appendix C.

Tunica (ISO 639-3: tun) is a language isolate, meaning that it has no known linguistic relatives. However, Tunica does share a number of features common to the languages of the southeastern United States, e.g., the Muskogean languages, Chitimacha, Natchez, Atakapa, Yuchi (also spelled Euchee), Tonkawa, and Biloxi and Ofo (Siouan). Tunica has Subject–

Object–Verb (SOV) basic word order, and there is a strong preference for the verb (**taya**) to be the last element in the phrase. As an SOV language, Tunica also has postpositions, unlike English which has prepositions (e.g., 'home - at' vs. 'at - home'). However, unlike many other SOV languages, Tunica does not have morphological case, where the functions of nouns are explicitly marked on those nouns. Also, like many of the languages of the Southeast, Tunica verbs exhibit active-stative alignment, where the subjects of most intransitive verbs (**taya oni sahku**) are marked in the same way as the subjects of transitive verbs (**taya nachu**), but a lexical class of about forty stative verbs (**taya wana** and 'static' in Haas) have subjects which are marked in the same way as objects of transitive verbs.

Another important feature of Tunica grammar is that there are two ways to cross-reference the subject of an active (non-stative) verb: the use of bound, personal suffixes, or the use of the various auxiliary verbs, which are conjugated and follow the main verb stem. The first strategy is used for habitual and completive aspects, while the latter is used for perfective and durative aspects, as well as to add semantic effects associated with those auxiliary verbs (e.g., 'come while _____ing' or 'go while _____ing'). Only the use of personal suffixes ('endings') is introduced in this book. Syntactically, certain postfixes (e.g., the future **-k'ahcha**) can only be attached to stems with bound, completive suffixes.

The auxiliary verbs **una** 'sit' and **ura** 'lie' are also used with nouns to indicate their position. This positional classification system is fairly straightforward for inanimates, where most are considered to be 'lying down', and for most animals, which are assigned a position (e.g., snakes are 'lying' but frogs are 'sitting'). Humans can either be sitting or lying down, but the choice of **una** versus **ura** is more complicated when humans are standing (**kal'ura** vs. **kal'una**), or when using **una** and **ura** in durative constructions, where the choice depends on both number and gender.

In addition to being divided into active versus stative categories, verbs are also divided by class, which we have simply called 'Class I' and 'Class II' (Haas's 'non-causative' and 'causative'). Class I verbs inflect as described above, with either bound personal suffixes or periphrastic (auxiliary verb) inflection. Class II verbs, on the other hand, only take the auxiliary **-uta**, properly inflected for person and number. Tunica verbs can agree with two arguments at most; the less animate of two potential objects (patients, recipients) simply appears in the clause without being cross-referenced on the verb (see 5 and 15).

Tunica has a few other small verbal categories associated with valency, i.e., that are used to express a different relationship between the subject/object and the action (e.g., 'active' vs. 'passive' verbs in English). In Tunica, this includes impersonal and 'transimpersonal' verbs. Impersonals appear when there is no overt or even implied person or thing causing the action. They are marked only for a third person feminine singular expletive subject (essentially a neutral place holder, since Tunica verbs must always have marking for subject). 'Transimpersonal' constructions are the closest Tunica comes to a passive (e.g., the English 'I got hit by a car', as opposed to 'a car hit me'), where the recipient of the action is more salient to the speaker than whatever caused the action. Morphologically, transimpersonals are impersonals that also take object marking for an animate patient. The verbal categories are fairly rigid; while there are some ways to move between categories (change valency), the only productive process is causation (with **-uta**). These verbal categories will be formally introduced in the second textbook.

Turning now to nouns, Tunica has several nominal-related features which will be unfamiliar to English speakers. First, Tunica has four grammatical number categories: singular, dual (for groups of two), plural, and collective (groups of non-count items, treated as one collective entity, e.g., **wishi** 'water'). Tunica also has grammatical gender, meaning that all nouns are assigned a 'gender', which in Tunica is a binary distinction between either masculine or feminine. While humans have individual genders in the singular (a mixed group of humans are masculine in the plural), the gender of most animals and inanimates depends primarily on how many you are talking about: animals and inanimates are masculine in the singular and dual, but feminine in the plural and collective. Gender is indicated both in verbal and nominal morphology, where nouns are optionally marked for gender and number with enclitics ('gender-number endings'), and verbs mandatorily index nominal gender for both second and third persons, for both the subject and the object (when present).

As is clear from the explanation above, the animacy of nouns in Tunica is important to the workings of Tunica grammar. Tunica has three animacy categories: human animate, non-human animate (i.e., animals), and inanimate. Things which are not regarded living or being aware are considered to be inanimate. The animacy of a noun influences a number of other grammatical properties, like the noun's gender, its positional classification, and whether that noun is cross-referenced on the verb when it is an object (i.e., differential object marking, where less animate nouns are less likely to be cross-referenced on the verb). Animacy categories are somewhat fluid, particularly in traditional narratives where animals are personified and people can shape-shift (therianthropy).

The final nominal property which appears in Tunica, but not in English, is a distinction between alienable and inalienable nouns. Inalienable nouns are a closed class of nouns that are always possessed, which in Tunica includes kinship terms, body parts, clothing items that include body part terms, and the terms for 'name' and 'friend/kin'. All other nouns take alienable prefixes, which are formed by the adding **-hk-** to the inalienable prefixes. Like other languages of the Southeast, the possessive prefixes in Tunica are the same set(s) of prefixes which appear as verbal markers for the subjects of stative verbs and the objects of transitive verbs.

## William Ely Johnson's Tunica, Sesostrie Youchigant's Tunica, and modern Tunica

Tunica was recorded at various points in time by different people. William Ely Johnson worked with Albert Gatschet to document Tunica in the 1880s, and then again with Volsin Chiki and John R. Swanton between 1907 and 1910. Decades later, Sesostrie Youchigant worked with Mary Haas to create the most complete record of Tunica in the 1930s, which was also the last data we have from native speakers. Over that span of approximately 50 years, we can see that the Tunica language changed, such that the different documentations represent the language at different stages. Modern Tunica has continued this trajectory of change. In the process of standardization, it has been necessary to reconcile these differences in the record of Tunica, as well as to fill in some of the gaps where aspects of Tunica were not documented. These forces and decisions have naturally resulted in modern Tunica being somewhat different from the versions of Tunica which exist in the notes of Haas, Gatschet, and Swanton. This section briefly summarizes some of the major ways in which modern Tunica differs from William Ely Johnson's Tunica and Sesostrie Youchigant's Tunica.

The biggest decisions that have had to be made deal with Tunica phonology. The phonological rules described by Haas for Sesostrie Youchigant's Tunica do not match all of the data in the earlier documentation, and also are not entirely consistent across the materials Haas collected. After much discussion, **Kuhpani Yoyani Luhchi Yoroni** felt that the solution which would benefit our new learners most would be to err on the side of morphological completeness, meaning that phonological processes that obscure morpheme boundaries or result in the loss of final vowels/syllables would not be a regular part of modern Tunica. This applies to all productively formed words, excluding compounds and other lexicalizations. This principle also led to the omission in modern Tunica of what Haas called 'phrase-final melodies', where **n**, or **vowel-n** for monosyllables, appears for phonological reasons at phrasal boundaries.

Morphological completeness and the differences between documentary sources both come into play when talking about the Tunica verbal system and the possessive prefixes. Tunica has active verbs and stative verbs, where stative verbs appear with the series of prefixes that function as possessive prefixes on nouns, while all active verbs mandatorily take suffixes. Which series of possessive prefixes seems to appear on stative verbs, or even if there are two series of prefixes, is a point of departure for the older (1880s/1910) dataset versus the newer dataset (1930s). To further complicate matters, Haas originally described Tunica as having one series of possessive prefixes for alienable possession, and another for inalienable possession in her 1940 grammar, but by 1946 she had decided that Tunica does not have an alienable/inalienable distinction, and that there was only one set of prefixes. After considering the data, we decided to adopt Haas's 1940 alienable/inalienable distinction for possession, and to use one series (the alienable set of prefixes) for the inflection of stative verbs (and objects of transitive verbs).

The final major topic which merits mention here is grammatical gender. In Tunica, every inanimate noun is (more or less arbitrarily) assigned a 'gender', masculine or feminine. However, because the gender of inanimate nouns is often not indicated overtly anywhere in the sentence (due in part to differential object marking), the gender of many inanimate nouns was not recorded. This is true for about half of the entries for inanimate nouns in Haas's *Tunica Dictionary*, where the lack of information about their gender is indicated by '*g.?*'. Because it is important grammatically to know the gender of these nouns, we decided to assign all inanimate nouns the same 'default' gender pattern, which is exhibited by many of the inanimate nouns for which we do have gender information. As a result, all inanimate, non-personified nouns in modern Tunica are masculine in the singular and dual, but feminine in the plural and collective.

Many new words have also entered the language. In working meetings and during the immersion workshops and language camps, a regular activity of **Kuhpani Yoyani Luhchi Yoroni** is the coinage of new words to fill lexical gaps. For example, children at the summer camps have invented words for *penguin*, *astronaut*, and *dinosaur*. We now have words for *computer*, *cell phone*, and *smartboard*. Tunica revitalization embodies the tribal motto: "Cherishing our Past, Building for our Future."

# Online pronunciation guide

The introductory chapter of this textbook, Chapter 0: Tunica Basics (pp. 1–8), familiarizes learners with Tunica sounds, the Tunica writing system, and other basics necessary to confidently read and pronounce all of the Tunica words presented in the rest of the textbook. To help with pronunciation, the Tunica words in Chapter 0 have been recorded and made available online via the Indiana University Libraries Media Collections Online service.

If you visit the link following each word below in your web browser, you will be able to hear that word pronounced by the Tunica language instructor whose name is listed after it. The words are presented here alphabetically but are cross-referenced with the pages where they appear in the text.

**arhilani**, *Teyanna Pierite-Simon*, p. 5
(https://purl.dlib.indiana.edu/iudl/media/791s45x25g)

**chɔha**, *Teyanna Pierite-Simon*, pp. 2, 3
(https://purl.dlib.indiana.edu/iudl/media/v73b98t88q)

**disu sahku**, *Juston Broussard*, p. 4
(https://purl.dlib.indiana.edu/iudl/media/g35445k82d)

**eruku**, *Elisabeth Pierite*, p. 2
(https://purl.dlib.indiana.edu/iudl/media/m117629b2r)

**esiku**, *Elisabeth Pierite*, p. 2
(https://purl.dlib.indiana.edu/iudl/media/x719608442)

**etikumashi**, *Teyanna Pierite-Simon*, pp. 4, 6
(https://purl.dlib.indiana.edu/iudl/media/d76r96dz9r)

**eyumayisahu**, *Elisabeth Pierite*, p. 6
(https://purl.dlib.indiana.edu/iudl/media/q37v63nz5m)

**hahkari**, *Elisabeth Pierite*, p. 6
(https://purl.dlib.indiana.edu/iudl/media/z40k81rk8n)

**Halibamu**, *Juston Broussard*, p. 4
(https://purl.dlib.indiana.edu/iudl/media/f95j33923k)

**harati**, *Sidney Barbry*, p. 6
(https://purl.dlib.indiana.edu/iudl/media/r26x919t88)

**harawi**, *Juston Broussard*, p. 3
(https://purl.dlib.indiana.edu/iudl/media/603q87jt0q)

**hayihku**, *Elisabeth Pierite*, p. 2
(https://purl.dlib.indiana.edu/iudl/media/n203963b7n)

**hɛ'ɛsh**, *Teyanna Pierite-Simon*, p. 3
(https://purl.dlib.indiana.edu/iudl/media/831c586s4n)

**hɛma**, *Elisabeth Pierite*, p. 1
(https://purl.dlib.indiana.edu/iudl/media/c38653f42k)

**hichut'ɛ**, *Teyanna Pierite-Simon*, p. 1
(https://purl.dlib.indiana.edu/iudl/media/s65h349z01)

**hinto**, *Elisabeth Pierite*, p. 4
(https://purl.dlib.indiana.edu/iudl/media/r171887s59)

**hipu**, *Ryan Lopez*, p. 5
(https://purl.dlib.indiana.edu/iudl/media/m90d86w52s)

**hipukani**, *Sidney Barbry*, p. 7
(https://purl.dlib.indiana.edu/iudl/media/w62f26g20t)

**hotun**, *Teyanna Pierite-Simon*, p. 4
(https://purl.dlib.indiana.edu/iudl/media/989r07bw5d)

**igachi**, *Sidney Barbry*, p. 5
(https://purl.dlib.indiana.edu/iudl/media/s95643hz4n)

**ihchahchi**, *Elisabeth Pierite*, p. 6
(https://purl.dlib.indiana.edu/iudl/media/s65h349x9j)

**ihktira**, *Elisabeth Pierite*, p. 6
(https://purl.dlib.indiana.edu/iudl/media/s75d37cn09)

**ingrasa**, *Elisabeth Pierite*, p. 4
(https://purl.dlib.indiana.edu/iudl/media/t74c683p1g)

**Johnku**, *Sidney Barbry*, p. 2
(https://purl.dlib.indiana.edu/iudl/media/c48356gv4h)

**kafi**, *Summer LeLeux*, p. 4
(https://purl.dlib.indiana.edu/iudl/media/d86n99hb5j)

**kochu**, *Teyanna Pierite-Simon*, pp. 3, 5
(https://purl.dlib.indiana.edu/iudl/media/158b49b58d)

**kohchu**, *Teyanna Pierite-Simon*, p. 5
(https://purl.dlib.indiana.edu/iudl/media/j62s16775x)

**kɔhta**, *Summer LeLeux*, p. 5
(https://purl.dlib.indiana.edu/iudl/media/r46q97fv7r)

**kɔta**, *Summer LeLeux*, p. 5
(https://purl.dlib.indiana.edu/iudl/media/m60q77p17v)

**kɔta**, *Teyanna Pierite-Simon*, p. 2
(https://purl.dlib.indiana.edu/iudl/media/148f46833j)

**lap'ɔhɔ**, *Teyanna Pierite-Simon*, p. 3
(https://purl.dlib.indiana.edu/iudl/media/m117629b9x)

**lɔtakani**, *Teyanna Pierite-Simon*, p. 3
(https://purl.dlib.indiana.edu/iudl/media/613m90mv8b)

**mahka**, *Juston Broussard*, p. 5
(https://purl.dlib.indiana.edu/iudl/media/168752db4d)

**maka**, *Juston Broussard*, p. 5
(https://purl.dlib.indiana.edu/iudl/media/q08554fv18)

**mili**, *Sidney Barbry*, p. 5
(https://purl.dlib.indiana.edu/iudl/media/q08554fv0z)

**nara**, *Teyanna Pierite-Simon*, p. 3
(https://purl.dlib.indiana.edu/iudl/media/t15049pj34)

**nisara**, *Juston Broussard*, p. 4
(https://purl.dlib.indiana.edu/iudl/media/712m21bn1h)

**ɔmahka**, *Elisabeth Pierite*, pp. 3, 5
(https://purl.dlib.indiana.edu/iudl/media/g64t54sd7b)

**ɔmaka**, *Teyanna Pierite-Simon*, p. 5
(https://purl.dlib.indiana.edu/iudl/media/j430103460)

**pahka**, *Teyanna Pierite-Simon*, p. 5
(https://purl.dlib.indiana.edu/iudl/media/d76r96f00g)

**paka**, *Teyanna Pierite-Simon*, p. 5
(https://purl.dlib.indiana.edu/iudl/media/f26811sg31)

**pihtu**, *Teyanna Pierite-Simon*, p. 5
(https://purl.dlib.indiana.edu/iudl/media/039k12g720)

**pitakani**, *Juston Broussard*, p. 3
(https://purl.dlib.indiana.edu/iudl/media/425k328f82)

**pitu**, *Teyanna Pierite-Simon*, p. 5
(https://purl.dlib.indiana.edu/iudl/media/9504952j57)

**po'in**, *Elisabeth Pierite*, pp. 5, 6
(https://purl.dlib.indiana.edu/iudl/media/h44079c88m)

**pokani**, *Elisabeth Pierite*, p. 7
(https://purl.dlib.indiana.edu/iudl/media/f16c08qp2h)

**rahpu**, *Juston Broussard*, p. 5
(https://purl.dlib.indiana.edu/iudl/media/v33r86j64s)

**rapu**, *Juston Broussard*, p. 5
(https://purl.dlib.indiana.edu/iudl/media/r26x919t7z)

**rasht'ɛ**, *Ryan Lopez*, pp. 3, 7
(https://purl.dlib.indiana.edu/iudl/media/g74q57vh6m)

**risan**, *Teyanna Pierite-Simon*, p. 4
(https://purl.dlib.indiana.edu/iudl/media/059c18mj7j)

**rɔwa**, *Ryan Lopez*, p. 2
(https://purl.dlib.indiana.edu/iudl/media/x91366d83c)

**sahku**, *Teyanna Pierite-Simon*, pp. 2, 5
(https://purl.dlib.indiana.edu/iudl/media/k32237qp89)

**sak'iti**, *Summer LeLeux*, p. 3
(https://purl.dlib.indiana.edu/iudl/media/z10w72j87g)

**saku**, *Teyanna Pierite-Simon*, p. 5
(https://purl.dlib.indiana.edu/iudl/media/f65v242r25)

**sinkshruka**, *Teyanna Pierite-Simon*, p. 4
(https://purl.dlib.indiana.edu/iudl/media/415p295w9v)

**sinku**, *Elisabeth Pierite*, p. 4
(https://purl.dlib.indiana.edu/iudl/media/435g35bh5f)

**taharani**, *Elisabeth Pierite*, p. 7
(https://purl.dlib.indiana.edu/iudl/media/m60q77p16j)

**tarkuku**, *Teyanna Pierite-Simon*, p. 5
(https://purl.dlib.indiana.edu/iudl/media/8418618p4p)

**teti**, *Teyanna Pierite-Simon*, p. 5
(https://purl.dlib.indiana.edu/iudl/media/j13900vz8d)

**tikahch**, *Elisabeth Pierite*, p. 7
(https://purl.dlib.indiana.edu/iudl/media/2676833w0x)

**tipuli**, *Sidney Barbry*, p. 6
(https://purl.dlib.indiana.edu/iudl/media/386020031r)

**uhkkosu**, *Elisabeth Pierite*, p. 6
(https://purl.dlib.indiana.edu/iudl/media/178455g614)

**uhkwanani**, *Elisabeth Pierite*, p. 6
(https://purl.dlib.indiana.edu/iudl/media/9407920605)

**ukiku**, *Elisabeth Pierite*, p. 6
(https://purl.dlib.indiana.edu/iudl/media/445c38db8r)

**wɛkakati**, *Elisabeth Pierite*, p. 1
(https://purl.dlib.indiana.edu/iudl/media/v13z80ct12)

**wɛsaku**, *Elisabeth Pierite*, p. 3
(https://purl.dlib.indiana.edu/iudl/media/465544jf7w)

**yanakati**, *Juston Broussard*, p. 3
(https://purl.dlib.indiana.edu/iudl/media/851564bt65)

**Yoroniku**, *Elisabeth Pierite*, pp. 2, 6
(https://purl.dlib.indiana.edu/iudl/media/f85n306q0w)

**yukati**, *Juston Broussard*, p. 3
(https://purl.dlib.indiana.edu/iudl/media/247d76zv0t)

# Chapter 0: Tunica Basics

## About the Tunica letters

You will recognize most of the letters of Tunica; they are also used for Spanish, French, and English. This section tells you how Tunica sounds are pronounced and introduces you to some of the new characters we use to write Tunica.

### Vowels

In English the letters *a, e, i, o*, and *u* are pronounced in a number of different ways, depending on what other sounds and letters surround them. English has more vowels than Tunica, though it uses fewer letters to spell them. This leads to the same sound often being spelled in different ways in English. The *a* of *bat* sounds like the *a* of *that*, but different from the *a* in *announce*, and different too from the *a* in *cape*.

Tunica vowels are easier. Each one has its own letter and is always written with that letter, so you can always sound out a Tunica word and pronounce it correctly.

Tunica has two vowel letters that do not appear in these other alphabets; **ɛ** and **ɔ**. Some varieties of English have these sounds, but English writing does not have special symbols for them.

**ɛ**: In Tunica, **ɛ** is always pronounced like the vowel of *bet*. Here are some examples:

| | |
|---|---|
| **hɛma** | 'you (feminine singular)' |
| **wɛkakati** | '(the moon) is waning' |
| **hichut'ɛ** | 'eagle' |

**ɛ** sounds the same in all these words.

**ɔ**: This letter represents a sound that is similar to the sound that is usually spelled in English with *aw*, as in *hawk*, *flaw*, and *caw*. English also sometimes spells this sound with *ou*, as in *bought*, *ought*, and *sought*. Some varieties of English do not have this vowel. In Tunica this vowel is always spelled with **ɔ**, as in:

**chɔha** 'chief'

**rɔwa** 'white'

**kɔta** 'gray'

The following table shows the Tunica letter on the left and then various words in English that use approximately the same sound. Notice the different English spellings.

| Tunica letter | Possible English spellings |
|---|---|
| **i** | k**ey**, p**ea**, s**ee**, L**eigh** |
| **e** | h**ay**, w**eigh**, **ai**d, caf**é** |
| **ɛ** | b**e**t, h**ea**lth |
| **a** | f**a**ther, t**o**p |
| **ɔ** | t**au**ght, f**ou**ght, c**aw**, sl**o**th |
| **o** | b**oa**t, n**o**te, sn**ow**, g**oe**s |
| **u** | b**oo**t, wh**o**, ch**ew**, fl**u** |

Each letter represents a single sound, one way of pronouncing the vowel. The vowels of Tunica are more like the vowels of Spanish: **a** as in *taco*, **e** as in *queso*, **i** as in *sí*, **o** as in *San Francisco*, and **u** is like the *u* of *Santa Cruz*.

**A special u**: Most of these vowels sound exactly the same wherever you find them, but **u** has a special form when it comes at the end of a word after **k** or **hk**, where it is whispered (voiceless). Since many words end in **-ku**, you hear this whispered **u** often. You'll barely hear it; it sounds mostly like a faint puff of air.

| | | | |
|---|---|---|---|
| **esiku** | 'my father' | **Johnku** | 'John' |
| **yoroniku** | 'Tunica man' | **sahku** | 'one' |
| **eruku** | 'he laughed' | **hayihku** | 'strange' |

## Consonants

For the most part, Tunica consonant letters and letter combinations are like their English counterparts, meaning you can read them as you would in English. Tunica has the following consonant sounds which are also found in English:

| Tunica Letter | Examples |
|---|---|
| **p** | as in *pig*, or Tunica **pitakani** 'I walk' |
| **t** | as in *table*, or Tunica **yukati** 'she arrived' |
| **ch** | as in *check*, or Tunica **chɔha** 'chief' |
| **k** | as in *kiss*, or Tunica **kochu** 'short' |
| **h** | as in *hot*, or Tunica **harawi** 'he sang' |
| **l** | as in *lake*, or Tunica **lɔtakani** 'I run' |
| **w** | as in *wet*, or Tunica **wɛsaku** 'he jumps' |
| **y** | as in *yes*, or Tunica **yanakati** 'she speaks' |
| **m** | as in *mother*, or Tunica **ɔmahka** 'alligator' |
| **n** | as in *nail*, or Tunica **nara** 'snake' |

In addition to these English sounds and letters, Tunica also has the letter **'**. This symbol represents glottal stop, the closure of the vocal cords. English uses this sound in words like *uh_oh* and the negative expression *unh_unh*; the glottal stop is the space between the two words. Some people also use a glottal stop instead of a *t* in *sentence*, *button*, and *mountain*. Some speakers of British English replace the *tt* of *bottle* with a glottal stop. English, then, sometimes spells glottal stop with *h* and sometimes with *t* or *tt*. In Tunica, glottal stop is always spelled **'**. **'** occurs in the middle of words like the following:

| | |
|---|---|
| **hɛ'ɛsh** | 'today' |
| **rasht'ɛ** | 'with great effort; difficult' |
| **lap'ɔhɔ** | 'not good; bad; wrong; unpleasant' |
| **sak'iti** | 'we ate' |

Glottal stops in Tunica can appear between vowels or after a consonant. When a glottal stop comes after a **p**, **t**, or **k**, there is no puff of air after the **p**, **t**, or **k** (unaspirated), so they sound like you would say them at the end of a word in English. Tunica words do not end in **'**.

Like English, Tunica has the sound **s** (as in *silence*), and the sound **sh** (as in *share*). For some speakers of Tunica, however, **s** and **sh** are made with the tongue a bit further back in the mouth, meaning that they sound more 'hissed' than *s* and *sh* in English. This feature was present in the Tunica we see in the texts and is a feature of many Native southeastern languages, including Muskogean languages and Natchez. Sample Tunica words with **s** and **sh** include **etikumashi** 'my parent-in-law' and **nisara** 'young person'.

Tunica has several other letters/sounds which only show up in borrowed words. So, while these are sometimes letters used in Tunica, they are not native Tunica sounds. These are:

| Tunica letter | Tunica example | English translation |
|---|---|---|
| **b** | **Halibamu** | 'Alabama Indian' |
| **d** | **disu sahku** | 'dime' |
| **g** | **ingrasa** | 'Englishman' |
| **f** | **kafi** | 'coffee' |

Additionally, like with the vowel **u**, some consonants are whispered (voiceless) in some contexts in Tunica. These include **n**, **l**, and **r**.

**N** is whispered when it is the last sound in a phrase. The most common context for this is when the yes/no question marker **-n** is attached to the end of a word:

**Hotun?** 'All?' 'Everyone?'

**Risan?** 'Is it multi-colored?'

**N** is also whispered before **ch**, **h**, **k**, **p**, **s**, **sh**, and **t**, in which case the preceding vowel is heavily nasalized. This is the case in the following examples:

**sinkshruka** 'they *(two women)* are afraid'

**sinku** 'five'

**hinto!** 'Come here!'

The Tunica **r** is more like the Spanish *r* in *perro* 'dog', than the *r* of English *rabbit*. It is a trilled or rolled **r**. Both **l** and **r** in Tunica work just like **n**, where they are voiced like the English *l* and *r* at the beginnings of words, between vowels, and before **'**, but they are whispered before **ch**, **h**, **k**, **p**, **s**, **sh**, and **t**. **L**'s and **r**'s do not appear as the last sounds in a phrase in modern Tunica.

**arhilani** 'story'

**tarkuku** 'the woods'

Lastly, the Tunica **h** by itself is a slight exhalation of air, just like in English words like *help* and *hello*. However, when **h** is before **p**, **t**, **ch**, and **k**, it gets a little extra strength. It is important to pronounce the **h** because it makes a meaningful distinction:

| | | | |
|---|---|---|---|
| **mahka** | 'expensive' | **maka** | 'grease, fat, lard, oil' |
| **ɔmahka** | 'alligator' | **ɔmaka** | 'sorcerer, sorceress' |
| **kohchu** | 'to devour' | **kochu** | 'short' |
| **kɔhta** | 'to build a fence' | **kɔta** | 'gray, tawny' |
| **pahka** | 'to dress up' | **paka** | 'to answer, to reply' |
| **pihtu** | 'crazy' | **pitu** | 'to get lost' |
| **rahpu** | 'to put on clothing' | **rapu** | 'to sleep' |
| **sahku** | 'one' | **saku** | 'eat' |

## Syllables

Syllables in Tunica are frequently consonant + vowel (CV). Noun and verb roots tend to be composed of two syllables, so CVCV. This means that generally speaking, words start in consonants and end in vowels.

**hipu** 'to dance'

**teti** 'road, path'

**mili** 'red'

However, this is not a hard and fast rule, as some Tunica words start with vowels or end in consonants. This is mostly the result of adding elements to the root of the word (for example **i** + **gachi** 'my mother', or **po** + **i** + **n** 'look! *(2ms)*').

It is common to have series of consonants in Tunica which involve **h**, **s**, **sh**, **l**, **n**, and **r** to appear before **p**, **t**, **ch**, and **k**. **'** can come after any consonant except itself. Two of the same consonant or vowel never appear next to each other within a root in Tunica. However, two of the same consonant can come to be next to each other. When this happens, we write both of them, even though they only get pronounced once, e.g. in **uh*kk*osu** 'its color'.

## Stress

For most Tunica words, the stress or accent falls on the first syllable of the root (shown in the following examples in italics). You will learn to recognize Tunica roots in the following chapters.

| | |
|---|---|
| ***Yo*roniku** | 'Tunica' |
| ***ha*rati** | 'she sang' |
| ***po*'in!** | '(you, m.) look!' |
| **ihk*ti*ra** | 'my clothes' |
| **uhk*wa*nani** | 'he wants, it is said' |

If the word is four or more syllables long, these are generally compounds, and the stress falls where it would on the words independently.

| | |
|---|---|
| **-*e*yu*ma*yi*sa*hu** | 'left arm' |
| **-*e*tiku*ma*shi** | 'parent-in-law' |

Generally speaking, the last syllables of words in Tunica are not stressed. However, there are a handful of exceptions, like when a root is only one syllable, like in ***ha*hka*ri*** 'barn', which is a combination of **hahka** 'corn' and the single-syllable word **ri** 'house'.

A small group of Tunica roots, which mostly include kinship terms, are always possessed and are always stressed on the syllable *before* the root. These words are listed in Mary Haas's *Tunica Dictionary* with an accent before the root (e.g. **´-hcha** 'grandparent').

| | |
|---|---|
| ***i*hchahchi** | 'my grandmother' |
| ***u*kiku** | 'his uncle' |
| ***ti*puli** | 'her feathers' |

Additionally, some prefixes (elements that attach to the beginning of words) are always stressed. For example, the agentive **ta-** 'doer, instrument' is always stressed:

***ta*****harani** 'fiddle', lit. 'the song-maker'

Lastly, endings or suffixes (elements that attach to the ends of words) that are more than one syllable have their own stress. For example, when a two-syllable ending like **-*ka*ni** 'I am _____ing' is added to a verb, you get a word with with two stressed syllables:

***hi*****pu*****ka*****ni** 'I dance.'
***pi*****ta*****ka*****ni** 'I walk.'

However, because it is not possible to have two stressed syllables in a row, if **-*ka*ni** were to attach itself to a one-syllable verb like **po** 'see', only the root is stressed: ***po*** + ***ka*****ni** = ***po*****kani**.

Because stress is mostly predictable, it is not written or indicated with italics in the rest of this textbook. If you are unsure how something should be pronounced, ask your Tunica teacher, consult a Tunica dictionary or the other resources available through the tribe, or contact the Tunica-Biloxi Language & Culture Revitalization Program.

## Tikahch!

**Tikahch** (thank you) for reading! Through the following examples, dialogues, and practice exercises you will understand how these rules and language features are applied. **Rasht'ɛ**, with great effort, and practice you will become a confident Tunica language learner.

# Chapter 1: Heni!

*Greetings!*

**TOPICS:**

# Taheni

*Greetings*

## Yoluyana

*Vocabulary*

| | |
|---|---|
| **apo'inan** | *See you later!* *(lit. let us (d) see each other)* |
| **eti** | *my friend* |
| **-etisa** | *to be named* |
| **etisa** | *I am named* |
| **-hat** | *on (one's) part* |
| **-hchi** | *gender-number ending (fs)* |
| **heni** | *hello! greetings!* |
| **hetisa** | *you (fs) are named* |
| **hɛma** | *you (fs)* |
| **hɛmat** | *you (fs), on your part* |
| **hita** | *take care!* |
| **kanahku** | *what* |
| **ko'o** | *great!* |
| **-ku** | *gender-number ending (ms)* |
| **lapu** | *good* |
| **ma** | *you (ms)* |
| **mahat** | *you (ms), on your part* |
| **-n** | *yes/no question* |
| **taheni** | *greetings* |
| **tikahch** | *thank you* |
| **wetisa** | *you (ms) are named* |

## Yanalepini

*Dialogue*

**Aiyannahchi:** Heni! Eti, hɛma lapun?
**Alicehchi:** Lapu. Hɛmat?
**Aiyannahchi:** Lapu, tikahch. Kanahku hetisa?
**Alicehchi:** Alice etisa. Hɛmat, kanahku hetisa?
**Aiyannahchi:** Aiyanna etisa.
**Alicehchi:** Lapu.

**Merlinku:** Heni! Eti, ma lapun?
**Chrisku:** Lapu. Mahat?
**Merlinku:** Lapu, tikahch. Kanahku wetisa?
**Chrisku:** Chris etisa. Mahat, kanahku wetisa?
**Merlinku:** Merlin etisa.
**Chrisku:** Lapu.

**Merlinku:** Eti, hɛma lapun?
**Aiyannahchi:** Lapu. Mahat?
**Merlinku:** Lapu, tikahch. Kanahku hetisa?
**Aiyannahchi:** Aiyanna etisa. Mahat, kanahku wetisa?
**Merlinku:** Merlin etisa.
**Aiyannahchi:** Ko'o! Hita!
**Merlinku:** Apo'inan!

## Lutamashu

*Grammar*

The **yanalepini** 'dialogues' show how to greet people in Tunica. You notice as you read through them that the words change a bit depending on who you are talking to. First, it matters whether you are talking to a male or a female. This is because Tunica has what we call grammatical gender, which means that the language categorizes every word as either masculine or feminine. So if you are saying 'you' and that refers to a female, then you use a different form than if 'you' refers to a male. This is also true of 'he' and 'she', just like in English. There is no gender distinction for 'I/we'.

Second, you'll notice that Tunica has different pronouns (he, they, we, you) that are used mainly when clarifying who you're talking about. We call 'I/me' and 'we/us' 1st person, 'you' and 'y'all' 2nd person, and 'he/him', 'she/her', and 'they/them' 3rd person. 'I' in Tunica is **ima**, and 'you' can be either **ma** or **hɛma**, depending on whether 'you' is a male or female. 'He/him' is **uwi**, while 'she/her' is **tihchi**. Pronouns in Tunica only refer to humans; there is no Tunica equivalent to 'it' for things. You always use one of these pronouns when greeting someone.

For example, **eti, ma lapun** is literally, 'my friend, are you well?' to a male, and **eti, hɛma lapun** is literally 'my friend, are you well?' to a female.

Lastly, like English, Tunica distinguishes singular (one thing) from plural (many things). However, Tunica also has an extra category called dual, which is for talking specifically about two things. The plural in Tunica is only used for three or more things. So, saying 'them two' in Tunica is **unima**, which is different than saying 'them three', which is **sɛma**.

When a word is specifically used to refer to one gender or the other, it will be followed by *(f)* for feminine and *(m)* for masculine. When it refers to a specific number of people, it will be followed by *(s)* for singular, *(d)* for dual, or *(p)* for plural. In the **yoluyana** 'vocabulary', you saw that **hɛma** means 'you *(fs)*'. This means that **hɛma** is feminine singular; it is used when referring to one woman.

The following table provides all of the forms of the pronouns in Tunica. This table format, with columns for singular, dual, and plural and rows for 1st person, 2nd person masculine and feminine, and 3rd person masculine and feminine, will be used throughout this textbook.

| | | SINGULAR | | DUAL | | PLURAL | |
|---|---|---|---|---|---|---|---|
| *1st person* | | **ima** | *I* | **inima** | *we two* | **inima** | *we all* |
| *2nd person* | *feminine* | **hɛma** | *you* | **hinima** | *you two* | **hinima** | *you all* |
| | *masculine* | **ma** | *you* | **winima** | *you two* | **winima** | *you all* |
| *3rd person* | *feminine* | **tihchi** | *she* | **sinima** | *they two* | **sinima** | *they all* |
| | *masculine* | **uwi** | *he* | **unima** | *they two* | **sɛma** | *they all* |

If you look at the pronouns, you'll notice that all of the dual forms are also the plural forms, except in the 3rd person masculine, where **unima** is the dual and **sɛma** is the plural. This is a pattern found throughout Tunica.

You might be asking yourself, what gender should I use if I'm talking about a mixed group of people, males and females? The answer is the masculine. If you are talking about people, then the whole group is considered masculine if there are any males in the group. Only groups or pairs of only females are considered feminine.

It is often the case that when pronouns are used in Tunica, they appear with the ending **-hat**, which can be translated as 'on his part; on her part'. While sometimes you see the full form of **-hat** like in **mahat** 'you *(ms)*, on your part', often the **h** of **-hat** is lost and the final vowel of the pronoun combines with the **a** of **-hat** (like in **uwɛt** 'he, on his part'). You will learn the rules about how and why this happens in later chapters. For, now, it is fine to recognize **-hat** in these forms, and how that is pronounced with the different pronouns:

| | | | | |
|---|---|---|---|---|
| **ima** | + | **-hat** | = | **imat** |
| **hɛma** | + | **-hat** | = | **hɛmat** |
| **ma** | + | **-hat** | = | **mahat** |
| **tihchi** | + | **-hat** | = | **tihchɛt** |
| **uwi** | + | **-hat** | = | **uwɛt** |

All of the other pronouns end in **a** and act like **hɛmat** (**sinimat**, **inimat**, etc.).

## Hinu 1

*Practice*

**1.1.1. Molɔtaki** (Fill it):
Fill in the blanks below. Remember to pay attention to who is talking to whom.

***Example:*** *Lapu,* *tikahch.*

1. Merlinku, Aiyannahchi:

**Merlinku:** Eti, hɛma lapun?

**Aiyannahchi:** Lapu, ________?

**Merlinku:** Lapu, tikahch. Kanahku ________?

**Aiyannahchi:** Aiyanna etisa. Kanahku ________?

**Merlinku:** Merlin ________.

**Aiyannahchi:** Lapu.

2. Aiyannahchi, Alicehchi:

**Aiyannahchi:** Eti, ________ lapun?

**Alicehchi:** Lapu, ________?

**Aiyannahchi:** Lapu, tikahch. ________ hetisa?

**Alicehchi:** Alice etisa. Hɛmat, kanahku ________?

**Aiyannahchi:** Aiyanna etisa.

**Alicehchi:** ________.

### 1.1.2. **Chu'ɔki** (Multiple choice):

Choose the correct response to the question in Tunica.

***Example:*** *Heni!*

***a. Heni!*** *b. Lapu.* *c. Tikahch!*

1. Eti, ma lapun?
   a. Mahat? b. Lapu. c. Kanahku hetisa?
2. Kanahku hetisa?
   a. Tikahch! b. Alice etisa. c. Kanahku wetisa?
3. Eti, hɛma lapun?
   a. Lapu, tikahch. b. Merlin etisa. c. Apo'inan!
4. Mahat, kanahku wetisa?
   a. Ko'o! b. Aiyanna etisa. c. Chris etisa.
5. Lapu, hɛmat?
   a. Lapu. b. Apo'inan! c. Heni!

## Kanahku tetisa?

*What's her name?*

### Yoluyana

*Vocabulary*

| | | | |
|---|---|---|---|
| **aha** | *no* | **tetisa** | *her name is* |
| **apo'itin** | *See you later!* (*lit. let us (p) see each other*) | **tihchɛt** | *she, on her part* |
| **enti** | *our friend* | **uwɛt** | *he, on his part* |
| **hon** | *yes* | **wentisa** | *your (md/p) names are* |
| **otisa** | *his name is* | **winimat** | *you (md/p), on your part* |

### Yanalepini

*Dialogue*

**Merlinku:** Chris, kanahku tetisa?
**Chrisku:** Tihchɛt, Aiyannahchi tetisa.
**Merlinku:** Aiyannahchi tetisan? Lapu.
**Chrisku:** Lapu.
**Merlinku** *to Aiyannahchi:* Aiyanna hetisan?
**Aiyannahchi:** Hon. Aiyanna etisa. Mahat?
**Merlinku:** Merlin etisa.

**Merlinku:** Heni! Eti, winima lapun?

**Alicehchi, Augustinku:** Lapu, mahat?

**Merlinku:** Lapu, tikahch. Kanahku wentisa?

**Alicehchi:** Alice etisa. Uwɛt, Augustinku otisa.

**Augustinku:** Winimat, Alice, Albert wentisan?

**Merlinku:** Aha, Merlin etisa.

**Augustinku:** Lapu. Apo'itin!

**Merlinku:** Eti, hɛma lapun?

**Alicehchi:** Lapu. Tikahch!

**Merlinku:** Uwi eti. Chrisku otisa.

**Alicehchi:** Chrisku otisa.

**Merlinku:** Hon. Kanahku hetisa?

**Alicehchi:** Alice etisa.

**Merlinku:** Ko'o! Hita!

**Alicehchi:** Apo'inan!

## Lutamashu

*Grammar*

Just like when using pronouns in Tunica, how you say 'what is your name?' changes based on the gender of the person you are talking to, and if you are talking to one, two, or more people. In Tunica 'to be named/called' is a verb (also like in Spanish *me llamo*). The basic form of the verb 'to be called' is **-etisa**, and the front of the word changes based on who or what is being named. The full set of forms for the verb **-etisa** is given in the following chart.

| | | SINGULAR | | DUAL | | PLURAL | |
|---|---|---|---|---|---|---|---|
| *1st person* | | **etisa** | *I am called* | **entisa** | *we (d) are called* | **entisa** | *we (p) are called* |
| *2nd person* | *feminine* | **hetisa** | *you (fs) are called* | **hentisa** | *you (fd) are called* | **hentisa** | *you (fp) are called* |
| | *masculine* | **wetisa** | *you (ms) are called* | **wentisa** | *you (md) are called* | **wentisa** | *you (mp) are called* |
| *3rd person* | *feminine* | **tetisa** | *she is called* | **sentisa** | *they (fd) are called* | **sentisa** | *they (fp) are called* |
| | *masculine* | **otisa** | *he is called* | **ontisa** | *they (md) are called* | **setisa** | *they (mp) are called* |

Like with pronouns, notice that the dual and the plural forms of **-etisa** are the same everywhere except the 3rd person masculine (**ontisa** 'they *(md)* are called' vs. **setisa** 'they *(mp)* are called'). You can also tell that these dual and plural forms are related to each other: the dual/plural form is usually the singular form plus an extra **n**. For example, **wetisa** 'you *(ms)* are called' becomes **wentisa** 'you *(md/p)* are called'. This is the case for all forms except the 3rd person feminine, where **tetisa** becomes **sentisa**. **-eti** works similarly: for instance, the 1st person plural form of **-eti** becomes **enti**, the same way that **-etisa** in the first person plural becomes **entisa**.

In the **yanalepini**, you saw that sometimes **-etisa** has an **-n** on the end. This indicates that this is a question. For example, **Alicehchi tetisa** is a statement: 'Her name is Alice'. However, **Alicehchi tetisan** with an **n** makes it a question: 'Is her name Alice?'. This **-n** is used to ask questions when the answer is going to be either **hon** 'yes' or **aha** 'no'. If the question is an information question, like questions with **kanahku** 'what', then you don't need the **-n**, because **kanahku** already tells you that it's going to be a question. So it is correct to say **Kanahku wetisa?** 'what is your *(ms)* name?' without the **-n**.

## Hinu 2

*Practice*

**1.2.1. Molɔtaki** (Fill it)**:**
Fill in the blanks below with the correct form of **-etisa** that matches the person or people being asked about. The answer to each question should be **hon**!

***Example:*** *Tihchi Aiyannahchi* ***tetisan*** ?

1. Inimat, Alice, Naomi _________?
2. Mahat, Merlin _________?
3. Uwɛt, Chrisku _________?
4. Hinimat, Alice, Aiyanna, Naomi _________?
5. Imat, Augustin _________?
6. Unimat, Augustinku, Merlinku _________?
7. Sinimat, Naomihchi, Aiyannahchi, Alicehchi _________?
8. Winimat, Chris, Augustin _________?
9. Sɛmat, Augustinku, Chrisku, Merlinku _________?
10. Hɛmat, Aiyanna _________?

**1.2.2.** **Luhchi pirɛtaki** (Translate):

Translate the following sentences into Tunica. Use the chart on page 16 if you need help.

***Example:*** *What is my name?* ***Kanahku etisa?***

1. What is your name? *(a boy)*

 ______

2. What are their names? *(2 girls)*

 ______

3. What are their names? *(3 boys)*

 ______

4. What is his name?

 ______

5. What is her name?

 ______

6. What are our names?

 ______

# Gender-number endings

## Yoluyana

*Vocabulary*

| | | | |
|---|---|---|---|
| **nuhchi** | *woman* | **-sinima** | *gender-number ending (fd/p)* |
| **oni** | *person; man* | **ta-** | *the; some* |
| **-sɛma** | *gender-number ending (mp)* | **-unima** | *gender-number ending (md)* |

## Yanalepini

*Dialogue*

**Alicehchi:** Heni! Eti, hinima lapun?

**Aiyannahchi, Naomihchi:** Lapu, hɛmat?

**Alicehchi:** Lapu, tikahch. Toniku, kanahku otisa?

**Naomihchi:** Daveku otisa. Tanuhchisinima, kanahku sentisa?

**Alicehchi:** Summerhchi, Rosehchi sentisa.

**Naomihchi:** Tikahch.

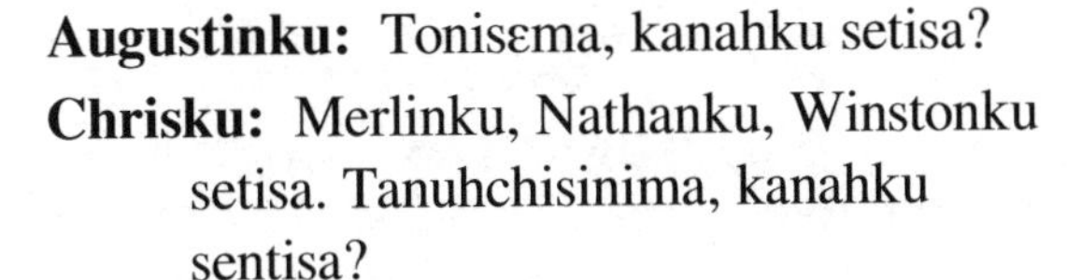

**Augustinku:** Tonisɛma, kanahku setisa?

**Chrisku:** Merlinku, Nathanku, Winstonku setisa. Tanuhchisinima, kanahku sentisa?

**Augustinku:** Alicehchi, Rosehchi, Emmahchi sentisa.

**Chrisku:** Lapu, tikahch.

**Alicehchi:** Naomi, ton'unima, kanahku ontisa?

**Naomihchi:** Ton'unimat, Merlinku Alfredku ontisa.

**Alicehchi:** Lapu. Tihchɛt? Tanuhchihchi, kanahku tetisa?

**Naomihchi:** Tanuhchihchɛt Cyndihchi tetisa.

## Lutamashu

*Grammar*

You have probably noticed that the names in the **yanalepini** and **hinu** in this chapter have things like **-ku** and **-hchi** added to the end. These are what we call gender-number endings, and they are there to give more information about the noun, namely how many there are and what the gender is. So **Aiyannahchi** gets **-hchi** because she is one woman, while **Augustinku** gets **-ku** because he is one man. While we have mostly seen these singular endings in this chapter, there are also dual and plural forms which will show up more as we learn more Tunica.

| | SINGULAR | DUAL | PLURAL |
|---|---|---|---|
| *feminine* | **-hchi** | **-sinima** | **-sinima** |
| *masculine* | **-ku** | **-unima** | **-sɛma** |

These endings can go on any noun, not just names. In the **yanalepini** we saw the forms **toniku**, **tonisɛma**, **ton'unima**, **tanuhchihchi**, and **tanuhchisinima**. The **t-** on the front of the words that start with **oni** is from **ta-**, meaning 'the'; it shortens to **t-** before words that start with vowels, so **t-** and **oni** form **toni**. Then the gender-number endings tell us how many people we are talking about and what their gender is. For example, in **ton'unima**, **-unima** tells us that there are two people and they are either both male or a mixed group (in this instance, one male and one female).

The other important thing to notice is that these endings are added when one is talking *about* someone, not when one is talking *to* someone. So, when someone asks **Kanahku tetisa?**, the reply is **Aiyannahchi tetisa**, with **-hchi**. However, when you are talking about yourself (for example, **Merlin etisa**) or using someone's name when talking to them (for example, **Alice, kanahku setisa?**), you don't get any gender-number endings.

## Hinu 3

*Practice*

**1.3.1. Luhchi pirɛtaki** (Translate)**:**
Write how you would refer to the groups of people below. Use **oni** and **nuhchi** with the appropriate gender-number endings (use the chart on the previous page for help). Remember that groups with both men and women use **oni** and the masculine gender-number endings.

***Example:*** *Merlinku, Alicehchi, Augustinku* ***onisɛma***

1. Chrisku ____________________
2. Alicehchi, Rosehchi ____________________
3. Merlinku, Chrisku ____________________
4. Aiyannahchi ____________________
5. Aiyannahchi, Alicehchi, Naomihchi ____________________
6. Chrisku, Daveku, Augustinku ____________________

**1.3.2. Molɔtaki** (Fill in the blank)**:**
Write the correct form of **-etisa** that would be used based on the pronoun.

***Example:*** *Uwi* ***otisa***

1. Ima __________
2. Sɛma __________
3. Unima __________
4. Tihchi __________
5. Inima __________

## Tetimili: Tunica names to know

*Culture*

**Tayoroniku-Halayihku**, Tunica-Biloxi people, preserve our language and culture in many ways. Recognizing the gifts and lives of our ancestors through names is a common way of maintaining our identity. The first and most influential gift to a child is their name. In naming children after grandparents, aunts, and uncles, we preserve the old stories and the work of their lives. Like the many place names of Indigenous origin in Louisiana, the names of our ancestors are a map of our own tribal history. We name three ancestors below on whose work we build our knowledge of our Tunica language today.

The first was William Ely Johnson, also known as Etienne Chiki. Johnson spoke many languages, including Tunica, Biloxi, Choctaw, French, and English. He worked to record the Tunica language in the 1880s.

The second was the Tunica chief Volsin Chiki. He was chief from 1900 to 1911, and worked on the Tunica language in the early 1910s. Among other contributions, Chief Chiki and William Ely Johnson provided descriptions of the Fête du Blé, a festival we will discuss in later chapters. In fact, he helped revive this tradition in the 1870s.

Chief Chiki's **ohtohku** ('nephew', 'his sister's son'), Sesostrie Youchigant, also known as Sam Young, also worked to preserve the Tunica language. Sesostrie Youchigant worked with two different linguists to record the language: John R. Swanton (in 1930 and 1931), and Mary R. Haas (from 1933 to 1938). Sesostrie Youchigant's work with Haas is where we get most of the Tunica examples you are learning today.

## Tetimili wiralepini

*Culture questions*

1. Names are one way we honor and continue our culture and language: can you think of something you do or your community does to celebrate these things? How might you want to include the Tunica language in these traditions and celebrations?

# Chapter 2: Hil'itiki!

*Let's move!*

**TOPICS:**

# Singular habitual endings

## Yoluyana

*Vocabulary*

| | | | |
|---|---|---|---|
| **hara** | *to sing* | **pita** | *to walk* |
| **hipu** | *to dance* | **rapu** | *to sleep* |
| **lapuhch** | *it is a good thing* | **wɛsa** | *to jump* |
| **lɔta** | *to run* | **ya** | *to do; to make* |

## Yanalepini

*Dialogue*

**Aiyannahchi:** Kanahku yaka?
**Alicehchi:** Hipukani. Kanahku yaka?
**Aiyannahchi:** Harakani.
**Alicehchi:** Harakan?
**Aiyannahchi:** Hon. Harakani.
**Alicehchi:** Lapuhch.

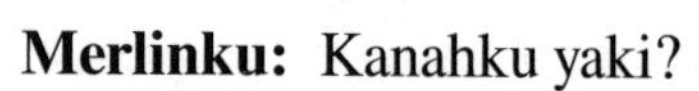

**Merlinku:** Kanahku yaki?
**Chrisku:** Pitakani. Kanahku yaki?
**Merlinku:** Lɔtakani.
**Chrisku:** Lɔtakin?
**Merlinku:** Hon. Lɔtakani.
**Chrisku:** Lapuhch.

**Merlinku:** Chrisku kanahku yaku?
**Aiyannahchi:** Wɛsaku. Alicehchi kanahku yakati?
**Merlinku:** Lɔtakati. Kanahku yaka?
**Aiyannahchi:** Harakani. Kanahku yaki?
**Merlinku:** Rapukani.
**Aiyannahchi:** Lapuhch.

## Lutamashu

*Grammar*

**Taya oni sahku** (intransitive verbs in English) are verbs like 'walk', 'run', 'play', 'jump', and 'swim' which only involve one person, a subject, who is doing the action. In Tunica, the subjects of **taya oni sahku** appear directly on the verb as endings (like **-kati** and **-ku**). Just like the pronouns that we saw in Chapter 1, the right ending to use with **taya oni sahku** depends on the gender, number, and person (1st, 2nd, 3rd) of the person doing the action. A summary of the singular endings is given below.

| | | | |
|---|---|---|---|
| **-kani** | *I am _____ing* | **-kati** | *she is _____ing* |
| **-ka** | *you (fs) are _____ing* | **-ku** | *he is _____ing* |
| **-ki** | *you (ms) are _____ing* | | |

All of the endings in this chapter are used to indicate habitual actions or events, which are things that are either happening now or happen regularly. They can be translated as 'I am _____ing', e.g., 'I am walking' for **pitakani**. Notice that all of these endings start with **k**.

## Hinu 1

*Practice*

**2.1.1. Atehpɛtaki** (Join together)**:**
Write the letter of the verb with the correct form to answer the question in the blanks below.

***Example:*** ***a*** *Kanahku yaka?* *a. Hipukani.*

1. _____ Kanahku yaku? a. Harakati
2. _____ Kanahku yaka/yaki? b. Rapuka
3. _____ Kanahku yakati? c. Lɔtaku
4. _____ Kanahku yakani? *(if male)* d. Pitakani
5. _____ Kanahku yakani? *(if female)* e. Wɛsaki

**2.1.2. Luhchi pirɛtaki** (Translate)**:**
Translate the following into Tunica. Use the chart on the previous page if you need help.

***Example:*** *He is sleeping.* **Rapuku.**

1. She is running. ____________________
2. You *(fs)* are singing. ____________________
3. I am jumping. ____________________
4. You *(ms)* are walking. ____________________
5. He is dancing. ____________________

**2.1.3. Luhchi pirɛtaki** (Translate)**:**
Translate the following into English. Use the chart on page 27 if you need help.

***Example:*** *Kanahku yakati?* ***What is she doing?***

1. Wɛsaku. ______________________________
2. Hipuki. ______________________________
3. Harakani. ______________________________
4. Kanahku yaka? ______________________________
5. Lɔtakatin? ______________________________

# Plural habitual endings

## Yoluyana

*Vocabulary*

| | | | |
|---|---|---|---|
| **eru** | *to laugh* | **shimi** | *to play* |
| **saku** | *to eat* | **woyu** | *to swim* |

## Yanalepini

*Dialogue*

**Merlinku, Chrisku, Daveku:** Kanahku yahkhiti?

**Aiyannahchi, Alicehchi, Rosehchi:** Eruhkiti. Kanahku yahkwiti?

**Merlinku, Chrisku, Daveku:** Shimihkiti.

**Aiyannahchi, Alicehchi, Rosehchi:** Shimihkwitin?

**Merlinku, Chrisku, Daveku:** Hon. Shimihkiti.

**Aiyannahchi, Alicehchi, Rosehchi:** Lapuhch.

**Aiyannahchi:** Chrisku, Merlinku, Daveku kanahku yakata?

**Alicehchi:** Sakukata.

**Aiyannahchi:** Augustinku, Henryku, Clydeku kanahku yakata?

**Alicehchi:** Woyukata.

**Aiyannahchi:** Lapuhch.

**Merlinku:** Alicehchi, Aiyannahchi, Rosehchi kanahku yahksiti?
**Chrisku:** Woyuhksiti.
**Merlinku:** Eruhksitin?
**Chrisku:** Aha. Woyuhksiti.
**Merlinku:** Lapuhch.

## Lutamashu

*Grammar*

Just like the singular **taya oni sahku** endings, the plural **taya oni sahku** endings vary based on the gender, number, and person of the person doing the action. A summary of the plural endings is given below.

| | | | |
|---|---|---|---|
| **-hkiti** | *we are _____ing* | **-hksiti** | *they (fp) are _____ing* |
| **-hkhiti** | *you all (fp) are _____ing* | **-kata** | *they (mp) are _____ing* |
| **-hkwiti** | *you all (mp) are _____ing* | | |

Notice that all of the plural endings start with an **hk** and end with **iti**, except for **-kata**. Also, as with pronouns in Chapter 1, the masculine plural is used for groups of men as well as groups of men and women. The feminine plural is only used when the group is all women.

## Hinu 2

*Practice*

**2.2.1. Atehpɛtaki** (Join together)**:**
Write the letter of the verb with the correct form to answer the question in the blanks.

***Example:*** ***a*** *Kanahku yakati?* *a. Hipukati.*

1. _____ Kanahku yakata? a. Shimihkwiti
2. _____ Kanahku yahkhiti/yahkwiti? b. Eruhkiti
3. _____ Kanahku yahksiti? c. Pitahkhiti
4. _____ Kanahku yahkiti? *(if females)* d. Woyukata
5. _____ Kanahku yahkiti? *(if males)* e. Sakuhksiti

**2.2.2. Luhchi pirɛtaki** (Translate)**:**
Translate the following into Tunica. Use the chart on the previous page if you need help.

***Example:*** *We are eating.* ***Sakuhkiti.***

1. They *(fp)* are swimming. ______________________
2. We are walking. ______________________
3. What are you all *(mp)* doing? ______________________
4. They *(mp)* are laughing. ______________________
5. You all *(fp)* are playing. ______________________

### 2.2.3. **Luhchi pirɛtaki** (Translate):

Translate the following into English. Use the chart on page 31 if you need help.

***Example:*** *Erukata.* ***They are laughing.***

1. Hipuhkiti. ____________________
2. Shimikatan? ____________________
3. Kanahku yahksiti? ____________________
4. Eruhkhiti. ____________________
5. Woyuhkwiti. ____________________

# Dual habitual endings

## Yoluyana

*Vocabulary*

| | | | |
|---|---|---|---|
| **hina** | *to write* | **niyu** | *to think; to consider* |
| **huwa** | *to wash oneself* | **wachi** | *to fight* |
| **lap'ɔhɔ** | *not good; bad* | **waha** | *to cry* |

## Yanalepini

*Dialogue*

**Naomihchi:** Kanahku yahkwina?
**Chrisku, Augustinku:** Niyuhkina.
**Naomihchi:** Hinahkwinan?
**Chrisku, Augustinku:** Aha. Niyuhkina. Kanahku yaka?
**Naomihchi:** Huwakani.
**Chrisku, Augustinku:** Lapuhch.

**Merlinku, Naomihchi:** Kanahku yahkhina?
**Alicehchi, Rosehchi:** Wachihkina. Kanahku yahkwina?
**Merlinku, Naomihchi:** Hinahkina.
**Alicehchi, Rosehchi:** Hinahkwinan?
**Merlinku, Naomihchi:** Hon. Hinahkina.
**Alicehchi, Rosehchi:** Lapuhch.

**Merlinku:** Chrisku, Henryku kanahku yahkuna?

**Aiyannahchi:** Sakuhkuna. Rosehchi, Alicehchi kanahku yahksina?

**Merlinku:** Niyuhksina. Daveku, Annahchi kanahku yahkuna?

**Aiyannahchi:** Wahahkuna.

**Merlinku:** Wahahkunan?

**Aiyannahchi:** Hon. Wahahkuna.

**Merlinku:** Lap'ɔhɔ.

## Lutamashu

*Grammar*

Recall from Chapter 1 that Tunica has an additional number distinction which English lacks: the dual. Dual refers to exactly two people doing an action. Rough English equivalents would be 'us two', 'you two', or 'them two'. So in Tunica, you have to specify whether there is only one, exactly two, or more than two people or objects involved in the action. **Taya oni sahku** have special forms for the dual. Here is a summary of the dual **taya oni sahku** habitual endings:

| | | | |
|---|---|---|---|
| **-hkina** | *we two are _____ing* | **-hksina** | *they two (fd) are _____ing* |
| **-hkhina** | *you two (fd) are _____ing* | **-hkuna** | *they two (md) are _____ing* |
| **-hkwina** | *you two (md) are _____ing* | | |

Like the plural **taya oni sahku** endings, the dual habitual endings start with **hk**. They also all end in **ina**, except for **-hkuna**.

At this point all of the regular forms of habitual **taya oni sahku** have been presented. A table showing all of these forms together is given in the table on the next page.

| | | SINGULAR | DUAL | PLURAL |
|---|---|---|---|---|
| *1st person* | | **-kani** | **-hkina** | **-hkiti** |
| *2nd person* | *feminine* | **-ka** | **-hkhina** | **-hkhiti** |
| | *masculine* | **-ki** | **-hkwina** | **-hkwiti** |
| *3rd person* | *feminine* | **-kati** | **-hksina** | **-hksiti** |
| | *masculine* | **-ku** | **-hkuna** | **-kata** |

## Hinu 3

*Practice*

**2.3.1. Atehpɛtaki** (Join together)**:**
Write the letter of the response to the question.

***Example:*** __*a*__ *Kanahku yakata?*     *a. Sakukata.*

1. _____ Kanahku yahkina? *(if males)*     a. Wahahksina.
2. _____ Kanahku yahkuna?     b. Wachihkina.
3. _____ Kanahku yahkina? *(if females)*     c. Niyuhkhina.
4. _____ Kanahku yahksina?     d. Huwahkwina.
5. _____ Kanahku yahkhina/yahkwina?     e. Hinahkuna.

**2.3.2. Molɔtaki** (Fill it)**:**
In each of the questions below, change the verb ending from singular or plural to dual. Leave the rest of the ending the same!

***Example:*** *Shimikani.* __***shimihkina.***__

1. Huwahkhiti. ______________________
2. Wahakani. ______________________
3. Wachihkwitin? ______________________
4. Niyukati. ______________________
5. Hinaku. ______________________

**2.3.3. Pakεtaki** (Question and Answer):

You and your friends are playing on the playground. Using some of the vocabulary we've learned in this chapter, respond to the following questions from your friends Thomas and Sara. Pick whichever verb you'd like but be sure to use the correct verb endings! Use the chart on the previous page if you need help.

***Example:** Kanahku yakati?* **Hipukati.**

1. Kanahku yahkina? ____________________
2. Kanahku yahksina? ____________________
3. Kanahku yahkuna? ____________________
4. Kanahku yahkhina/yahkwina? ____________________

## Tetimili: Rahp'itiki!

*Culture: Let's play ball!*

Our Choctaw relatives know stickball as the "Little Brother of War" because the game was used to settle disputes between tribes rather than resorting to war. The Mississippi Band of Choctaw Indians annually hosts the World Series of Stickball in which the various communities compete for top honors. For **Tayoroniku-Halayihku**, our ball-playing tradition is part of our ceremonial tradition of *Fête du Blé*. This ceremony will be discussed further later in the book.

Our last traditional chief and medicine man, Chief Joseph Alcide Pierite, Sr., excelled at stickball:

"I played it and I was perfect in my days with it 'cause I had practiced at 14 years everyday, everyday and if you gon' be good at anything that's the way to be good at it" (Chief Joseph Alcide Pierite Sr., Medford tapes, ca. 1970s).

"Racquet ball," as Chief Pierite referred to the game, was played by both men and women. The men on the team would use two **punatarahpani** 'stickball sticks', while the women could use their hands to pick up the **puna** 'ball', which was made from tightly wrapped cloth covered in deer hide. A **palatohku** 'point' was scored when a team member touched the ball to the post. Although stickball was only played during the day, a lantern would hang from the post to light the field for the night's dances.

Stickball is described as the "father of all field sports." Games played between Indigenous nations of the Southeast and Gulf South had political, social, and ceremonial implications. In the story of Thunder, one **Tawaka** 'commander' gambled his whole family away on a single ball game. The traditional *Fête du Blé* tested the endurance of our ancestors who danced all night and played ball all day.

Our tribe, with many others in the Gulf South, still play stickball. If you would speak your language while playing, **lapuhch** 'it would be a good thing'.

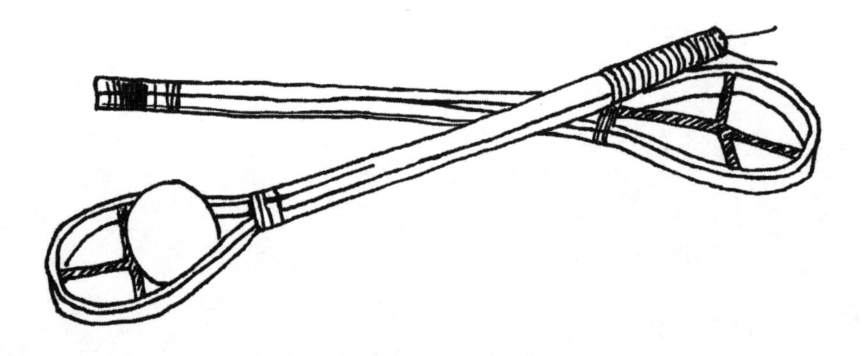

## Tetimili yoluyana

*Culture vocabulary*

| | | | |
|---|---|---|---|
| **pala** | *to win* | **rahpa** | *to play ball* |
| **palatohku** | *goal; point; score* | **tarahpani** | *ballplayer* |
| **puna** | *ball* | **punatarahpani** | *stickball (game); ball sticks* |

## Tetimili wiralepini

*Culture questions*

1. If you were to play stickball with your friends, what kinds of things might you want to be able to say in Tunica while you play?

2. Draw a **puna** and a **tarahpani** for your favorite type of ballgame. If you can't remember what these words mean, be sure to look at the **yoluyana** after the **tetimili**!

# Chapter 3: Kanahku ya'iti?

*What did we do?*

**TOPICS:**

# Singular completive endings

## Yoluyana

*Vocabulary*

| | | | |
|---|---|---|---|
| **ami** | *to leave; to go (from)* | **pata** | *to fall* |
| **kɔra** | *to drink* | **sara** | *to pray; sorry* |
| **lapuya** | *well* | **yuka** | *to arrive; to go (to)* |
| **lawushi** | *yesterday; the day before; at night* | | |

## Yanalepini

*Dialogue*

**Aiyannahchi:** Chrisku, kanahku yawi?
**Merlinku:** Kɔrawi. Diamondhchi, kanahku yati?
**Aiyannahchi:** Sarati.
**Merlinku:** Saratin?
**Aiyannahchi:** Hon. Sarati.
**Merlinku:** Lapuhch.

**Merlinku:** Lawushi kanahku ya'a?
**Naomihchi:** Pitani. Lawushi kanahku ya'i?
**Merlinku:** Lawushi patani.
**Naomihchi:** Pat'in?! Lap'ɔhɔ.

**Augustinku:** Dave, amikin? Lawushi yuk'i!
**Daveku:** Hon, sara. Lapuya rapuni!
**Augustinku:** Lapuhch. Imat, lawushi lapuya rapuni.
**Daveku:** Tikahch. Amikani!

## Lutamashu

*Grammar*

In Chapter 2, we learned how habitual endings are used with **taya oni sahku** to describe ongoing or repetitive actions. Another set of endings, the completive set, is used to describe actions that are over and done with. The closest English has to this completive meaning is the past tense, as in 'he walked'. As with habitual **taya oni sahku**, the form of the completive that gets used depends on the person, number, and gender of the person or thing doing the action. The following table gives the five singular completive endings you saw in the **yanalepini** above.

| | | | |
|---|---|---|---|
| **-ni** | *I _____ed* | **-ti** | *she _____ed* |
| **-a** | *you (fs) _____ed* | **-wi** | *he _____ed* |
| **-i** | *you (ms) _____ed* | | |

Notice in the second **yanalepini** that 'you *(ms)* fell' in Tunica is **pat'i**. This comes from the combination of **pata** and **-i**. In Tunica, when two vowels meet, usually only one of them can stick around. The vowel that remains is generally preceded by a glottal stop. You might remember an exception to this from Chapter 1: **ta-** + **oni** became **toni**, with no glottal before the o. In fact, when **ta-** is used to mean "the" before a word starting with a vowel, it usually becomes **t-** without a glottal! Sometimes, you may see words like **ta'oni**, where there is no vowel blending, but this is less common.

Tunica has rules that dictate whether one vowel wins or whether the vowels combine into an entirely new vowel. Pay particular attention to **-a** and **-i** rules below since they are used by completive endings.

| | | |
|---|---|---|
| a + a → a | i + a → ɛ | u + a → ɔ |
| a + i → i | i + i → i | u + i → i |
| a + u → u | i + u → u | u + u → u |
| a + ɔ → ɔ | | |

For a full list of all the vowel blends you'll find in this book, look to the quick reference in the back!

You can see that the order of the vowels matters. If **i** or **u** is the second vowel, it always wins. However, if **a** is the second vowel, it usually blends to form a new vowel. We refer to this process throughout the textbook as vowel blending. Here are some examples of vowels that blend with verbs we have learned so far.

**rapu** + **-a** = **rap'ɔ**
**rapu** + **-i** = **rap'i**

**sara** + **-a** = **sar'a**
**sara** + **-i** = **sar'i**

**wachi** + **-a** = **wach'ɛ**
**wachi** + **-i** = **wach'i**

When one vowel is lost, a glottal stop appears in place of the first vowel, like in **rap'ɔ**. This lets you know that a vowel has been assimilated into the following vowel. However, there are times when both vowels remain. If the main part of the verb is only one syllable, like **ya** 'to do', then its vowel can never be lost. Instead, both vowels remain, as in **kanahku ya'i?** 'what did you *(ms)* do?'. However, they still will get separated by a glottal stop, since Tunica does not allow two vowels to be next to each other. Practice using completive forms in the following exercises.

## Hinu 1

*Practice*

**3.1.1. Molɔtaki** (Fill it):

Fill in the blanks below. Remember to pay attention to the pronouns and which vowels are coming together.

***Example:*** *Ma rap'i. (rapu)*

1. Hɛma lɔt'_____. (lɔta)
2. Hɛma wach'_____. (wachi)
3. Hɛma niy'_____. (niyu)
4. Ma wah'_____. (waha)
5. Ma sak'_____. (saku)
6. Ma shim'_____. (shimi)

**3.1.2. Pas'aki** (Split it)**:**
For each of the following verb forms, provide the verb, the ending, and the pronoun that corresponds to that conjugation. In the last column, write a sentence using the pronoun and the verb.

***Example:***

| | | | | |
|---|---|---|---|---|
| *pat'a* | ***pata*** | ***-a*** | ***hɛma*** | ***hɛma pat'a*** |

| | VERB | VERB | ENDING | PRONOUN | SENTENCE |
|---|---|---|---|---|---|
| 1. | lɔt'a | _____ | _____ | _____ | _____ |
| 2. | sak'i | _____ | _____ | _____ | _____ |
| 3. | wach'i | _____ | _____ | _____ | _____ |
| 4. | am'ɛ | _____ | _____ | _____ | _____ |
| 5. | rap'ɔ | _____ | _____ | _____ | _____ |
| 6. | shim'i | _____ | _____ | _____ | _____ |
| 7. | wach'ɛ | _____ | _____ | _____ | _____ |
| 8. | sak'ɔ | _____ | _____ | _____ | _____ |

**3.1.3. Luhchi pirɛtaki** (Translate)**:**
Translate the following into English.

***Example:*** *Wachiwi.* **He fought.**

1. Yuk'ɛ. ______
2. Kɔr'i. ______
3. Sarani. ______
4. Amiti. ______
5. Patawi. ______

**3.1.4. Luhchi pirɛtaki** (Translate)**:**
Translate the following into Tunica.

***Example:*** *I fell.* **Patani.**

1. I arrived. ______
2. He drank. ______
3. You *(ms)* departed. ______
4. You *(fs)* prayed. ______
5. She fell. ______

# Plural completive endings

## Yoluyana

*Vocabulary*

| | | | |
|---|---|---|---|
| **-aha** | *not* | **le** | *to get lost* |
| **aka** | *to enter; to go in* | **raha** | *to comb one's hair* |
| **yaka** | *to come back* | **inkrish** | *to our house* |
| **yana** | *to talk; to speak; word* | **lawumihta** | *day before yesterday* |

## Yanalepini

*Dialogue*

**Aiyannahchi:** Lawumihta kanahku yawiti?

**Chrisku, Merlinku, Augustinku:** Lawumihta le'iti.

**Aiyannahchi:** Lewitin? Sara. Lawumihta inkrish yakani.

**Chrisku, Merlinku, Augustinku:** Lawumihta, Diamondhchi, Summerhchi, Genesishchi kanahku yasiti?

**Aiyannahchi:** Yanasiti, rahasiti. Lapuhch.

**Rosehchi, Naomihchi, Aiyannahchi:**
Chrisku, Merlinku, Henryku kanahku yata?

**Alicehchi, Diamondhchi, Lisahchi:**
Yanata. Kanahku yahiti?

**Rosehchi, Naomihchi, Aiyannahchi:**
Le'iti. Inkrish ak'it'ɛhɛ. Lawushi kɔritin?

**Alicehchi, Diamondhchi, Lisahchi:** Aha. Sar'iti.

**Rosehchi, Naomihchi, Aiyannahchi:**
Lapuhch.

## Lutamashu

*Grammar*

The plural completive endings in Tunica are used when three or more people did something. Remember that the masculine plural is used for mixed groups of people. The feminine plural is only used when you're talking about a group of only women.

| | | | |
|---|---|---|---|
| **-iti** | *we _____ed* | **-siti** | *they (fp) _____ed* |
| **-hiti** | *you all (fp) _____ed* | **-ta** | *they (mp) _____ed* |
| **-witi** | *you all (mp) _____ed* | | |

When a verb is followed by **-iti**, two vowels end up next to each other just like with **-i** and **-a** in the singular. The same vowel rules described above apply to **-iti** as well, so that you get one vowel and a glottal stop, like in **rah'iti**.

You might have noticed in the **yanalepini** that sometimes when **-hiti** is added to a word ending in a vowel that the **h** disappears and the vowels combine. For example, **kɔra** + **-hiti** is **kɔriti**, *not* **kɔrahiti**. This is because **h** is a weak sound, so it often gets lost. This is just like what happens to **-hat** (e.g. in **hɛmat**), which was discussed in Chapter 1. However, if you want to use the complete, unabbreviated form, this too is acceptable. Nonetheless, just like with vowels, the **h** is not lost when the word before it is only one syllable. This is why in the **yanalepini** you see **yahiti**, *not* **yiti**.

### Negation

As we learned in Chapter 1, the word for 'no' in Tunica is **aha**. In fact, **aha** can also be used at the end of words to mean 'not', like in **lap'ɔhɔ** 'not good'. For example, you can add **-aha** to **ima** to say 'not I, not me', in which case you say **im'aha**. **-aha** can also be used at the ends of verbs to mean that someone didn't do something. In the **yanalepini**, we saw the form **ak'it'ɛhɛ**, which means 'we did not enter'. **-aha** always attaches to something that is already a complete word (like **ak'iti**). Because **h** is a weak sound, *both* the vowels in **-aha** change, based on the vowel blending rules in the previous section. So, for example, 'they *(mp)* are not talking' would be **yana** + **kata** + **-aha**, which is **yanakat'aha**, and 'you all *(mp)* didn't come back' would be **yaka** + **witi** + **-aha**, which is **yakawit'ɛhɛ**. This same process happens in **lap'ɔhɔ** 'not good', which is **lapu** + **-aha**. Here the **u** contracts with the **a** to create **-ɔhɔ**, which spreads across both vowels.

If the element before **-aha** is only a single vowel (like **-a** or **-i**), then there isn't any contraction (just like in **yahiti**). However, **-aha** is special. Even though one of the vowels is not lost, the two **a**'s in **-aha** both change based on what the vowel right before **-aha** is. For example, 'you *(ms)* did not talk' would be **yana** + **-i** + **-aha**, which is **yan'i'ɛhɛ**. You also still get glottal stops in between every time two vowels are next to each other.

## Hinu 2

*Practice*

**3.2.1. Atehpɛtaki** (Join together)**:**
Write the letter of the verb with the correct form to answer the questions in the blanks.

***Example:*** *a* *Kanahku yasiti?* *a. Rahasiti.*

1. _____ Kanahku yata? a. Le'iti.
2. _____ Kanahku ya'iti?*(if mixed)* b. Akiti.
3. _____ Kanahku yahiti/yawiti? c. Yanata.
4. _____ Kanahku yasiti? d. Rahawiti.
5. _____ Kanahku ya'iti? *(if female)* e. Yakasiti.

**3.2.2. Luhchi Pirɛtaki** (Translate):
Translate the following into English.

***Example:*** *Sariti.* ***You (fp) prayed.***

1. Yakawiti. ____________________
2. Akata. ____________________
3. Lesiti. ____________________
4. Rah'it'ɛhɛ. ____________________
5. Yanit'ɛhɛ. ____________________

**3.2.3. Luhchi Pirɛtaki** (Translate):
Translate the following into Tunica.

***Example:*** *We got lost.* ***Le'iti.***

1. We came back. ____________________
2. You all *(mp)* combed your hair. ____________________
3. They *(fp)* spoke. ____________________
4. They *(mixed group)* didn't enter. ____________________
5. You all *(fp)* didn't get lost. ____________________

# Dual completive endings

## Yoluyana

*Vocabulary*

| | | | |
|---|---|---|---|
| **hapa** | *to stop* | **woru** | *to learn; to study* |
| **hotu** | *to finish* | **yoyani ya** | *to work* |
| **uki** | *to sit; to dwell; to remain* | **yɔla** | *to leave* |

## Yanalepini

*Dialogue*

**Aiyannahchi, Rosehchi:** Lawushi yoyani yawinan?

**Merlinku, Chrisku:** Hon, lawushi yoyani ya'ina. Lawushi kanahku yahina?

**Aiyannahchi, Rosehchi:** Lawushi wor'ina.

**Merlinku, Chrisku:** Lapuhch. Hotinan?

**Aiyannahchi, Rosehchi:** Aha. Hotuwinan?

**Merlinku, Chrisku:** Hon. Lapuhch.

**Augustinku:** Lawumihta, Aiyanna, Alicehchi kanahku yasina?

**Rosehchi:** Yɔlasina. Hapasina, yoyani yasin'aha.

**Augustinku:** Chrisku, Daveku yɔl'unan?

**Rosehchi:** Aha. Chrisku, Daveku uk'una.

**Augustinku:** Lapuhch.

## Lutamashu

*Grammar*

Recall from previous chapters that Tunica has specific ways of talking about two people doing things. This is also the case in the completive. The dual completive endings are given below.

| | | | |
|---|---|---|---|
| **-ina** | *we two _____ed* | **-sina** | *they two (fd) _____ed* |
| **-hina** | *you two (fd) _____ed* | **-una** | *they two (md) _____ed* |
| **-wina** | *you two (md) _____ed* | | |

Because **-ina** and **-una** start with vowels, they interact with the vowels at the end of words just like **-iti**, **-i**, and **-a**. So 'they two *(md)* left' is **yɔl'una**, and 'we two studied' is **wor'ina**. Also, **-hina** acts just like **-hiti** in that the **h** gets lost and the vowels combine. So 'you two *(f)* finished' is **hotina** (**hotu** + **hina**), though the full form, **hotuhina**, is also acceptable.

We have now learned all of the regular completive endings for Tunica verbs! A summary table of endings is given below, so you can see the relationship between the singular, dual, and plural forms.

| | | SINGULAR | DUAL | PLURAL |
|---|---|---|---|---|
| *1st person* | | **-ni** | **-ina** | **-iti** |
| *2nd person* | *feminine* | **-a** | **-hina** | **-hiti** |
| | *masculine* | **-i** | **-wina** | **-witi** |
| *3rd person* | *feminine* | **-ti** | **-sina** | **-siti** |
| | *masculine* | **-wi** | **-una** | **-ta** |

In fact, you may have noticed that many of the completive endings are similar to the habitual set you already know. In fact, most of the habitual endings are formed by adding **ka** or **hk** to the beginning of the completive form, e.g. completive **-ina** and habitual **-hkina**. Compare the differences in form and meaning between the habitual and completive forms below.

| | | | |
|---|---|---|---|
| **pitakani** | *I am walking* | **pitani** | *I walked* |
| **rapuka** | *you (fs) are sleeping* | **rap'ɔ** | *you (fs) slept* |
| **saraki** | *you (ms) are praying* | **sar'i** | *you (ms) prayed* |
| **lekati** | *she gets lost* | **leti** | *she got lost* |
| **niyuku** | *he believes* | **niyuwi** | *he believed* |

| | |
|---|---|
| **wachihkina** | *we two are fighting* |
| **sakuhkhina** | *you two (fd) are eating* |
| **patahkwina** | *you two (md) are falling* |
| **rahahksina** | *they two (fd) are combing their hair* |
| **wɛsahkuna** | *they two (md) are jumping* |

| | |
|---|---|
| **wach'ina** | *we two fought* |
| **sakina** | *you two (fd) ate* |
| **patawina** | *you two (md) fell* |
| **rahasina** | *they two (fd) combed their hair* |
| **wɛs'una** | *they two (md) jumped* |

| | |
|---|---|
| **shimihkiti** | *we are playing* |
| **yɔlahkhiti** | *you all (fp) are leaving* |
| **hipuhkwiti** | *you all (mp) are dancing* |
| **woruhksiti** | *they (fp) are learning* |
| **erukata** | *they (mp) are laughing* |

| | |
|---|---|
| **shim'iti** | *we played* |
| **yɔliti** | *you all (fp) slipped* |
| **hipuwiti** | *you all (mp) danced* |
| **worusiti** | *they (fp) learned* |
| **eruta** | *they (mp) laughed* |

## Hinu 3

*Practice*

**3.3.1. Chu'ɔki** (Multiple choice):
Choose the right response to the question about what people are doing.

***Example:*** *Kanahku ya'una?*
***a. Yɔl'una.*** *b. Yɔlawi.* *c. Yɔlata.*

1. Kanahku ya'ina? *(if females)*
   a. Hot'iti. b. Hotiti. c. Hotusina.
2. Kanahku yawina?
   a. Ukiwina. b. Uki'iti. c. Uk'ina.
3. Kanahku yasina?
   a. Woruhksina. b. Worusina. c. Wor'iti.
4. Kanahku ya'ina? *(if males)*
   a. Yoyani yawina. b. Yoyani ya'ina. c. Yoyani yata.
5. Kanahku yahina?
   a. Hapasiti. b. Hap'ina. c. Hapina.

**3.3.2. Molɔtaki** (Fill it):
In each of the questions below, change the verb from habitual to completive. Leave the gender and number of the ending the same! Use the chart on page 50 if you need help.

***Example:*** *Yakahkwiti.* ***Yakawiti.***

1. Akakata. ________
2. Lehksiti. ________
3. Rahahkit'ɛhɛ. ________
4. Yanahkiti. ________
5. Sarahksiti. ________

**3.3.3. Molɔtaki** (Fill it):
In each of the questions below, change the verb ending from singular to plural. Leave the rest of the ending the same! Look at the chart on page 50 if you need help.

***Example:*** *Sarawi.* ***Sarata.***

1. Yan'i. ________
2. Le'ɛ. ________
3. Akati. ________
4. Yakani. ________
5. Rahati. ________

## Tetimili: Tuwatasiwat'ɛ

*Culture: The Owl-Mammoth*

This is the story of **Tuwatasiwat'ɛ**, the Owl-Mammoth, adapted from the *Tunica Texts*. This story can be interpreted in many different ways. One could say that it means "never go into the woods at night because you never know who you are going to meet" or simply that "there is strength in numbers." We love the ingenuity of the two boys in this story. It's their cleverness that ultimately saves them from the Owl-Mammoth. We know this by the ninth line that says "**Uhknɛhtali kichu rihku ili raw'una. Pih'una.**" This is where the boys put the logs in their beds and hide. It is further solidified that this trick worked in the thirteenth line that says **tarihku ili tapiwihch, tɔkatɛkah'unima howɛsawihch uhkshuch'una**, where the boys outsmart the Owl-Mammoth and successfully shoot him until "he exploded." We are reminded in this story that it takes courage and strength to overcome any obstacles that may come your way.

**Aparush Tahch'ihchi mili piratihch, usa. TASIWAKU.**
When the sun got red in the sky, he would come. TASIWA.

**Har'usa: "Tasiwa hiwa yonahe. Tasiwa hiwa yonahe, Tasiwa hiwa yonahe. UWA."**
He came singing: "Tasiwa hiwa yonahe.Tasiwa hiwa yonahe, Tasiwa hiwa yonahe. UWA."

**Lawutɛpan, kaku hal'ukini kichu uk'unaku uhksakuwan yakaku.**
Every night, he would come back to eat someone living in the village.

**Hal'ukini rɔhpant ɔkatɛkaha uk'una.**
Two orphan boys lived on the edge of the village.

**Ashuhki sahku onti hal'ukini kichu uk'ɛrasɛma sihkpowan yak'una.**
One day they came to see their friends in the village.

**Hinahkushkan yuk'unahch, Ta'uchɛhkatonayi, "Winkonisɛma hotu sihksakuwi."**
But when they arrived Old Toad Woman told them, "Tasiwa ate all your people."

**"Hinahkushkan ihksakupokuhch, ihklehuku," niti.**
"But when he tries to eat me, he spits me out."

**Ta'uchɛhkatonayi tɔkatɛkah'unima wishkatahi, alakuhpa unkyuwati.**
Old Toad Woman gave the boys bows and arrows.

**Unknɛhtali kichu rihku ili raw'una. Pih'una.**
They put two logs in their bed and hid.

**Tasiwaku unksakuwan yakawi. Ripokuni hayihta ukiwiman eruwi.**
Tasiwa came to eat them. He perched on the roof of the house and laughed.

**Rasht'ɛ eruwi. Tari hilawi.**
He laughed so hard he made the house move.

**Tasiwaku tari kichu powihch, tɔkatɛkaha rap'un'unima unkpowi niyuwi.**
When Tasiwa looked into the house, he thought that he saw the two sleeping orphan boys.

**Tarihku ili tapiwihch, tɔkatɛkah'unima howɛsawihch uhkshuch'una.**
As he grabbed the logs, the boys jumped out and shot him.

**Amari uhkshuch'una. Tasiwa tihkati.**
They shot him so much that he exploded.

**Ushtosu tarihkush chir'aki. Rihku osint'ɛ unkpir'aki.**
His eyes splattered on the trees and today we see them as tree knots.

## Tetimili yoluyana

*Culture vocabulary*

| | | | |
|---|---|---|---|
| **ɔkatɛkaha** | *orphan* | **Ta'uchɛhkatonayi** | *Old Toad Woman* |
| **shuchi** | *to shoot (with a bow and arrow)* | **Tuwatasiwat'ɛ (Tasiwa)** | *Owl-Mammoth* |

## Tetimili wiralepini

*Culture questions*

1. Can you find any of the vocabulary we've learned over our first three chapters here? What are some of those words? How about verb endings?

2. There are a few different beings mentioned in this story. Who are they and what roles do they play?

3. The story of **Tasiwa** is an old and frightening one. Did you grow up with any stories like this? What were they?

# Chapter 4: Wirakashi

## *Numbers*

**TOPICS:**

# Wir'intaki!

*Let's count!*

## Yoluyana

| | |
|---|---|
| **ahomu** | *divided by* |
| **kashku** | *how many* |
| **kolu** | *minus* |
| **namu** | *many; much* |
| **sinkshku** | *equals* |
| **taworuni** | *teacher* |
| **(-)tɛya** | *plus* |
| **tihika** | *year; summer* |
| **wirakashi** | *numbers* |
| **yahki** | *times (multiplied by)* |
| **ihkyuk'aki** | *I'm (___ years old)* |
| **hihkyuk'aki** | *you (fs) are (___ years old)* |
| **wihkyuk'aki** | *you (ms) are (___ years old)* |
| **tihkyuk'aki** | *she is (___ years old)* |
| **uhkyuk'aki** | *he is (___ years old)* |

## Yanalepini

**Billku:** Tihika kashku hihkyuk'aki?

**Aiyannahchi:** Tihika michu sahkutɛya enihku ihkyuk'aki. Mahat, tihika kashku wihkyuk'aki?

**Billku:** Tihika michu tohkusahkutɛya tohkusahku ihkyuk'aki.

**Aiyannahchi:** Tihika namu! Lapuhch!

**Alicehchi:** Tihika kashku wihkyuk'aki?

**Daveku:** Tihika michu mankutɛya tayihku ihkyuk'aki. Hɛmat, tihika kashku hihkyuk'aki?

**Alicehchi:** Tihika michu enihkutɛya tisihku ihkyuk'aki!

**Daveku:** Lapuhch! Summerhchɛt, tihika kashku tihkyuk'aki?

**Alicehchi:** Tihika michu ilitɛya masahki tihkyuk'aki. Jameskɔt, tihika kashku uhkyuk'aki?

**Daveku:** Tihika michu ilitɛya sinku uhkyuk'aki.

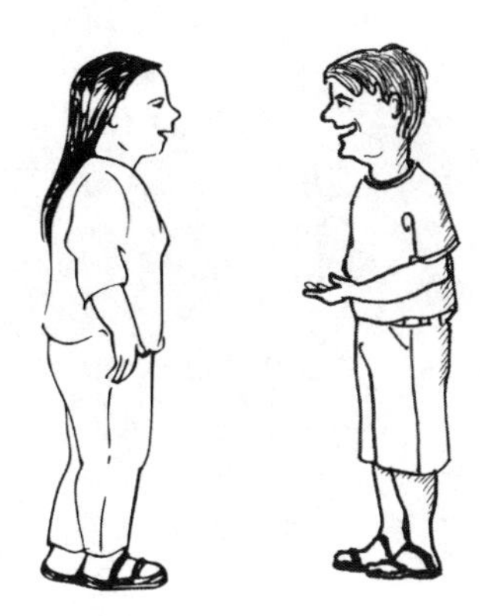

**Naomihchi:** Augustin, kashku enihku tɛya sinku?

**Augustinku:** Tisihku.

**Naomihchi:** Hon. Tisihku. Rose, kashku michu sahku kolu sahku?

**Rosehchi:** Tohkusahku.

**Naomihchi:** Hon. Tohkusahku. Merlin, kashku manku yahki manku?

**Merlinku:** Michu sahkutɛya manku.

**Naomihchi:** Aha. Michu sahkutɛya mank'ɔhɔ. Alice, kashku?

**Alicehchi:** Manku yahki manku michu sahkutɛya masahki sinkshku.

**Naomihchi:** Hon. Michu sahkutɛya masahki sinkshku. Merlin, kashku michu sahkutɛya sinku ahomu enihku?

**Merlinku:** Sinku sinkshku.

**Naomihchi:** Hon. Sinku sinkshku.

**Wirakashi:**
*Numbers*

| | | | |
|---|---|---|---|
| **sahku** | *1* | **michu sahkutɛya sahku** | *11* |
| **ili** | *2* | **michu sahkutɛya ili** | *12* |
| **enihku** | *3* | **michu sahkutɛya enihku** | *13* |
| **manku** | *4* | **michu sahkutɛya manku** | *14* |
| **sinku** | *5* | **michu sahkutɛya sinku** | *15* |
| **masahki** | *6* | **michu sahkutɛya masahki** | *16* |
| **tayihku** | *7* | **michu sahkutɛya tayihku** | *17* |
| **tisihku** | *8* | **michu sahkutɛya tisihku** | *18* |
| **tohkusahku** | *9* | **michu sahkutɛya tohkusahku** | *19* |
| **michu sahku** | *10* | **michu ili** | *20* |

| | | | |
|---|---|---|---|
| **michu ilitɛya sahku** | *21* | **michu enihkutɛya sahku** | *31* |
| **michu ilitɛya ili** | *22* | **michu enihkutɛya ili** | *32* |
| **michu ilitɛya enihku** | *23* | **michu enihkutɛya enihku** | *33* |
| **michu ilitɛya manku** | *24* | **michu enihkutɛya manku** | *34* |
| **michu ilitɛya sinku** | *25* | **michu enihkutɛya sinku** | *35* |
| **michu ilitɛya masahki** | *26* | **michu enihkutɛya masahki** | *36* |
| **michu ilitɛya tayihku** | *27* | **michu enihkutɛya tayihku** | *37* |
| **michu ilitɛya tisihku** | *28* | **michu enihkutɛya tisihku** | *38* |
| **michu ilitɛya tohkusahku** | *29* | **michu enihkutɛya tohkusahku** | *39* |
| **michu enihku** | *30* | **michu manku** | *40* |

| | | | |
|---|---|---|---|
| **michu sinku** | *50* | **michu tisihku** | *80* |
| **michu masahki** | *60* | **michu tohkusahku** | *90* |
| **michu tayihku** | *70* | **polun sahku** | *100* |

## Lutamashu

The Tunica number system follows a regular pattern. In the chart above, you can see that there is a different word for each number one to ten. However, you might have noticed that the word for ten, **michu**, is followed by the word for one, **sahku**. Whenever the word **michu** appears, it must always be followed by another number to indicate how many tens there are. So **michu ili** is 'twenty', **michu enihku** is 'thirty', and so on.

To count past ten, we need another word: **-tɛya**. This word is equivalent to the English 'plus'. For example, the word for eleven is **michu sahkutɛya sahku**. The whole word literally translated means 'one ten plus one'. All numbers from one to ninety-nine follow this pattern.

When speaking with Mary Haas, Sesostrie Youchigant used shortened forms for numbers over ten. The number counting the tens loses the final **-ku**, so **michu sahkutɛya enihku** becomes **michu sahtɛya enihku**. The textbook contains the longer forms, but you can use either.

To ask how old someone is requires a special construction: **Tihika kashku _____yuk'aki**. This starts with **tihika** 'year' plus **kashku** 'how many'. A noun must always come before **kashku**, which represents whatever you are counting. The last word is at its core the verb **yuka** 'to reach; to arrive'. So although the most common translation for **tihika kashku _____yuk'aki** in English is 'how old is X?', a more literal translation would be something like 'how many years have reached X?'.

The beginning of **yuk'aki** changes based on who you are talking to: **ihk-** for talking about yourself, **hihk-** for talking to a woman, **wihk-** for talking to a man, **tihk-** for talking about a woman, and **uhk-** for talking about a man. So **tihika X wihkyuk'aki** would be 'you *(ms)* are X years old' or 'X years have reached you *(ms)*', while **tihika X ihkyuk'aki** would be 'I am X years old' or 'X years have reached me'. These forms will become more familiar as we learn more types of verbs.

## Hinu 1

**4.1.1. Kashku?**

Use the following exercise to practice with numbers and become familiar with how to express how old you are.

**Example:** *Tihika kashku uhkyuk'aki? (27)*
*Tihika* ***michu iliteya tayihku*** *uhkyuk'aki.*

1. Tihika kashku hihkyuk'aki? (15)

   Tihika ______________________ ihkyuk'aki.

2. Tihika kashku tihkyuk'aki? (67)

   Tihika ______________________ tihkyuk'aki.

3. Tihika kashku wihkyuk'aki? (22)

   Tihika ______________________ ihkyuk'aki.

4. Tihika kashku uhkyuk'aki? (79)

   Tihika ______________________ uhkyuk'aki.

5. Tihika kashku ihkyuk'aki? *(a female)* (8)

   Tihika ______________________ hihkyuk'aki.

**4.1.2. Pakɛtaki** (Answer it)**:**

Solve the following math problems by writing the answers out in Tunica.

***Example:*** *12 + 2 =* ***michu sahkutɛya manku***

1. $8 - 5 =$ ______________
2. $6 + 3 =$ ______________
3. $6 \times 10 =$ ______________
4. $4 + 3 =$ ______________
5. $9 - 8 =$ ______________
6. $34 - 5 =$ ______________
7. $29 + 6 =$ ______________
8. $45 \div 9 =$ ______________
9. $4 \times 5 =$ ______________
10. $80 \div 8 =$ ______________

### 4.1.3. Molɔtaki:

Solve the following math problems by writing the answers out in Tunica.

***Example:*** *manku tɛya tisihku* **_michu sahkutɛya ili_** *sinkshku*

1. Michu ili ahomu michu sahku ________________ sinkshku.
2. Tisihku yahki tayihku ________________ sinkshku.
3. Ili yahki manku ________________ sinkshku.
4. Masahki kolu sahku ________________ sinkshku.
5. Sinku yahki ili ________________ sinkshku.
6. Michu sahku tɛya tisihku ________________ sinkshku.
7. Tohkusahku ahomu enihku ________________ sinkshku.
8. Michu enihku kolu manku ________________ sinkshku.

## Wirakashihta

*Ordinal numbers*

### Yoluyana

| | | | |
|---|---|---|---|
| **chɔha** | *chief* | **kaku** | *who; which* |
| **-hta** | *-st, -rd, -th (ordinal)* | **Tayoroniku-Halayihku** | *Tunica-Biloxi* |
| **inkara** | *we have* | **wirakashihta** | *ordinal numbers* |

### Yanalepini

**Merlinku:** Tachɔhaku Tayoroniku-Halayihku sahkuhta, kanahku otisa?

**Rosehchi:** Tachɔha Paulku, niyukani.

**Merlinku:** Aaaa. Brides les Boeufsku tachɔhaku ilihtan?

**Rosehchi:** Aha. Brides les Boeufsku tachɔhaku enihkuhta.

**Merlinku:** Kaku tachɔhaku ilihta?

**Rosehchi:** Cahura Joligoku tachɔhaku ilihta.

**Merlinku:** Inima Tayoroniku-Halayihku tachɔhasɛma namu inkara!

### Lutamashu

Numbers like **sahku**, **ili**, **enihku** 'one, two, three', which you've seen in the previous section, are used to count things and to do math problems. These numbers are called **wirakashi** (or cardinal numbers in English). Numbers like **sahkuhta**, **ilihta**, **enihkuhta** 'first, second, third' are used to put things in order, like when numbering objects or putting ideas or people in a series. These ordering numbers are called **wirakashihta** (or ordinal numbers in English). To make ordinal numbers in Tunica, you just add **-hta** to the regular number, so to say "the sixth one," you would combine **masahki** + **-hta** to get **masahkihta**.

## Hinu 2

**4.2.1. Wirakashihta mashuwitiki:**
Write the ordinal number in Tunica for each of the following.

***Example:*** *enihku* ***enihkuhta***

1. sahku ______________________
2. michu sahku ______________________
3. tayihku ______________________
4. tisihku ______________________
5. tohkusahku ______________________
6. manku ______________________
7. sinku ______________________

### 4.2.2. Wirakashi mashuwitiki:

Write the cardinal number for each of the following.

***Example:*** *sahkuhta* **sahku**

1. ilihta ______
2. michu sahkutɛya sahkuhta ______
3. enihkuhta ______
4. masahkihta ______
5. michu ilihta ______
6. polun sahkuhta ______

## Tahch'a

*Months*

## Yoluyana

| | |
|---|---|
| **ashuhki** | *day* |
| **ashutayi** | *week* |
| **-hch** | *when; during; while* |
| **sinkara** | *they (f) have* |

| | |
|---|---|
| **tahch'a** | *moon; month* |
| **-t'ɛ** | *big* |
| **tihkara** | *she (it) has* |
| **tihkashuhki** | *her (its) day* |

| | |
|---|---|
| **ipirashu** | *my birthday* |
| **hipirashu** | *your (fs) birthday* |
| **wipirashu** | *your (ms) birthday* |

| | |
|---|---|
| **tipirashu** | *her birthday* |
| **upirashu** | *his birthday* |

## Yanalepini

**Naomihchi:** Kanahku tahch'ahch hipuhkina?

**Alicehchi:** Tahch'ahipuhch hipuhkina.

**Naomihchi:** Kanahku tahch'ahch woyuhkina?

**Alicehchi:** Tihikatahch'a, Tihikatahch'a Tehukuma, Tahch'aruwinahch, woyuhkina.

**Chrisku:** Tihika kashku wihkyuk'aki? Kanahku tahch'ahch wipirashu?

**Augustinku:** Tihika michu tohkusahkutɛya tohkusahku ihkyuk'aki. Ipirashu Tahch'aruwina ashuhki michu ilitɛya manku. Mahat?

**Chrisku:** Tihika michu sahkutɛya sahku ihkyuk'aki. Ipirashu Tahch'asap'arahch.

**Aiyannahchi:** Kanahku tahch'a ashuhki michu ilitɛya tisihku tihkara?

**Merlinku:** Tahch'awɛka Tehukuma ashuhki michu ilitɛya tisihku tihkara.

**Aiyannahchi:** Kanahku tahch'a ashuhki michu enihkutɛya sahku tihkara?

**Merlinku:** Tahch'awɛka, Komelitahch'a, Tahch'ahipu, Tihikatahch'a Tehukuma, Tahch'aruwina, Tahch'awɛra, Tahch'asap'ara ashuhki michu enihkutɛya sahku sinkara.

**Chrisku:** Ashutayi ashuhki kashku tihkara?

**Augustinku:** Ashuhki tayihku tihkara.

**Chrisku:** Ashutayi tihkashuhki sahkuhta kanahku tetisa?

**Augustinku:** Ashut'ɛ tetisa.

**Tahch'a:**
*Months*

| **Tahch'awɛka** | *January* | spoiled month; waning moon month |
|---|---|---|
| **Tahch'awɛka Tehukuma** | *February* | waning moon month's little sister |
| **Komelitahch'a** | *March* | hackberry tree month |
| **Tahch'atapa** | *April* | planting month |
| **Tahch'ahipu** | *May* | Powwow month |
| **Tihikatahch'a** | *June* | summer month |
| **Tihikatahch'a Tehukuma** | *July* | summer month's little sister |
| **Tahch'aruwina** | *August* | hot month |
| **Tahch'aruwina Tehukuma** | *September* | hot month's little sister |
| **Tahch'awɛra** | *October* | hunting month |
| **Tahch'asap'aratohku** | *November* | little winter month |
| **Tahch'asap'ara** | *December* | winter month |

**Ashutayi:**
*The week*

| | |
|---|---|
| **Ashut'ɛ** | *Sunday* |
| **Rapusahku** | *Monday* |
| **Rap'ili** | *Tuesday* |
| **Rap'onihku** | *Wednesday* |
| **Rapumanku** | *Thursday* |
| **Rapusinku** | *Friday* |
| **Samdi / Ashut'ɛ Tehukuma** | *Saturday* |

## Lutamashu

Tunica month names all contain the word **tahch'a** 'moon'. Modern Tunica uses lunar month names to approximate the solar months of the western calendar. The Tunica formerly marked time according to full moons and the seasons and activities associated with each. For example, 'April' in Tunica is **Tahch'atapa**, 'planting month' because April is when the Tunica would typically sow their crops. Tunica month names can also be descriptive. 'August' is **Tahch'aruwina**, meaning 'hot month'. A final interesting aspect of Tunica month names is that certain ones contain the element **Tehukuma**, 'younger same-gender sibling'. We know that the Tunica view the moon as feminine, therefore months like **Tahch'aruwina Tehukuma** 'September' is literally 'August's little sister'. Since months are feminine, their verbs are also marked as feminine; **Tahch'awɛka Tehukuma ashuhki michu ilitɛya tisihku tihkara** literally means 'Spoiled month's younger sister (February) days twenty-eight she-has', or "February has twenty-eight days."

Most of the Tunica day names are a combination of **rapu** 'sleep' and a number. The first day of the week, **Ashut'ɛ** 'Sunday', is composed of **ashuhki** 'day' and **-t'ɛ** 'big'. So 'Monday' is one sleep after **Ashut'ɛ**, or **Rapusahku**. 'Saturday' has two names: **Samdi** is borrowed from French *samedi*, while **Ashut'ɛ Tehukuma** means 'Sunday's little sister'.

You may have noticed above that the different words for different people's birthdays have similar beginnings as the different forms of **-etisa** in Chapter 1. This is because both of these are things that always belong to someone. This type of word, called an inalienable noun, includes body parts and family members because all of these have an inherent relationship with one (or more) particular person that can't be given or taken away from them. For example, you can't give away your name or your birthday the same way that you could give away a book. In Tunica, these things that can't be given away form a special group of nouns that have different possessive prefixes than other nouns. These can be seen in the examples below, but remember that sometimes the vowels can change depending on what's after them (like with **-etisa**).

**i + pirashu** = my birthday
**hi + pirashu** = your *(fs)* birthday
**wi + pirashu** = your *(ms)* birthday
**ti + pirashu** = her birthday
**u + pirashu** = his birthday

For other nouns, there is a separate set of prefixes. You will learn the full set for this type of possession in Chapters 8 and 11–12.

## Hinu 3

**4.3.1. Tawiralepini pakawintaki:**
Answer the following questions.

***Example:*** *Ashuhki kashku ashutayi tihkara?* ***Tayihku.***

1. Ashutayi tihkashuhki sahkuhta Ashut'ɛ. Kanahku ashuhki ilihta? ______
2. Tihika sahku tahch'a kashku tihkara? ______
3. Tahch'awɛka ashuhki kashku tihkara? ______
4. Ashutayi tihkashuhki enihkuhta kanahku tetisa? ______
5. Tahch'a masahkihta kanahku tetisa? ______
6. Kanahku tahch'ahch hipirashu/wipirashu? ______
7. Kanahku tahch'ahch George Washingtonku upirashu? ______
8. Ashutayi tihkashuhki sinkuhta kanahku tetisa? ______

### 4.3.2. Atehpɛtaki:

Match the following holidays and events to the month they are in.

***Example:*** __**a**__ *Leap day* *a. Tahch'awɛka Tehukuma*

| | | | |
|---|---|---|---|
| 1. | _____ Tahch'awɛka | a. | Christmas |
| 2. | _____ Tahch'awɛka Tehukuma | b. | Fourth of July |
| 3. | _____ Komelitahch'a | c. | Saint Patrick's Day |
| 4. | _____ Tahch'atapa | d. | Tunica-Biloxi Powwow |
| 5. | _____ Tahch'ahipu | e. | Thanksgiving |
| 6. | _____ Tihikatahch'a | f. | Deer season opens for rifle hunting |
| 7. | _____ Tihikatahch'a Tehukuma | g. | Valentine's Day |
| 8. | _____ Tahch'aruwina | h. | New Year's Day |
| 9. | _____ Tahch'aruwina Tehukuma | i. | April Fool's Day |
| 10. | _____ Tahch'awɛra | j. | Father's Day |
| 11. | _____ Tahch'asap'aratohku | k. | Labor Day |
| 12. | _____ Tahch'asap'ara | l. | Fall start of school |

### 4.3.3. Molɔtaki:

Fill in the blanks with the number of days in each month in Tunica. Write them out completely, as in the example below.

***Example:*** *Tahch'asap'aratohku* **_Michu enihku_**

1. Tahch'awɛka __________
2. Tahch'awɛka Tehukuma __________
3. Komelitahch'a __________
4. Tahch'atapa __________
5. Tahch'ahipu __________
6. Tihikatahch'a __________
7. Tihikatahch'a Tehukuma __________
8. Tahch'aruwina __________
9. Tahch'aruwina Tehukuma __________
10. Tahch'awɛra __________
11. Tahch'asap'ara __________

## Tetimili: Tihika Nisa

*The New Year*

Today, we celebrate New Year's Eve on December 31st and New Year's Day on January 1st. However, the traditional New Year was likely during the summer, similar to other tribes of the Southeast, during Green Corn time. This is the reason why the word for both 'year' and 'summer' is **tihika** in Tunica.

In ***Hichut'una Awachihk'unanahch*** 'Fighting Eagles', Sesostrie Youchigant describes the behavior of the Tunica chief who became the one who whoops above:

> **Hinyatihch, tihikatɛpan pan'u'uwani hayishi.**
> Every year he passes above.
>
> **Hɛlawu panuwihch sehitihch tihika nisa pirakatɛni.**
> The night that he passes is the dawn of the new year.
>
> (Haas, *Tunica Texts*, text 8B, p. 76)

Sesostrie Youchigant clarified this when talking with Mary Haas (Haas, *Tunica Texts*, text 8A, p. 75, footnotes 17–21). He said that the chief, as an eagle, flies from pole to pole, passing over Marksville heading south at midnight on New Year's Eve and passing back over on his way north at midnight on New Year's Day. Sesostrie Youchigant himself heard **Hayishta'uruni** 'the one who whoops above' calling "Ku ku" every two acres as he passes, whooping like a man and making a noise similar to an airplane. He noted that after the whites moved into the area, **Hayishta'uruni** had to fly higher and became harder to hear.

Today, the fireworks that we hear starting at the stroke of midnight commemorate his whooping.

## Tetimili wiralepini

1. We see the word **hayishi** in the first line of the story and in the name of the Tunica chief who whoops above (**Hayishta'uruni**). What do you think **hayishi** means?

2. Initially, **Hayishta'uruni** flew in the summer during the Green Corn time. What are the names of those months in Tunica?

3. Now **Hayishta'uruni** flies on New Year's Eve and New Year's Day: what are the Tunica words for the months those are celebrated in today?

# Chapter 5: Taya Nahchu

*Transitive Verbs*

**TOPICS:**

# Taya nahchu

*Transitive verbs*

## Yoluyana

| | | | |
|---|---|---|---|
| **arhilani** | *story* | **rohina** | *letters; alphabet* |
| **chuyaka** | *to bring* | **kichu** | *in; inside* |
| **sa** | *dog* | **leyu** | *to point at something* |
| **saku** | *food* | **minu** | *cat* |
| **tapi** | *to grab; to catch* | **po** | *to look at; to watch; to see; to read* |
| **weni** | *to find; to discover* | **puna** | *ball* |
| **wishi** | *water* | **rihkuyahoni** | *tree branch* |
| **wiya** | *to throw* | | |

## Yanalepini

**Daveku:** Naomi, kanahku poka?
**Naomihchi:** Minu wenini.
**Daveku:** Minu pokan'ɛhɛ.
**Naomihchi:** Taminu leyukani.
**Daveku:** Taminu pokani!

*Daveku rihkuyahoni tapiku, chuyakaku.*
*Taminu tarihkuyahoni tapikuhch,*
*Daveku taminu tapiku.*
*Naomihchi taminu tapikati.*

**Naomihchi:** Tikahch, Dave!

**Rosehchi:** Heni, Augustin! Kanahku yaki?

**Augustinku:** Saku sakukani. Wishi kɔrakani. Kanahku yaka? Rohina pokan?

**Rosehchi:** Aha, arhilani hinakani.

**Augustinku:** Ko'o!

**Rosehchi:** Tarhilani kichu oni, sa shimihkuna. Toniku puna tapiku, wiyaku. Tasa minu poku, tapuna pok'ɔhɔ. Toni tapuna leyuku. Tasa tapuna weniw'ɛhɛ.

**Augustinku:** Arhilani lapu!

**Rosehchi:** Tikahch.

## Lutamashu

**Taya nahchu**, or transitive verbs, are verbs that have both a subject (someone who is doing the action) and an object (someone or something that the action is being done to). Take a look at the following sentence:

**Tanuhchihchi arhilani hinakati.**
Subject Object Verb
'The woman is writing a story.'

In this sentence, **hina** not only has a subject (**tanuhchihchi**), it also has an object (**arhilani**). We learned in Chapter 2 that the noun in Tunica comes before the verb, so you can say **tanuhchihchi hinakati** 'the woman is writing', with only a subject that appears before the verb. When there is an object, the object appears after the subject but before the verb. This is not like English, where the object comes after the verb ('the woman is writing *a story*' vs. **tanuhchihchi** ***arhilani*** **hinakati**). All sentences in Tunica follow this same pattern: Subject–Object–Verb.

A few of the verbs that we have already learned can be either **taya oni sahku** or **taya nahchu**, depending on whether it makes sense for them to have an object. Some examples appear on the next page.

| With just a subject: | | With a subject and an object: | |
|---|---|---|---|
| **Sakukani** | 'I am eating' | **Saku sakukani** | 'I am eating food' |
| **Pokani** | 'I am watching' | **Taminu pokani** | 'I am watching the cat' |
| **Hinakani** | 'I am writing' | **Arhilani hinakani** | 'I am writing a story' |

Any verb that can be a transitive verb can also be translated using 'it', without any changes. This means that **sakukani** can mean either 'I am eating' or 'I am eating it'.

## Hinu 1

**5.1.1. Chu'ɔki:**
Choose the correct translation of the following statements.

***Example:*** *Saku sakuki.*
***a. You (ms) are eating food.*** *b. You (ms) are eating.* *c. You (ms) ate it.*

1. Rihkuyahoni tapini.
   a. She grabbed a branch. b. I grabbed a cat. c. I grabbed a branch.

2. Wishi chuyakakati.
   a. She is bringing water. b. She is taking water. c. She brought a branch.

3. Taminu weniwiti.
   a. I found a cat. b. They *(mp)* lost their cat. c. You *(mp)* found the cat.

4. Tasa pohkina.
   a. I am looking for a dog. b. We *(d)* are looking at the dog.
   c. We *(d)* looked at a dog.

5. Arhilani hinahksina.
   a. They *(fd)* write stories. b. They *(md)* write books. c. They *(fd)* read stories.

### 5.1.2. Chu'ɔki:

Choose the correct translation of the following statements.

***Example:*** *I am reading it.*

***a. Rohina pokani.*** *b. Rohina poni.* *c. Arhilani poni.*

1. The teacher wrote the story.
   a. Taworuni arhilani chuyakati. b. Taworuni arhilani hinati.
   c. Tanuhchi arhilani poti.
2. They *(md)* ate it.
   a. Sak'una. b. Saku sakuhkuna. c. Sak'ina.
3. We *(p)* brought food.
   a. Saku tapiwi. b. Saku sakukani. c. Saku chuyak'ina.
4. A man read it.
   a. Oni weniwi. b. Oni rohina powi. c. Rohina poku.
5. The dog is bringing a branch.
   a. Sa rihkuyahoni tapiku. b. Tasa wishi chuyakaku. c. Tasa rihkuyahoni chuyakaku.

### 5.1.3. Luhchi pirɛtaki:

Translate the following into Tunica.

***Example:*** *I throw the ball.* ***Puna wiyakani.***

1. You *(md)* wrote a story. ______________________
2. They *(fp)* bring the cat. ______________________
3. He found a dog. ______________________
4. We *(p)* grab a dog. ______________________
5. You *(fs)* make food. ______________________

### 5.1.4. Luhchi pirɛtaki:

Translate the following into English.

***Example:*** *Rohina poni.* ***I read it.***

1. Saku wenihkuna. ____________
2. Arhilani hinahkwiti. ____________
3. Taminu tapikati. ____________
4. Saku yata. ____________
5. Tasa positi. ____________

## Tetimili: Tinikowihchi

*The Clawed Witch*

Who are the witches? They live in isolation, away from our people. They have hunted our people and devoured them. In the fragment of a story told by Sesostrie Youchigant below, the Clawed Witch stalks around her hunting grounds.

**Tinikowihchi a'akɛni.**
The Clawed Witch used to be around, they say.

**Lɔta rihkɛni.**
She ran swiftly, they say.

**Lɔt'ahch, kanahku tapikatɛni.**
When she ran, she would catch something, they say.

**Tishuma sam'atahch sakukatɛni.**
Then she would cook the meat and eat it, they say.

(Haas, *Tunica Texts*, text 42C, p. 166)

We also know of Tanap who scratches at the window of all children who would defeat him in a wrestling match or who learn about all the plants of the woods. Then there's the Stone

Witch who is a master of disguise. She took on the characteristics of a human and ate her prey. It is said she is to return (come back) in two thousand years.

Although they are ferocious, we have also known these witches to care for our people. They teach us certain medicine. Our **ariyasɛma** 'medicine people' were both healers and protectors. We call upon them to heal us of our ailments as well as protect us in battles and ensure the success of a hunt. Is the Stone Witch an icon of feminine strength? Is the Clawed Witch a reference to having loved and lost? Only the old stories echo secrets from the times long past.

## Tetimili wiralepini

1. We see the ending **-ɛni** on the last word of every phrase in the story (e.g., **Lɔt'a rihkɛni.** 'She ran swiftly, they say.'). Using the translation and the vocabulary you already know, what do you think it means?

2. The witches in stories like these sometimes hunt our people, but sometimes care for them. What do you think about the two sides of witches?

# Chapter 6: Taya waka

## *Commands*

**TOPICS:**

## -ki

*Positive commands*

### Yoluyana

| | | | |
|---|---|---|---|
| **ɛpa** | *to open* | **rowina** | *book; paper* |
| **hɛ'ɛsh** | *today* | **sehinta** | *tomorrow* |
| **-ki** | *command suffix* | **tishuhki** | *door* |
| **lehpi** | *to close* | **taya waka** | *command* |
| **me** | *to search for; to look for* | | |

### Yanalepini

**Alicehchi:** Am'itiki!

**Merlinku:** Hon! Henry, tasa po'iki!

**Henryku:** Tasa pokani.

**Merlinku:** Wor'iki!

**Henryku:** Hon, worukani.

**Merlinku:** Lapu. Hot'ihch, lapuya rap'iki!

**Henryku:** Hon. Yɔlawinaki!

**Merlinku:** Yɔlahkina. Alice, rowina me'ɛki!

**Alicehchi:** Rowina wenini.

**Merlinku:** Lapu, tarowina chuyak'aki! Yɔl'inaki!

**Daveku:** Akawinaki! Tatishuhki ɛpawinaki!

**Chrisku, Naomihchi:** Tikahch. Shim'itiki!

**Daveku:** Aha, hɛ'ɛsh yoyani yakani. Sehinta yakawinaki!

**Chrisku, Naomihchi:** Awww, lap'ɔhɔ.

**Daveku:** Yɔlawinahch, tatishuhki lehpiwinaki! Sehinta shim'itiki!

## Lutamashu

When you tell someone to do something, this is called **taya waka**, or a command in English. There are several ways to tell someone to do something in Tunica. The easiest is to add **-ki** to the completive form of the verb. For example, **shim'i** means 'you *(ms)* played'. To tell a boy to play you say **shim'iki**, which is simply **shim'i** + **-ki**. Likewise, 'you *(fs)* played' is **shim'ɛ**. To tell a girl to play you say **shim'ɛki**. Even though the ending makes it look like the action is happening in the past, **taya waka** don't have any past meaning.

You can express the desire to have anyone do an action using this same **-ki** ending.

| | | | |
|---|---|---|---|
| **shim'ɛ** | you *(fs)* played | **shim'ɛki!** | you *(fs)* play! |
| **shim'i** | you *(ms)* played | **shim'iki!** | you *(ms)* play! |
| **shimina** | you *(fd)* played | **shiminaki!** | you *(fd)* play! |
| **shimiwina** | you *(md)* played | **shimiwinaki!** | you *(md)* play! |
| **shimiti** | you *(fp)* played | **shimitiki!** | you *(fp)* play! |
| **shimiwiti** | you *(mp)* played | **shimiwitiki!** | you *(mp)* play! |
| **shim'ina** | we *(d)* played | **shim'inaki!** | let's *(d)* play! |
| **shim'iti** | we *(p)* played | **shim'itiki!** | let's *(p)* play! |

## Hinu 1

**6.1.1. Luhchi mash'ɔki:**
Fill in the correct form of each verb below based on who you are ordering to do the action.

***Example:***

| | Verb | to a girl | to a boy | to many girls | to many boys / to a mixed gro |
|---|---|---|---|---|---|
| | *hara* | ***har'aki*** | ***har'iki*** | ***haritiki*** | ***harawitiki*** |
| 1. | lehpi | ______ | ______ | ______ | ______ |
| 2. | ɛpa | ______ | ______ | ______ | ______ |
| 3. | me | ______ | ______ | ______ | ______ |
| 4. | wiya | ______ | ______ | ______ | ______ |
| 5. | po | ______ | ______ | ______ | ______ |
| 6. | hotu | ______ | ______ | ______ | ______ |
| 7. | woru | ______ | ______ | ______ | ______ |
| 8. | weni | ______ | ______ | ______ | ______ |
| 9. | aka | ______ | ______ | ______ | ______ |
| 10. | yana | ______ | ______ | ______ | ______ |

### 6.1.2. Luhchi pirɛtaki:

Translate the following into Tunica.

***Example:*** *Point! (to a boy)* **Ley'iki!**

1. Look! *(to a girl)* ____________________
2. Close it! *(to a boy)* ____________________
3. Sit! *(to two boys)* ____________________
4. Let's read! ____________________
5. Grab it! *(to two girls)* ____________________
6. Stop! *(to a group of girls)* ____________________
7. Leave! *(to everyone)* ____________________
8. Find the book! *(to a girl)* ____________________
9. Open it! *(to a boy)* ____________________
10. Bring the books! *(to everyone)* ____________________

# -tan

*Polite commands*

## Yoluyana

| | | | |
|---|---|---|---|
| **hahchi** | *now* | **taworu** | *student* |
| **hatika** | *again* | **tohkuhch** | *please* |
| **hinu** | *practice* | **yana** | *word* |
| **-tan** | *polite command* | **yoyani** | *work* |

## Yanalepini

**Taworuni:** Rowina tapiwitiki! Taworusɛma, tayana hinawititan, tohkuhch: Hinu, Yoyani, Rowina…

*Taworusɛma hinakata. Hotukata.*

**Taworuni:** Ko'o! Aiyanna, tarowina tap'ɛtan, tohkuhch.

**Aiyannahchi:** Hon. Yakani.

**Taworuni:** Tikahch!

**Naomihchi:** Chris, tatishuhki ɛp'itan, tohkuhch.

**Chrisku:** Hatika yan'atan, tohkuhch?

**Naomihchi:** Tatishuhki ɛp'iki!

**Chrisku:** Yakakani.

**Naomihchi:** Hahchi!

## Lutamashu

The affirmative commands we have learned so far using **-ki** are strong commands. These can be given among friends. Also, where there is a difference in status, the higher ranked person (the older person, the teacher, the group leader) can use these forms to lower ranked people (younger folk, students, group members). However, to show respect, one can soften the command and use a polite form: The polite forms, like the **-ki** commands, use the completive stem and add **-tan** after the subject ending.

**Hap'itan.** Stop. *(to a man)*

**Hap'atan.** Stop. *(to a woman)*

Because it is a polite command, this form is often accompanied by **tohkuhch** 'please', as we saw in the **yanalepini**.

## Hinu 2

**6.2.1. Pirɛtaki:**
Change the following from commands addressed to two people to commands addressed to just one person. If the original command is strong, keep it strong. If the original is polite, keep it polite. Change only the number of the addressee.

***Example:*** *Lɔtawinaki* **Lɔt'iki!**

1. Ɛpawinatan. ____________
2. Arhilani hininatan. ____________
3. Rihkuyahoni chuyakawinatan. ____________
4. Lehpinaki! ____________
5. Rowina pohinatan. ____________

### 6.2.2. Pirɛtaki:

Change the following commands to three or more people to commands to just one person. Keep the polite forms polite. Keep the strong forms strong.

***Example:*** *Woyuwitiki* ***Woy'iki!***

1. Ɛpawititan. ____________
2. Mehititan. ____________
3. Rowina lehpiwitiki! ____________
4. Shimititan. ____________
5. Huwitiki! ____________

### 6.2.3. Pirɛtaki:

Change the following polite commands to strong commands, and the strong commands to polite commands.

***Example:*** *Wɛsinatan.* ***Wɛsinaki!***

1. Tishuhki lehp'itan. ____________
2. Ɛp'atan. ____________
3. Sakuwititan. ____________
4. Lehpinatan. ____________
5. Mewititan. ____________
6. Har'aki! ____________
7. Rapuwitiki! ____________
8. Lapuya rapitiki! ____________
9. Hipinaki! ____________
10. Shimiwitiki! ____________

# -ahatan

*Negative commands*

## Yoluyana

| | | | |
|---|---|---|---|
| **-ahatan** | *negative command ("Don't ____!")* | **laspi** | *metal; money* |
| **chu** | *to take* | **laspi ri** | *bank* |
| **hila** | *to move* | **oni laspi ri** | *bank teller* |
| **hinyatihch** | *then; now; so; after that* | **tanira** | *thief* |

## Yanalepini

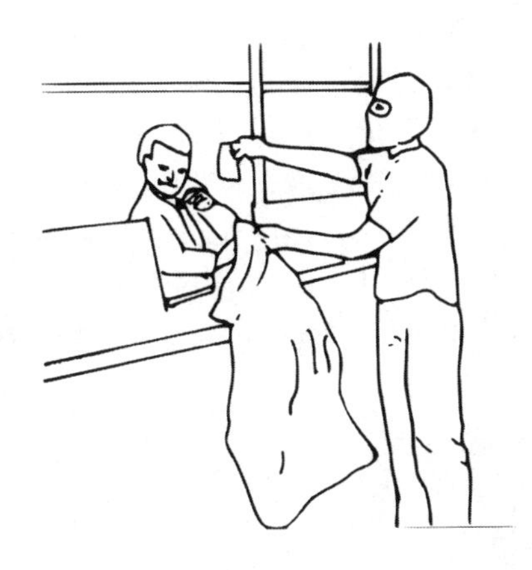

**Taniraku:** Hil'ahatan! Talaspi chukani.

**Oni laspi ri:** Aha! Talaspi chu'ahatan!

**Taniraku:** Ɛp'iki!

**Oni laspi ri:** Hilakan'ɛhɛ! Talaspi ri yɔl'iki! Onisɛma yakakata.

*Tonisɛma talaspi ri akakata.*

**Taniraku:** Yɔlakani!

**Alicehchi:** Chris, kanahku yaki?

**Chrisku:** Saku wiyakani.

**Alicehchi:** Ya'ahatan! Tasaku sak'iki!

**Chrisku:** Sakukan'ɛhɛ!

*Chrisku saku wiyaku. Hinyatihch, Henryku, Chrisku wachihkuna.*

**Alicehchi:** Lap'ɔhɔ! Wach'ɛhɛtan! Hotuwinaki!

**Henryku:** Chrisku yawi.

**Alicehchi:** Chris, "sara" yan'iki!

**Chrisku:** Sara, Henry.

**Alicehchi:** Lapu.

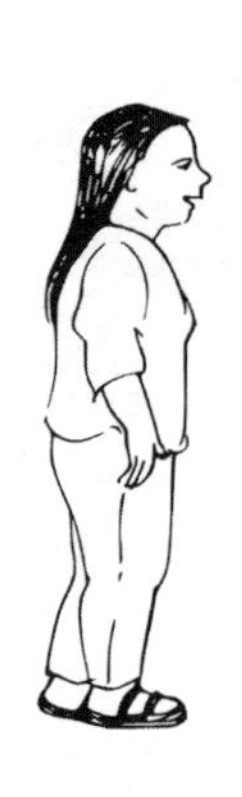

## Lutamashu

To tell someone *not* to do something, you always do the same thing: add **-aha** 'no, not' to the verb, and then add **-tan**. This means the negative command will look the same no matter who you're talking to; verb + **-ahatan** works for everyone. There is no completive ending like in the positive commands in the previous section. However, the **a**'s in **-aha** will still change depending on what comes before it, just like when **-aha** is by itself. The negative command is the same for both the polite and strong command forms. **hil'aki!** 'move!', and **hil'atan** 'finish quickly' may both be negated by saying **hil'ahatan**. Compare the positive and negative commands below.

| | | | |
|---|---|---|---|
| **me'ɛki!** | *look for it (2fs)!* | **me'ɛhɛtan!** | *don't (2fs) look for it!* |
| **ɛp'aki!** | *open it (2fs)!* | **ɛp'ahatan!** | *don't (2fs) open it!* |
| **lehp'ɛtan!** | *please close it (2fs)!* | **lehp'ɛhɛtan!** | *don't (2fs) close it!* |
| **ley'ɔtan!** | *please point to it (2fs)!* | **ley'ɔhɔtan!** | *don't (2fs) point to it!* |

The table above shows second person feminine singular examples, but it works the same regardless of gender and number.

## Hinu 3

### 6.3.1. Luhchi mash'ɔki:

Give the negative command forms of the following verbs.

***Example:*** *pita* **pit'ahatan**

1. hila ________
2. eru ________
3. woru ________
4. wiya ________
5. leyu ________
6. lehpi ________
7. wachi ________
8. me ________
9. chu ________
10. ɛpa ________

### 6.3.2. Luhchi pirɛtaki:

Translate the following sentences into Tunica.

***Example:*** *Don't point at it!* **ley'ɔhɔtan!**

1. Don't close the book! ________
2. Find the money! *(to many boys)* ________
3. Don't do it! ________
4. Look for the cat! *(to two girls)* ________
5. Don't open it! ________
6. Please grab the branch. *(to a boy)* ________
7. Don't take a dog! ________
8. Eat the food! *(to many people)* ________
9. Don't read the story! ________
10. Don't move! ________

## Tetimili: Ɛsha wakan'ɛhɛtan!

*Do not fell willows!*

In our storytelling, everything has a spirit and Tunica people are able to communicate with those spirits for protection or guidance. It is told that those spirits are the ancestors still watching over their families. There are many stories of the Tunica asking for guidance or help, but the story *Do not fell willows!* is a great example. It is also a good story for commands such as **-tan**. In the story, a mother asks a willow tree for protection from a panther hunting her and her children. The willow responds and cover the mother and her children to protect them from the panther's sight. Ever since, we do not chop down willows.

**Tanuhchihchi tehkusɛm'ama ɔnta.**
There was a woman and her children.

**Tarku rɔhpant ɔnta.**
They lived near the woods.

**Ashuhki sahku tarku kichu yuk'uk'ɛra.**
One day they went into the woods.

**Yaluhki mena'ara.**
They were looking for mushrooms.

**Tehkusɛma yaluhki sihk'ɛlu.**
Her children liked mushrooms.

**Lapu lisuti.**
They were tasty.

**Oni sahusɛma yaluhki hotu tarku uhktɛlahchu wen'ɔnta.**
Other people had found all the mushrooms at the edge of the woods.

**Hinyatihch, tɛhɛli mahkina tarku kichu yuk'uk'ɛra.**
So her family went deep in the woods.

**Yaluhki wenitahch, sihksh'ɛpa.**
When they found mushrooms, they were happy.

**Yaluhki marina'ara.**
They were picking mushrooms.

**Hɛrana'ar'aha.**
They weren't watching.

**Hikuwa hɛnt'ɛ wɛr'una rɔhpant.**
An enormous panther was hunting nearby.

**Uhkyahpasht'ɛ.**
He was very hungry.

**Sigachihchi tahikuwa uhkpotihch, rɔhpant uhki.**
When their mother saw the panther, he was close.

**Hinyatihch, tehkusɛma ɛsha haluhta sihkpih'ɔta hashupa.**
She quickly hid her children beneath a willow.

**"Ingachi Ɛsha, inkshihkɛtatan! Tahikuwa inkpowik'ɛhɛhch, lapuhch! Ɛsha, inkpihɔtatan, tohkuhch," niti.**
"Our mother Willow, help us! If the panther doesn't see us, it will be a good thing. Willow, please hide us," she said.

**"Ehkusɛma, yan'ahatan, hil'ahatan!" niti.**
"My children, don't speak, don't move!" she said.

**Tehkusɛma yanat'aha, hilat'aha.**
Her children didn't speak, they didn't move.

**Hinyatihch, Ta'ɛshahchi tihkrihkuyahoni tar'ata.**
Then, Willow stretched her branches.

**Ehkusɛma, sigachihch'ɛma sihkpih'ɔta.**
She hid the children and their mother.

**Hinahk'ɔhchat, hɛ'ɛsh ɛsha sinkrihkuyahoni yuru.**
For this reason, willow trees' branches are long and skinny to this day.

**Tahikuwa sihkpowishtuk'ɔhɔ.**
The panther couldn't see them.

**Tahikuwa uwa, histahahki uhkyahpa.**
The panther went away, still hungry.

**"Tikahch, Ɛsha. Ehkusɛma, ɛsha sinkrihkuyahoni poht'ɔhɔtan. Ɛsha enti," sigachihchi yanati.**
Their mother said, "Thank you, Willow. My children, don't cut the branches of willows. Willows are our friends."

**Hiyatira, tonisɛma ɛsha wak'ant'aha.**
Ever since, people do not fell willows.

**Ɛsha wakan'ɛhɛtan!**
Do not fell willows!

## Tetimili yoluyana

| | | | |
|---|---|---|---|
| **ɛsha** | *willow* | **hikuwa** | *panther* |
| **yaluhki** | *mushroom* | **sihkpih'ɔta** | *she hid them* |

## Tetimili wiralepini

1. Find some of the **taya waka** in this story. What command form is used when talking with each audience: the polite or the informal? Why do you think that is?

2. How is the role of the mother in the story similar to **ɛsha** 'the willow'?

# Chapter 7: Tayak'ahcha ɔsa sahusinim'ama

*The future and other endings*

**TOPICS:**

# Tayak'ahcha

*Future actions*

## Yoluyana

| | | | |
|---|---|---|---|
| **aha** | *nothing; nowhere (response to a question)* | **rahpa** | *to play ball* |
| **-ama** | *along with* | **ri** | *house; home; building* |
| **ashuhkitɛpan** | *every day* | **-sh** | *to; toward* |
| **hɛlawu** | *tonight* | **-shi** | *at; location of* |
| **-k'ahcha** | *will (future)* | **kata** | *where* |
| **wishipɛta** | *pond* | **nihkirhipu** | *powwow* |

## Yanalepini

**Taworunihchi:** Tihika yukatihch, kanahku ya'ak'ahcha, Alice?
**Alicehchi:** Tihika yukatihch, ashuhkitɛpan rohina pokanik'ahcha.
**Taworunihchi:** Rowina kashku po'ɔk'ahcha?
**Alicehchi:** Michu ilitɛya sinku.
**Taworunihchi:** Kanahku sahkuhta po'ɔkahcha?
**Alicehchi:** Sahkuhta *Harry Potter* pokanik'ahcha.
**Taworunihchi:** Lapuhch. Mahat, Dave, tihika yukatihch kanahku ya'ik'ahcha?
**Daveku:** Imat ashuhkitɛpan woyunik'ahcha.
**Taworunihchi:** Kata woy'ik'ahcha?

**Daveku:** Wishipɛtashi woyunik'ahcha.
**Taworunihchi:** Lapuhch. Aiyanna, kanahku ya'ak'ahcha?
**Aiyannahchi:** Nihkirhipush yukanik'ahcha. Hipunik'ahcha, haranik'ahcha.
**Taworunihchi:** Lapuhch. Hɛmat, Rose, kanahku ya'ak'ahcha?
**Rosehchi:** Rahpanik'ahcha.
**Taworunihchi:** Mahat, Chrisku, kanahku ya'ik'ahcha?
**Chrisku:** Imat rapunik'ahcha.

**Naomihchi:** Hɛlawu Alicehchi, Aiyannahchi, Chrisku, Daveku kanahku yatak'ahcha?
**Augustinku:** Hɛlawu rahpatak'ahcha.
**Naomihchi:** Rosehchi, Lisahchi rahpasinak'ahchan?
**Augustinku:** Aha, Rosehchi, Lisahchi rahpasinak'ahch'aha. Hɛlawu rishi ukisinak'ahcha. Hɛmat, hɛlawu rahp'ak'ahchan?
**Naomihchi:** Aha! Hɛlawu nihkirhipush Merlinku im'ama hip'itik'ahcha. Mahat?
**Augustinku:** Imat hipunik'ahch'aha. Nihkirhipush haranik'ahcha.
**Naomihchi:** Lapuhch!

## Lutamashu

**Tayak'ahcha**, verbs referring to future actions, are built on the completive form of the verb. To talk about these actions in the future, add the completive endings for the appropriate subject like you normally would to the verb, and then add **-k'ahcha**. Although **-k'ahcha** attaches to the completive forms, there is no past meaning, just future.

The following examples show how this works. Because **-k'ahcha** starts with a consonant, there is no vowel blending; the form remains the same.

**Hipuni** 'I danced' → **Hipunik'ahcha** 'I will dance'

**Rahpati** 'she played ball' → **Rahpatik'ahcha** 'She will play ball'

**Po'ɔ** 'you *(fs)* watched' → **Po'ɔk'ahcha** 'you *(fs)* will watch'

To make future verbs negative you simply add **-aha** at the end of the word. The **a** of **-aha** will blend with the **a** of **-k'ahcha** to yield **-k'ahch'aha**.

**Hipunik'ahcha** 'I will dance' → **Hipunik'ahch'aha** 'I will not dance'

**Rahpatik'ahcha** 'She will play ball' → **Rahpatik'ahch'aha** 'She will not play ball'

**Po'ɔk'ahcha** 'you *(fs)* will watch' → **Po'ɔk'ahch'aha** 'you *(fs)* will not watch'

## Hinu 1

**7.1.1. Yoluyana mash'ɔki:**
Make the following verbs future. You may have to change the ending!

***Example:*** *haraku* ***harawik'ahcha***

1. hot'iti ____________
2. rap'una ____________
3. rahpaku ____________
4. lehpikata ____________
5. hinati ____________
6. chuhksiti ____________
7. yasina ____________
8. tapiwiti ____________
9. wenikati ____________
10. wiyahkwina ____________

### 7.1.2. Luhchi pirɛtaki:

Make the following negative verbs future and negative, then translate them.

***Example:***

| VERB | NEGATIVE FUTURE | TRANSLATION |
|---|---|---|
| *ley'ɔhɔ* | ***ley'ɔk'ahch'aha*** | ***She will not point at it.*** |

| | VERB | NEGATIVE FUTURE | TRANSLATION |
|---|---|---|---|
| 1. | wɛs'it'ɛhɛ | ______ | ______ |
| 2. | wachit'aha | ______ | ______ |
| 3. | yat'ɛhɛ | ______ | ______ |
| 4. | hilaw'ɛhɛ | ______ | ______ |
| 5. | ɛp'aha | ______ | ______ |
| 6. | harit'ɛhɛ | ______ | ______ |
| 7. | mewin'aha | ______ | ______ |
| 8. | po'it'ɛhɛ | ______ | ______ |
| 9. | wenisin'aha | ______ | ______ |
| 10. | hinasit'ɛhɛ | ______ | ______ |

# Connections

## Yoluyana

| | | | |
|---|---|---|---|
| **a-** | *together; each other* | **kaha** | *to come upon; to meet* |
| **hinto!** | *come on!* | **-pa** | *too; also; even* |
| **hotu** | *all; every; everyone* | **punatarahpani** | *stickball (game); ball sticks* |
| **tarku** | *the woods; the forest* | | |

## Yanalepini

**Augustinku:** Naomi, Rose, Tihika Nisa yukatihch, kanahku yahinak'ahcha?

**Naomihchi, Rosehchi:** Times Squaresh yuk'inak'ahcha. Hip'inak'ahcha!

**Augustinku:** Imapa Times Squaresh yukanik'ahcha!

**Naomihchi, Rosehchi:** Ko'o! Akuhp'itiki! Hotu hip'itik'ahcha!

**Augustinku:** Lapuhch!

**Aiyannahchi:** Hɛlawu kanahku ya'inak'ahcha?

**Alicehchi:** Sahkuhta sak'inak'ahcha. Ilihta rohina po'inak'ahcha. Enihkuhta tarku kichu shim'inak'ahcha.

**Aiyannahchi:** Chriskɔt, kanahku yawik'ahcha?

**Alicehchi:** Rahpawik'ahcha.

**Aiyannahchi:** Hon, punatarahpani chuyakawi.

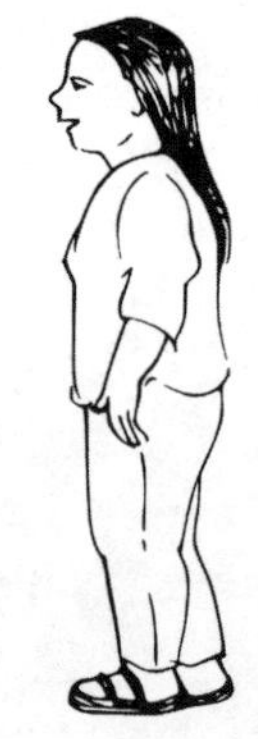

*Aiyannahchi, Alicehchi, Daveku, Chrisku akahakata.*

**Alicehchi:** Hɛlawu kanahku yawinak'ahcha?

**Daveku, Chrisku:** Rahp'inak'ahcha. Hinimat?

**Alicehchi:** Sak'inak'ahcha. Hinyatihch, rohina po'inak'ahcha, shim'inak'ahcha.

**Chrisku:** Rahp'inak'ahch'aha hinimapan?

**Aiyannahchi:** Lapuhch. Inima hotu arahp'itiki!

**Chrisku:** Ko'o! Arahp'itik'ahcha. Hinto!

## Lutamashu

In the **yanalepini** in this chapter, we saw two new useful endings: **-ama** 'and; along with', and **-pa** 'also'.

**-ama**. In English we can put 'and' between pretty much any two words of the same type ('slip and fall', 'Bert and Ernie', 'fast and furious'). Even though **-ama** can be translated as 'and; along with', in Tunica it can only be used to join two nouns. A series of three nouns, like "Merlin, Bill, and Harry" would *not* take **-ama**. In that case, the three nouns would simply be said one after the other: **Merlinku, Billku, Harryku**. When there are just two nouns, we can use **-ama**. It attaches to the end of the second noun. So, for example, 'Genesis and Lisa' would be **Genesishchi Lisahch'ɛma**. If the noun ends in a vowel, regular vowel blending rules apply (see Chapter 3), as in **taworunisɛma taworusɛm'ama** 'teachers and students', **Diamondhchi Alicehch'ɛma** 'Diamond and Alice', and **onisɛma nuhchisinim'ama** 'men and women'.

**-pa**. **-pa** means 'also', and can attach to any noun (e.g., **Merlinkupa** 'Merlin too') or pronoun (e.g., **imapa** 'me too'). Although a noun with **-pa** can go anywhere in the sentence that a noun or pronoun can go, it often appears at the end of the phrase. The following example is from the *Tunica Texts*:

> **Hinyatihch, sarakata sɛmapa.**
> 'Then they too would pray.'
>
> (Haas, *Tunica Texts*, text 22C:c, p. 142).

Lastly, although we learned **-hat** 'on X's part' in Chapter 1, we have thus far mostly seen it used with pronouns (e.g., **imat** 'on my part', **uwɛt** 'on his part'). **-hat**, like **-pa**, can also attach to any noun. This includes regular nouns like **taworunihchɛt** 'the teacher, on her part', as well as proper nouns like **Merlinkɔt** 'Merlin, on his part'. As always, when **-hat** attaches to the end of a word ending with a vowel, regular blending rules apply. Check out these examples.

| | | | | |
|---|---|---|---|---|
| **inima + hat** | we + as for | → | **inimat** | as for us |
| **Alicehchi + hat** | Alice + as for | → | **Alicehchɛt** | as for Alice |
| **nihkirhipu + hat** | powwow + as for | → | **nihkirhipɔt** | as for the powwow |

## Hinu 2

**7.2.1. Atehpɛtaki:**
Join the following words with their endings.

***Example:*** *Lisa + hat* **Lisat**

1. Alicehchi Frankku + ama ______________
2. toniku tanuhchihchi + ama ______________
3. ima uwi + ama ______________
4. hɛma + pa ______________
5. chɔhaku +pa ______________
6. Aiyannahchi + pa ______________
7. sa + hat ______________
8. tihchi + hat ______________
9. Carriehchi + hat ______________

### 7.2.2. Luhchi pirɛtaki:

Translate the following sentences into Tunica.

***Example:*** *George is laughing. I am laughing too.* **Georgeku eruku. Erukani imapa.**

1. Jack and Jill are fighting (each other).

 ______________________________

2. The cat and the dog fought (each other).

 ______________________________

3. Tonight he will sleep. Tonight I, too, will sleep.

 ______________________________

4. Augustin slept as well.

 ______________________________

5. Aiyanna is writing. As for Jack, he is reading.

 ______________________________

6. Dave walked. As for Alice, she sang.

 ______________________________

7. You threw the branch. As for the dog, it grabbed it.

 ______________________________

8. You *(ms)* and I will meet up.

 ______________________________

9. They are also dancing.

 ______________________________

10. Henry and Samuel will play ball tonight.

 ______________________________

## Tetimili: Kana Tiyushɛlahchi tihkɔkali tihkyukati

*How Possum got her pouch*

Marsupials are mammals that are carried in the pouches of their mothers. While most marsupial species live in Australia and New Guinea, some, including possums, live in America.

The following story about possums was told by Sesostrie Youchigant to Mary Haas and recorded in the *Tunica Texts*. This is a traditional story explaining how possums came to have pouches, a feature that makes them unique among contemporary mammals in North America. As you read, ask yourself: could Terrapin's (Turtle's) gift to Possum be a reminder of the connection between **Tayoroniku-Halayihku** and other Indigenous nations? Do our animal kin learn from each other and have their own systems to change themselves?

**Wantaha Tiyushɛlahchi tihkri rihku kichu tihkara.**
Long ago, Possum had a home in a tree.

**Ashuhki sahku saku me'ata.**
One day, she left to look for food.

**Semitihch, Tachihchiruhchi wi'ɛta.**
When she came back, she heard Wren.

**"Chi man ta kiyu chi man ta le tu tan," harati.**
"Chi man ta kiyu chi man ta le tu tan,"[1] she sang.

**Tiyushɛlahchi tihkshruka namu.**
Possum was very scared.

**Yorum'aha waliti. "Ihkshihkawintatan, tohkuhch!"**
She called to the wild animals. "Help me, please!"

**Tachihchiruhchi hatika "Chi man ta kiyu chi man ta le tu tan," harati.**
Wren sang again: "Chi man ta kiyu chi man ta le tu tan."

**Tayorum'aha sihkshruka. Lɔtasiti.**
The wild animals were afraid. They ran away.

[1] This song consists of untranslatable vocables, which are groups of sounds that make up the melody. Vocables are common in indigenous songs that have been shared among tribes who speak different languages. The Wren's song may have come from a different tribe who shared it long ago with the Tunica, who incorporated it into this traditional story.

**Takohkuku pitahkuna.**
Terrapin was walking by.

**Tiyushɛlahchi "Ihkshihkawitatan, tohkuhch!" niti.**
"Help me, please!" Possum said.

**"Tarukaniku ihkri rɔhpant una. Ehkusinima yukanishtuk'ɔhɔ.**
"There is a monster near my house. I cannot get to my children.

**Kanahku yanik'ahcha erus'aha."**
I do not know what I shall do."

**Takohkuku "Ihknashi yuk'ak'ihch, lapu yanik'ahcha," niwi.**
Terrapin said: "If you lead me there, I will do a good thing."

**Tihkrishi yuk'una. Takohkuku tarihku ɛha pɛkawi.**
They arrived at her house. Terrapin kicked and punched the tree.

**Tachihchiruhchi nar'uwa. Tiyushɛlahchi tihkri akati.**
Wren flew away. Possum entered her house.

**Tehkusinima meruti. Tihksh'ɛpa panu.**
She hugged her children. She was very happy.

**Takohkuku "Hinahku, lapu hihkmashunik'ahcha," niwi.**
Terrapin said: "This way I will make it better for you."

**Tichihki warawi. Tehkusinima sinkchuwihch, tichihki kichu sinkukinuhki.**
He split open her belly. He took her children and placed them in her belly.

**Hɛ'ɛsh, Tiyushɛlahchi tehkusinima hishtahahki sinkerikati.**
Today, Possum always carries her children with her.

Adapted from Haas, *Tunica Texts*, text 18, pp. 120–123.

## Tetimili yoluyana

| | | | |
|---|---|---|---|
| **iyushɛla** | *possum* | **yorum'aha** | *wild animal* |
| **chihchiru** | *wren* | **kohku** | *turtle; terrapin* |

## Tetimili wiralepini

1. In this story, the names of the animals end with **-hchi** and **-ku** and begin with **ta-**. What do those markers mean? Why might we see those markers in stories like this but not, for example, when your friend talks about her pet dog?

2. Stories like this one are often allegories for real-world situations. What could Terrapin's gift to Possum represent to **Tayoronihku-Halayihku**?

# Chapter 8: Yoluyana-*ka* Taya wan'ama

## *Question words and stative verbs*

**TOPICS:**

# Yoluyana-*ka*

*Question words*

## Yoluyana

| | |
|---|---|
| **ka'ash** | *when* |
| **kaku** | *who; which* |
| **kana** | *how* |
| **kanahku** | *what* |
| **kashku** | *how many; how much* |
| **kata** | *where; somewhere; anywhere* |
| **kaya** | *why* |

| | |
|---|---|
| **pala** | *to win* |
| **palatohku** | *goal; point; score* |
| **panu** | *very* |
| **romantohku** | *slow; slowly* |
| **sahu** | *other* |
| **tewali** | *fast* |
| **yoluyana-*ka*** | *question word* |

## Yanalepini

**Alicehchi:** Aiyanna, kanahku yakata?

**Aiyannahchi:** Rahpakata.

**Alicehchi:** Kaku palaku?

**Aiyannahchi:** Inimat palahkiti!

**Alicehchi:** Palatohku kashku?

**Aiyannahchi:** Masahki.

**Alicehchi:** Sahusɛmat? Palatohku kashku?

**Aiyannahchi:** Manku. Tarahpanisɛma lapuya rahpakata.

**Alicehchi:** Lapu panu. Pal'itiki!

**Rosehchi:** Kata amiki?
**Chrisku:** Nihkirhipush yukakani.
**Rosehchi:** Kaya?
**Chrisku:** Hɛ'ɛsh hipukani!
**Rosehchi:** Lapu! Kana nihkirhipush yuk'ik'ahcha?
**Chrisku:** Ima Merlink'ɔma pit'inak'ahcha.
**Rosehchi:** Ka'ash amiwinak'ahcha?
**Chrisku:** Hɛlawu am'inak'ahcha.
**Rosehchi:** Tewali amiwinaki! Merlinku romantohku pitaku.
**Chrisku:** Hon. Tewali am'inak'ahcha.

## Lutamashu

So far we have seen a few ways to ask questions in Tunica. If a speaker wants to receive an answer of **hon** 'yes' or **aha** 'no', an **-n** ending would be added to the last word of the sentence, as in **Hipukatin?** 'Is she dancing?'. If the speaker wants more information than **hon** or **aha**, you would need to use a question word. English question words are usually called wh-words because many of them begin with 'wh', but in Tunica they are known as **yoluyana-*ka***, because they all begin with **ka**. We've seen **kanahku** 'what', **kashku** 'how many', **kaku** 'who, which', and **kata** 'where' already, but there are many different **yoluyana-*ka*** which will be helpful to you in building different kinds of questions. When you use **yoluyana-*ka***, you do not use **-n**.

**Kaku** 'who, which' is used to ask for information about people.

| | |
|---|---|
| **Kaku lɔtawi?** | 'Who ran?' |
| **Kaku pitati?** | 'Who *(fs)* walked?' |

Notice that you use **lɔtawi** when you don't know who ran or if you think the person who ran is a man. You use **lɔtati** only if you think the person who ran is a woman. **Kaku** means 'which' when used with another noun, like this:

| | |
|---|---|
| **Kaku tarahpaniku patawi?** | 'Which player *(ms)* fell?' |
| **Kaku tarahpanisinima shimihksiti?** | 'Which players *(fp)* are playing?' |

**Kata** 'where' is the question word for locations.

| | |
|---|---|
| **Kata lɔtati?** | 'Where did she run?' |
| **Kata rap'ɔ?** | 'Where did you *(fs)* sleep?' |

**Ka'ash** 'when' is used for questions about the time an event takes place.

| | |
|---|---|
| **Ka'ash lɔtati?** | 'When did she run?' |
| **Ka'ash harawi?** | 'When did he sing?' |

**Kana** 'how' is used in questions about the condition or manner of an action or event.

| | |
|---|---|
| **Kana lɔtati?** | 'How did she run?' |
| **Kana woyuwi?** | 'How did he swim?' |

**Kaya** 'why' is the word for asking about a purpose.

| | |
|---|---|
| **Kaya lɔtakati?** | 'Why is she running?' |
| **Kaya yakaw'ɛhɛ?** | 'Why didn't he come back?' |

**Kanahku** 'what, which' is the word for asking about a thing.

| | |
|---|---|
| **Kanahku otisa?** | 'What is his name?' |
| **Kanahku yaka?** | 'What are you *(fs)* doing?' |
| **Kanahku rowina pokati?** | 'Which book is she reading?' |

Notice that **kanahku** is used to mean 'which' when talking about objects, but **kaku** is 'which' when talking about people.

**Kashku** 'how many' asks for the number of something.

| | |
|---|---|
| **Ashuhki kashku ashutayi tihkara?** | 'How many days are in a week?' |
| **Oni kashku pitakata?** | 'How many people are walking?' |

Notice that **kashku** comes after the noun that is being counted.

These same words can be used for non-specific places, times, things, etc., roughly equivalent to 'any', '-ever' or 'every' for each quality. This is common for 'wherever/anywhere' and 'whenever, any time'.

| | |
|---|---|
| **Kata uk'iki!** | 'Sit *(ms)* anywhere!' |
| **Kata yukakani, worukani.** | 'Wherever I go, I am learning.' |
| **Ka'ash tishuhki lehpiku, sahu ɛpaku.** | 'Any time a door closes, another opens.' |

## Hinu 1

**8.1.1. Molɔtaki:**
For each of these answers, give the correct question word.

***Example:*** *tarku kichu* ***kata***

1. ili ____________
2. Merlinku ____________
3. romantohku ____________
4. Rapumanku ____________
5. tapuna ____________

**8.1.2. Pakɛtaki:**
Re-read the **yanalepini** with Aiyanna and Alice on page 110. Answer these questions in Tunica.

1. Kaku palaku?

   ____________________________________________

2. Tasahusɛma palatohku kashku yata?

   ____________________________________________

3. Kaku lapuya rahpakata?

   ____________________________________________

# Taya wana

*Stative verbs*

## Yoluyana

| | | | |
|---|---|---|---|
| **-aha** | *to not have* | **-sh'ɛpa** | *to be happy* |
| **-ara** | *to have* | **-shniyu** | *to be lonely* |
| **ehniyuwista** | *my sweetheart* | **-shtamar'ɛhɛ** | *to be rude; to be disrespectful* |
| **-elu** | *to like something* | **-shtamari** | *to be respectful; to be polite* |
| **-mahka** | *to love* | **-sipi** | *to be cold (person)* |
| **-niyulapu** | *to be smart* | **-tohkuni** | *to be tired* |
| **-p'ɛsha** | *to be sad; to be unhappy* | **-wana** | *to want* |
| **-sepi** | *to be in poor health* | **-yaru** | *to be curious* |
| **-sh'ɛlama** | *to be pitiable* | **-yashi** | *to be angry* |

## Yanalepini

**Naomihchi:** Dave, eti ma lapun?

**Daveku:** Lap'ɔhɔ. Ihkyashi.

**Naomihchi:** Kaya wihkyashi?

**Daveku:** Henryku Aiyannahch'ɛma yɔl'una. Ihkshniyu.

**Naomihchi:** Wihksh'ɛlam'aha. Hinto! Shim'inaki!

**Daveku:** Ihkwan'aha. Ihktohkuni.

**Naomihchi:** Hahchi ihkp'ɛsha.

**Daveku:** Lap'ɔhɔ. Shim'inaki!

**Alicehchi:** Aiyanna! Ehniyuwista ihkara! Samuelku otisa. Uhkniyulapu, uhkshtamari. Ihksh'ɛpa, ihkmahka.

**Aiyannahchi:** Ko'o!

**Alicehchi:** Hɛmat?

**Aiyannahchi:** Ehniyuwista ihkaha. Lawushi Fredku im'ama akuhp'ina. Uhkshtamar'ɛhɛ. Ihkel'ɔhɔ.

**Alicehchi:** Sara, lap'ɔhɔ.

**Naomihchi:** Aiyanna, hihksipi panu. Ihkyaru; kaya hihksipi?

**Aiyannahchi:** Ihksepi.

**Naomihchi:** Kaya hihksepi?

**Aiyannahchi:** Lawushi tarku kichu rapuni.

**Naomihchi:** Hihksh'ɛlama.

## Lutamashu

So far all the verbs we have discussed in Chapters 2–7 have been verbs that describe doing something. In this chapter we learn a new kind of verb, one that describes being in a state or condition. Some examples of these **taya wana** or stative verbs include **-niyulapu** 'to be smart, intelligent', **-sh'ɛpa** 'to be happy", **-shtamari** 'to be respectful, polite', **-sipi** 'to be cold', **-yashi** 'to be angry', and **-yaru** 'to be curious'. Often the closest words in English for these concepts are adjectives rather than verbs. Other words in this class are verbs in English too, for example **-ara** 'to have', **-mahka** 'to love', and **-wana** 'to want'.

**Taya wana** do not take the same endings that action verbs take. Instead, they use a prefix to show who is in the state or condition indicated by the verb. These prefixes that appear on **taya wana** in Tunica also have several other uses, which we will learn in Chapter 11. The basic forms are listed on the chart on the next page.

| | | SINGULAR | | DUAL | | PLURAL | |
|---|---|---|---|---|---|---|---|
| *1st person* | | **ihk-** | *I* | **ink-** | *we two* | **ink-** | *we all* |
| *2nd person* | *feminine* | **hihk-** | *you* | **hink-** | *you two* | **hink-** | *you all* |
| | *masculine* | **wihk-** | *you* | **wink-** | *you two* | **wink-** | *you all* |
| *3rd person* | *feminine* | **tihk-** | *she* | **sink-** | *they two* | **sink-** | *they all* |
| | *masculine* | **uhk-** | *he* | **unk-** | *they two* | **sihk-** | *they all* |

**Taya wana** must always appear with one of these prefixes in order to be a complete word. Unlike action verbs, they often appear without any endings at all.

The following are some examples of **taya wana**:

| | |
|---|---|
| **ihksh'ɛpa** | 'I'm happy' |
| **tihksepi** | 'she's in poor health' |
| **uhksh'ɛlama** | 'he's pitiable' |
| **winkshtamari** | 'you *(md/p)* are well-behaved' |
| **sinksipi** | 'they *(fd/p)* are cold' |
| **sihkyaru** | 'they *(mp)* are curious' |

In order to negate **taya wana**, the negative ending **-aha** simply attaches directly to the root, e.g., **ihktohkun'ɛhɛ** 'I am not tired' or **ihkshniy'ɔhɔ** 'I am not lonely'. When this happens, normal vowel blending rules for **-aha** apply. However, the verbs **ara** 'to have' and **aha** 'to not have' are special in that there is a separate form for not having something. Neither of these verbs can take **-aha**.

## Hinu 2

**8.2.1. Chu'ɔki:**
Choose the correct Tunica translation of the following English statements.

***Example:*** *She wants (it).*
***a. Tihkwana.*** *b. Uhksipi.* *c. Sihkmahka.*

1. They two *(md)* are lonely.
   a. Uhksepi. b. Wihkp'ɛsha. c. Unkshniyu.
2. I am respectful.
   a. Ihkshtamari. b. Tihkyahpa. c. Inkshtamar'ɛhɛ.
3. They *(fp)* are happy.
   a. Sihkyashi. b. Sinksh'ɛpa. c. Sihkelu.
4. We *(d)* are tired.
   a. Wihkwana. b. Ihkyaru. c. Inktohkuni.
5. You *(ms)* are smart.
   a. Wihkniyulapu. b. Unkshniyu. c. Winksh'ɛlama.

**8.2.2. Molɔtaki:**
Fill in the blanks with the correct pronoun so that the Tunica matches the English translation.

***Example:*** *__Uhk__ aha.* *He doesn't have it.*

1. _____yashi. I'm angry.
2. _____sh'ɛpa. She's happy.
3. _____shniyu. They *(fp)* are lonely.
4. _____mahka. You *(mp)* love.
5. _____p'ɛsha. They *(md)* are unhappy.
6. _____sipi. He is cold.
7. _____niyulapu. We are smart.

8. ______elu. You *(fs)* like (it).
9. ______shtamar'ɛhɛ. You *(fd)* are disrespectful.
10. ______yaru. You *(ms)* are curious.

### 8.2.3. Luhchi pirɛtaki:

Translate the following into English. Use the chart on page 116 if you need help.

***Example:*** *Uhksh'ɛlama.* ***He is pitiable.***

1. Unkyash'ɛhɛ. ______________________
2. Tihkara. ______________________
3. Sinkshtamari. ______________________
4. Hihkaha. ______________________
5. Hinkniyulap'ɔhɔ. ______________________

### 8.2.4. Luhchi pirɛtaki:

Translate the following into Tunica. Use the chart on page 116 if you need help.

***Example:*** *They (md) want (something).* ***Unkwana.***

1. You *(mp)* are cold. ______________________
2. We *(d)* are rude. ______________________
3. I am tired. ______________________
4. You *(fp)* are not lonely. ______________________
5. You *(fs)* are curious. ______________________

# Vowel-initial taya wana

## Yoluyana

| | | | |
|---|---|---|---|
| **-ehtini** | *to own* | **-shari** | *to have time* |
| **eht'ira** | *my clothes* | **-shpitu** | *to forget* |
| **-eht'ira** | *to be clothed* | **-shtahahki** | *only* |
| **-erusa** | *to know* | **-sihu** | *to be thirsty* |
| **-esahku** | *to be widowed* | **wiranitohku** | *second (unit of time)* |
| **hal'ukini** | *village* | **-yahpa** | *to be hungry* |
| **-hayi** | *to be old* | **-yari** | *to be ashamed* |

## Yanalepini

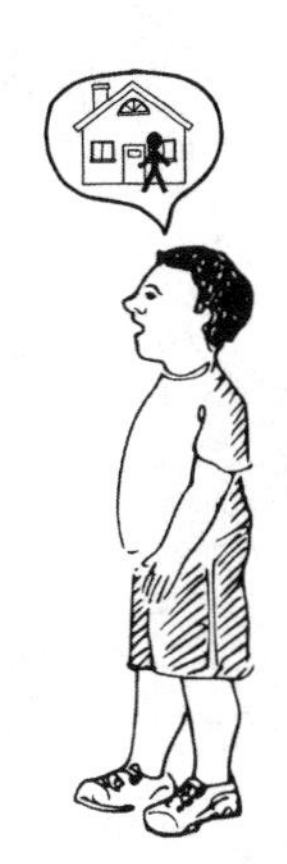

**Aiyannahchi:** Uwi werusan?
**Chrisku:** Hon, uwi erusa.
**Aiyannahchi:** Kanahku otisa?
**Chrisku:** Samuelku otisa. Osahku.
**Aiyannahchi:** Sara. Kata ukiku werusa?
**Chrisku:** Hal'ukini kichu ri ohtini.
**Aiyannahchi:** Ah, uwi erusa. Uhkhayi.
**Chrisku:** Hon. Tihika michu manku uhkyuk'aki.
**Aiyannahchi:** Lapuhch.

**Augustinku:** Ihkyahpa. Sak'inaki!

**Naomihchi:** Hon, ihkyahpa imapa. Ihksihu.

**Augustinku:** Hinto! Heht'iran?

**Naomihchi:** Aha, eht'ir'aha!

**Augustinku:** Kaya heht'ir'aha?

**Naomihchi:** Ihkshpitu. Wiranitohku sahkushtahahki!

**Augustinku:** Amikani, ihkshar'ɛhɛ. Heht'irahch, sak'inak'ahcha.

**Naomihchi:** Ihkyari…eht'ira weninik'ahcha.

## Lutamashu

Most **taya wana** use the full form of the prefixes we learned in the previous section to show who is happy, thirsty, etc. But a few verbs that start with the letter **e** take a shorter form of the pronouns that don't have an **hk** or **k** at the end. We already learned one of these verbs in Chapter 1: **-etisa** 'to be named'. **Taya wana** that start with **e** take the following prefixes:

| | | SINGULAR | | DUAL | | PLURAL | |
|---|---|---|---|---|---|---|---|
| *1st person* | | **i-** | *I* | **in-** | *we 2* | **in-** | *we all* |
| *2nd person* | *feminine* | **hi-** | *you (f)* | **hin-** | *you 2 (f)* | **hin-** | *you all (f)* |
| | *masculine* | **wi-** | *you (m)* | **win-** | *you 2 (m)* | **win-** | *you all (m)* |
| *3rd person* | *feminine* | **ti-** | *she* | **sin-** | *they 2 (f)* | **sin-** | *they all (f)* |
| | *masculine* | **u-** | *he* | **un-** | *they 2 (m)* | **si-** | *they all (m)* |

So **etisa** comes from **i** + **-etisa**, and **otisa** comes from **u** + **-etisa**.

$$i + e \rightarrow e \qquad u + e \rightarrow o$$

Notice in the examples on the following page that the dual and plural forms that have an **n** in them allow the blending vowel to jump over the **n** to join with the vowel of the pronoun.

**in** + **-ehtini** → **entini** 'we own'

**sin** + **-esahku** → **sensahku** 'they *(fd/p)* are widowed'

**un** + **-eht'ira** → **ont'ira** 'they *(md)* are clothed'

You are already familiar with these forms from using them for **-etisa**. Now we are simply learning more verbs that work the same way. The only additional thing to learn pertains to **-eht'ira** and **-ehtini**. The same vowel blending takes place, but the **h** is lost in the dual and plural forms that have **n**. This is because it is really hard to pronounce **nht** and **nhs**. Tunica makes it easier by dropping the **h**. This is why in the example above, **un** + **eht'ira** becomes **ont'ira**, *not* **onht'ira**.

Additionally, we learned the word **-elu** 'to like' in the previous section. Even though **-elu** starts with **e**, it is an exception: **-elu** always takes the prefixes with **k** and **hk**, and never takes the shortened prefixes. So we get **ihkelu** and **uhkelu**, *not* **elu** and **olu**.

The other word that is an exception is **-erusa** 'to know'. Although **-erusa** takes all of the shortened prefixes and looks just like you would expect in the singular, it has unexpected forms for talking about more than one person (except for **serusa**). These forms need to be memorized, since they only apply to this one word. However, there are some clues you can use: any form where you get an **-n** in the dual or plural, for **-erusa** these forms end in **-nasa**.

| | | SINGULAR | | DUAL | | PLURAL | |
|---|---|---|---|---|---|---|---|
| *1st person* | | **erusa** | *I know* | **erunasa** | *we (d) know* | **erunasa** | *we know* |
| *2nd person* | *feminine* | **herusa** | *you know* | **herunasa** | *you two know* | **herunasa** | *you all know* |
| | *masculine* | **werusa** | *you know* | **werunasa** | *you two know* | **werunasa** | *you all know* |
| *3rd person* | *feminine* | **terusa** | *she knows* | **serunasa** | *they two know* | **serunasa** | *they all know* |
| | *masculine* | **orusa** | *he knows* | **orunasa** | *they two know* | **serusa** | *they all know* |

## Hinu 3

### 8.3.1. Atehpɛtaki:

Join the indicated pieces together to make a complete word.

***Example:*** *i + -ehtini* ***ehtini***

1. hi + -eht'ira ________
2. win + -esahku ________
3. in + -etisa ________
4. sin + -ehtini ________
5. uhk + -elu ________
6. sink + -elu ________
7. sihk + -yahpa ________
8. sink + -sihu ________
9. i + -eht'ira ________
10. hin + -ehtini ________
11. ti + -eht'ira ________
12. wi + -etisa ________
13. un + -etisa ________
14. u + -erusa ________
15. win + -erusa ________
16. si + -erusa ________

### 8.3.2. Molɔtaki:

Choose the correct form (short or long) of the prefix for each of the following **taya wana**. Don't worry about showing how the vowels would blend.

***Example:*** ***hink*** *wana (hink-, hin-)*

1. _____yahpa (ihk-, i-)
2. _____yaru (hihk-, hi-)
3. _____eht'ira (wihk-, wi-)
4. _____shpitu (uhk-, u-)
5. _____etisa (tihk-, ti-)
6. _____mahka (ink-, in-)
7. _____sepi (hink-, hin-)
8. _____stamari (wink-, win-)
9. _____sipi (sink-, sin-)
10. _____ehtini (unk-, un-)
11. _____hayi (sihk-, si-)
12. _____elu (ihk-, i-)
13. _____ara (sink-, sin-)
14. _____aha (ink-, in-)

15. _____erusa (uhk-, u-)
16. _____yari (unk-, un-)
17. _____hayi (tihk-, ti-)
18. _____shari (sihk-, si-)
19. _____yashi (wink-, win-)
20. _____esahku (hihk-, hi-)

**8.3.3. Ey'ɔki** (Circle it)**:**
Circle the form that shows what happens when the short forms of the pronouns join the verb and the vowels blend.

| | | | | | |
|---|---|---|---|---|---|
| ***Example:*** | *si + -ehtini* | → | *siehtini* | ***sehtini*** | *sihetini* |
| 1. | sin + -etisa | → | sentisa | sinetisa | senetisa |
| 2. | u + -eht'ira | → | ueht'ira | oht'ira | oeht'ira |
| 3. | hi + -ehtini | → | heehtini | hihtini | hehtini |
| 4. | wi + -erusa | → | werusa | wierusa | werunasa |
| 5. | hin + -esahku | → | hinesahku | hensahku | hesahku |
| 6. | hin + -erusa | → | hinerusa | henrusa | herunasa |
| 7. | i + -etisa | → | ietisa | itisa | etisa |
| 8. | un + -erusa | → | onrusa | unerusa | orunasa |
| 9. | win + -eht'ira | → | wineht'ira | went'ira | winht'ira |
| 10. | in + -ehtini | → | enhtini | entini | inehtini |

# Tetimili: Nuhchi Tahch'i tihkarhilani

*Sun Woman Story*

Like many tribes in the Southeast, the Tunica-Biloxi revered the sun as a deity. We have two main stories of how **Nuhchi Tahch'i** or Sun Woman came to be. One comes from the Biloxi people and describes how the Ancient of Otters was shunned from a game for being too stinky. His grandmother then gave him some medicine which caused him to smell better. Upon returning to the game, the woman who shunned him from the game wanted to play with him but he refused. This caused her to become ashamed and she went up into the sky, thus becoming the Sun Woman.

In the Tunica version, the Kingfisher disguises himself as a handsome man in order to court a beautiful woman. He courted her at night at a dance till he married her. Upon waking up and finding out she was tricked, she became ashamed. The following excerpt adapted from the *Tunica Texts* explains the rest of the story:

**Sehitihch, tihkyahpa.**
At dawn she [the beautiful woman] was hungry.

**"Tasaku mewiy'ahch, lapuhch," uhkniti.**
"If you go find food, it would be a good thing," she told him [her husband, the kingfisher].

**Hinyatihch, tawishi hayihta narawihch, taninitohkusinima sinktapichuwi.**
So he flew off over the water, and he caught some fish.

**Tihkyuwawi.**
He brought them to her.

**Hinyatihch tihkyari.**
Then she was ashamed.

**"Ma, tawishi hayihta win'ahch, lapuhch," uhkniti.**
She said to him, "You, if you stay above the water, it would be a good thing."

**Tihchɛt tihkyari.**
(But) as for her, she was ashamed.

**Hinyatihch haratihch, hiputi.**
Then as she sang, she danced.

**Hapatihch, hayishwichin, ukitik'ahcha**
When she stopped, (she told him) that she would go above to live.

**Tahch'ihchi tihkpir'akɛni.**
She became the Sun, it is said.

Adapted from Haas, *Tunica Texts*, text 3, p. 20 and p. 22.

## Tetimili wiralepini

1. Find one example of a **taya wana** in this story: what does it mean and what are its parts?

2. Imagine you are Sun Woman realizing that Kingfisher is a bird: what's one question you might ask him using the Tunica question words you learned in this chapter? What's one question Kingfisher might want to ask Sun Woman?

# Chapter 9: Taka taritaworutohkushi

*Classroom objects*

## TOPICS:

# Hɛku, hiku

*This and that*

## Yoluyana

| | | | |
|---|---|---|---|
| **ashuhkitawirani** | *clock* | **rowinara** | *whiteboard* |
| **hayishi** | *above* | **tahina** | *pen; pencil; marker* |
| **hɛ-** | *this; these* | **takahpuni** | *scissors* |
| **hi-** | *that; those* | **tanahchuni** | *stickers* |
| **-hta** | *on; with* | **tasahchuni** | *glue* |
| **kosutahina** | *crayon; marker; colored pencil* | **tawɛhani** | *light* |
| **mashu** | *to make; to build* | **tiranit'ɛ** | *hour* |
| **mi-** | *that over there* | **teliy'oni** | *doll* |
| **pahitaniyu** | *computer* | **tɛrashki** | *page* |
| **rihkɔra** | *table* | **wirani** | *minute; time* |
| **ritaworu** | *school* | **wo** | *to build (a fire); to turn (something) on* |
| **ritaworutohku** | *classroom* | **lapu** | *good; correct* |

## Yanalepini

**Rosehchi:** Worukani.

**Aiyannahchi:** Imapa. Tɛrashki namu hinakani.

**Rosehchi:** Im'aha. Hɛpahitaniyu worukani.

**Aiyannahchi:** Pahitaniyu ihkwana.

**Rosehchi:** Taritaworu pahitaniyu namu uhkara.

*Taworunihchi taritaworutohku kichu akakati. Tawɛhani wokati. Taworusɛma akakata. Ukikata.*

**Taworunihchi:** Hɛ'ɛsh rowina teliy'oni mash'itik'ahcha. Rowina, tahina, kosutahina, tasahchuni, takahpuni tapiwitiki!

*Taworusɛma tarihkɔrash lɔtakata. Rowina teliy'oni mashukata.*

**Taworunihchi:** Henry, tanahchuni wihkwanan?

**Henryku:** Hon. Tanahchunisinima namu ihkwana.

*Taworunihchi tanahchunisinima mekati.*

**Henryku:** Mitanahchuni patawi.

**Taworunihchi:** Hɛtanahchunin?

**Henryku:** Hon.

*Taworunihchi tanahchuni tapikati.*

**Henryku:** Tikahch!

**Augustinku:** Kanahku wirani?

**Merlinku:** Erus'aha.

*Merlinku rowinara hayishi ashuhkitawirani poku. Leyuku.*

**Merlinku:** Po'iki! Wiranit'ɛ sinku.

**Augustinku:** Hi'ɛshuhkitawirani lap'ɔhɔ. Hɛ'ɛshuhkitawirani po'iki!

**Merlinku:** Hmm, hi'ɛshuhkitawiranihta wiranit'ɛ tayihku.

**Augustinku:** Hon, lapu.

## Lutamashu

Think about what the difference is between 'this book' and 'that book'. In English, we use 'this' to talk about objects closer to us, and we use 'that' to talk about objects farther away from us. Tunica has a similar system. However, instead of just having 'this' for close and 'that' for far, Tunica divides 'that' into 'that, not close by but in this general area' and 'that, way over there'. Tunica uses prefixes for 'this', 'that', and 'that way over there':

**hɛ-** 'here, this, these'

**hi-** 'there, that, those'

**mi-** 'way over there, that one way over there, those way over there'

Because **hɛ-**, **hi-**, and **mi-** are prefixes, they can't be used like 'this' and 'that' can in English by themselves. They always have to be attached to something. In Tunica, saying 'this crayon' or 'that student' is really simple: just add **hɛ-**, **hi-**, or **mi-** to the front of the noun. So 'this book' would be **hɛrowina**, and 'that *(f)* student' would be **hitaworuhchi**. Here are some more examples:

**Hitaworunihchi Alicehchi tetisa.**
That teacher is named Alice.

**Hɛrihkɔrashi ukikani.**
I am sitting at this table.

**Mi'oniku hipuku.**
That person *(ms)* way over there is dancing.

You might notice that even though **Mi'oniku** has two vowels coming together, there is no vowel blending. This is because the **hɛ-**, **hi-**, and **mi-** prefixes do not cause vowel blending. Instead, you just add a glottal between the prefix and the word to which it attaches.

The prefixes do not indicate how many things there are. All three prefixes stay the same no matter how many people/things there are. The number of objects is shown on the noun, or not at all. So **hiritaworu** by itself can mean either 'that school' or 'those schools', **hɛtaworunihchi** means 'this teacher *(fs)*', and **hɛtaworunisinima** means 'these teachers *(fd/p)*'.

## Hinu 1

**9.1.1. Luhchi pirɛtaki:**
Translate the following into Tunica.

***Example:*** *this sticker* **hɛtanahchuni**

1. that clock
   ______________________
2. those markers
   ______________________
3. those two tables way over there
   ______________________
4. those two crayons
   ______________________
5. these five papers
   ______________________
6. those four scissors way over there
   ______________________
7. this glue
   ______________________
8. these whiteboards
   ______________________
9. that doll
   ______________________
10. that light way over there
    ______________________

**9.1.2. Luhchi pirɛtaki:**
Translate the following into English.

***Example:*** *hikosutahina* **_that crayon_**

1. hitakahpuni sinku

   ____________________
2. mi'ɛshuhkitawirani

   ____________________
3. hɛrihkɔra

   ____________________
4. hɛtɛrashk'unima

   ____________________
5. hitahinasinima

   ____________________
6. mitaworunisɛma

   ____________________
7. hirowinara

   ____________________
8. mirowinarasinima

   ____________________

# 'This' and 'that' as people

## Yoluyana

| | | | |
|---|---|---|---|
| **chehkini** | *chair* | **pahitawali** | *phone* |
| **halanipahi** | *television* | **rihkɔratahina** | *desk* |
| **hayihta** | *on* | **rowinahina** | *notebook* |

## Yanalepini

**Augustinku:** Kaku mihchi?
**Naomihchi:** Mihchi taworunihchi.
**Augustinku:** Kaku hisɛma?
**Naomihchi:** Hisɛma taworusɛma. Chehkini hayihta ukikata, rihkɔratahina hayihta rowinahina kichu hinakata.
**Augustinku:** Hisɛma erukata. Lapuhch.

**Aiyannahchi:** Hi'unima, kanahku yahkuna?
**Merlinku:** Hi'unima halanipahi pohkuna.
**Aiyannahchi:** Hɛsinima, halanipahi pohksinan?
**Merlinku:** Aha, pahitawalihta yanahksina.
**Aiyannahchi:** Kaya? Yoyani yahksinan?
**Merlinku:** Hon.

## Lutamashu

If you don't know what something is, or if you are asking about someone, or just don't think it's necessary to say the noun (e.g., 'What is this? Who is that?'), you can ask this by adding the gender-number endings that you learned about in Chapter 1 to **hɛ-**, **hi-**, and **mi-**.

| | SINGULAR | DUAL | PLURAL |
|---|---|---|---|
| *feminine* | **-hchi** | **-sinima** | **-sinima** |
| *masculine* | **-ku** | **-unima** | **-sɛma** |

Remember that the correct ending depends on how many things you are talking about (one vs. two vs. three or more), and whether the person is male or female. So if you want to say 'who is that?', referring to a man, you'd use **hiku**, which is **hi-** 'that' + **-ku** for one male. If you wanted to ask 'who are those (women) way over there', you'd use **misinima**, which is **mi-** 'that, way over there' + **-sinima** for many females, and so on. A chart of the forms for talking about unnamed male and female people is given here:

| | | SINGULAR | DUAL | PLURAL |
|---|---|---|---|---|
| *near* | *feminine* | **hɛhchi** | **hɛsinima** | **hɛsinima** |
| | *masculine* | **hɛku** | **hɛ'unima** | **hɛsɛma** |
| *far* | *feminine* | **hihchi** | **hisinima** | **hisinima** |
| | *masculine* | **hiku** | **hi'unima** | **hisɛma** |
| *very far* | *feminine* | **mihchi** | **misinima** | **misinima** |
| | *masculine* | **miku** | **mi'unima** | **misɛma** |

There is an option to use a shorter form of the gender-number endings when used with **hɛ-**, **hi-**, and **mi-**: if you're speaking quickly, you can use only the first part of the gender-number ending, so for example **hi'unima** would be **hi'un**, and **misinima** would be **misin**.

## Hinu 2

**9.2.1. Molɔtaki:**
Using the form of the verb, fill in the correct form of 'this' or 'that' as a subject in the sentence. Use the prefix given in parentheses.

***Example:*** *__Hiku__ (hi-) wahaku.*

1. ____________ (hi-) mashukati.
2. ____________ (mi-) wokata.
3. ____________ (hɛ-) woruku.
4. ____________ (mi-) sensahku.
5. ____________ (hɛ-) uhkshpitu.
6. ____________ (mi-) sinkyahpa.
7. ____________ (hɛ-) tihkshtamari.
8. ____________ (mi-) sihkyaru.
9. ____________ (hi-) serusa.
10. ____________ (hɛ-) unktohkuni.

### 9.2.2. Pakɛtaki:

Answer the question 'Who is this/that?' using both **hɛ-**, **hi-**, or **mi-** and the noun given in parentheses. Don't forget to add gender-number endings to the nouns!

***Example:*** *Kanahku hɛku? (teacher)* **Hɛku taworuniku.**

1. Kanahku mi'unima? (*people*) ________________
2. Kanahku hɛsinima? (*women*) ________________
3. Kanahku hiku? (*man*) ________________
4. Kanahku misɛma? (*chiefs*) ________________
5. Kanahku hɛhchi? (*student*) ________________
6. Kanahku hi'unima? (*robbers*) ________________
7. Kanahku misinima? (*ball players*) ________________

# 'This' and 'that' as things

## Yoluyana

| | | | |
|---|---|---|---|
| **halani** | *picture* | **pahitaniyutohku** | *laptop* |
| **hinatamurini** | *eraser* | **pahitawirani** | *calculator* |
| **luhchi Yoroni** | *the Tunica language* | **ukitamashu** | *bench* |
| **pahitaniyu ɛsa** | *tablet* | | |

## Yanalepini

**Taworunihchi:** Hɛku, kanahku otisa?
**Taworusɛma:** Hiku pahitaniyutohku.
**Taworunihchi:** Hon. Hisinima rihkɔra hayihta, kanahku sentisa?
**Taworusɛma:** Pahitaniyu ɛsa sentisa.
**Taworunihchi:** Miku tishuhki hayishi, kanahku otisa?
**Taworusɛma:** Miku halani otisa.
**Taworunihchi:** Lapu!

*Taworusɛma ritaworutohku kichu shimikata. Taworuniku akaku.*

**Taworuniku:** Hi'ukitamashu hayihta ukiwitiki!

*Taworusɛma ukikata.*

**Taworuniku:** Tahina, hinatamurini, pahitawirani tapiwitiki! Aiyanna, rowinara hayihta hin'aki!

*Aiyannahchi rowinarash yukakati.*

**Taworuniku:** Hɛrowinahinasinima tapiwitiki! Clyde, arhila sahkuhta po'itan, tohkuhch. Aiyanna, luhchi Yoroni kichu tarhilani hin'ataki!

**Aiyannahchi, Clydeku:** Ko'o!

## Lutamashu

In the previous section, we learned how to use **hɛ-**, **hi-**, and **mi-** to talk about unnamed people and where they are relative to the speaker. But, what if we want to talk about things, and ask, 'what is that?' To talk about things, we also use **hɛ-**, **hi-**, and **mi-** plus gender-number endings, but unlike with people, all things take a single set of endings. These endings are already familiar to you, because the singular and dual forms are the same as the masculine forms (**-ku** and **-unima**), and the plural form is the same as the form for women (**-sinima**). This means that to refer to any and all objects, you'll use the following forms depending on how many there are and how far away they are from you:

| | SINGULAR | | DUAL | | PLURAL | |
|---|---|---|---|---|---|---|
| *near* | **hɛku** | *this* | **hɛ'unima** | *these (2)* | **hɛsinima** | *these (3+)* |
| *far* | **hiku** | *that* | **hi'unima** | *those (2)* | **hisinima** | *those (3+)* |
| *very far* | **miku** | *that way over there* | **mi'unima** | *those (2) way over there* | **misinima** | *those (3+) way over there* |

So if I were referring to 'this thing (near me)', I would use **hɛku**. 'That thing (further away from me)' would use **hiku**, and 'that thing I used to have in the 1st grade' would be **miku**. Similarly, I can talk about 'that (one) thing' with **hiku**, 'those two things' with **hi'unima**, or 'those (many) things' with **hisinima**.

## Hinu 3

**9.3.1. Luhchi pirɛtaki:**
Translate the following into English.

***Example:*** *Hɛsinima chehkini.* ***These are chairs.***

1. Miku rihkɔra. ______
2. Hisinima ukitamashu. ______
3. Hɛku ritaworutohku. ______
4. Hisɛma tarahpanisɛma. ______
5. Mi'unima pahitaniyutohku. ______

**9.3.2. Luhchi pirɛtaki:**
Translate the following into Tunica.

***Example:*** *That is a picture.* ***Hiku halani.***

1. This is a desk. ______
2. That over there is a book. ______
3. Those are erasers. ______
4. These are calculators. ______
5. Those over there are tablets. ______

**9.3.3. Atehpɛtaki:**
Write the letter of the English sentence next to its Tunica translation.

***Example:*** __*a*__ *Mi'unima ukitamashu.* *a. Those two over there are benches.*

1. _____ Hisinima tahina.
2. _____ Miku rihkɔratahina.
3. _____ Hɛ'unima rowinahina.
4. _____ Misinima halani.
5. _____ Hi'unima chehkini.
6. _____ Hɛku pahitaniyu.

a. That over there is a desk.
b. This is a computer.
c. Those over there are pictures.
d. Those two are chairs.
e. Those are pencils.
f. These two are notebooks.

# Tetimili: Ritaworu

*School*

Tunica-Biloxi children in Marksville were not allowed to attend White schools until about 1948, when Chief Horace Pierite and Sub-Chief Joseph Pierite Sr. successfully lobbied to change local school segregation policies toward Native children. Even then, Tunica-Biloxi children could only attend White schools if they had no discernible African-American ancestry, excluding a significant portion of our tribe. Elsewhere in Louisiana, Jena Choctaws secured integration in the early 1940s; Houmas were integrated in Lafourche Parish but not Terrebonne Parish; Choctaw-Apaches attended White schools regularly; Clifton-Choctaws had a K-6 community school that was designated as White but could not attend White high schools in Rapides Parish; Coushattas attended White high schools; and some Chitimachas went to a federal Indian school in 1906, while others attended a segregated Indian school in their community after that.

In other areas, the United States forced many Native children to attend Indian-only boarding schools far from their families. In these schools, students were forbidden to speak their languages, practice their religions, or wear their traditional clothes. In Marksville, our tribe faced the same pressures to assimilate and stop being Tunica-Biloxi.

Today Indigenous children in Louisiana attend school with their peers of other ethnicities. They can complete high school in their home communities before going off to college. Many earn bachelor's and graduate degrees. And even though the schools don't teach our language, no one can stop us from learning it and passing it down as our ancestors hoped we would.

## Tetimili wiralepini

1. Considering the history of tribal education in Louisiana and the United States, what drives you to continue your own education while incorporating the knowledge of indigenous culture and language?

2. How would you like to help your tribal community in the realms of education, health, business, or government? Are there other ways that you would like to support your community?

3. If you are non-indigenous, how can you be a good ally in helping preserve indigenous knowledge, traditions, and rights?

# Chapter 10: Taka halani

*Adjectives*

**TOPICS:**

# Takosu

*Colors*

## Yoluyana

| | |
|---|---|
| **ayi** | *fire* |
| **elu kayi yuru** | *banana* |
| **tehk'elukayi** | *orange (fruit)* |
| **kayi** | *yellow; gold; brown; orange* |
| **kɛra** | *speckled; spotted; mottled* |
| **kosu** | *color* |
| **kosuhki** | *crawfish* |
| **kɔta** | *gray* |
| **kuwatohku** | *bird* |
| **meli** | *black* |
| **mili** | *red* |
| **muhkini** | *smoke* |
| **-nahku** | *like; similar to* |
| **ɔshta** | *blue; green; purple* |
| **rihku** | *tree* |
| **risa** | *multi-colored; variegated; dappled* |
| **rɔwa** | *white* |
| **shimila** | *blue jay* |
| **tahkishi** | *skin; hide; bark; shell* |
| **uhkkosu** | *its color* |
| **wo** | *to build a fire* |
| **wosu** | *striped* |
| **yaluhki** | *mushroom* |
| **yanishi** | *bull; bovine* |
| **yanishi nuhchi** | *cow* |

## Yanalepini

**Merlinku:** Hɛkosuhki, kanahku uhkkosu?

**Chrisku:** Hikosuhki mili.

**Merlinku:** Hɛku melin?

**Chrisku:** Aha. Takosuhki mili.

**Merlinku:** Lapuhch. Takosuhki sakunik'ahcha!

**Chrisku:** Po'iki! Mikuwatohku mili uhkkosu, takosuhkinahku.

**Merlinku:** Hon. Takosuhkinahku.

**Aiyannahchi:** Hɛ'elu kayi yuru, kanahku uhkkosu?

**Alicehchi:** Hɛ'elu kayi yuru kayi.

**Aiyannahchi:** Tikahch. Himinu, kanahku uhkkosu?

**Alicehchi:** Himinu, uhkkosu kɔta.

**Aiyannahchi:** Kanahku minu rapuku?

**Alicehchi:** Himinu meli rapuku.

**Aiyannahchi:** Tikahch.

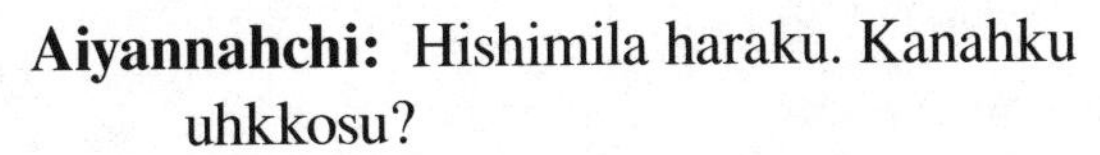

**Aiyannahchi:** Hishimila haraku. Kanahku uhkkosu?

**Alicehchi:** Tashimila ɔshta. Hiyanishi nuhchi, kanahku uhkkosu?

**Aiyannahchi:** Hiyanishi nuhchi kɛra. Shimila wosun?

**Alicehchi:** Hon. Minu risan?

**Aiyannahchi:** Hon, minu risa.

**Merlinku:** Tarihku, kanahku uhkkosu?

**Chrisku:** Tarihku ɔshta, uhktahkishi kayi.

**Merlinku:** Tikahch. Tayaluhki, kanahku uhkkosu?

**Chrisku:** Hiku kayi uhkkosu!

**Merlinku:** Tikahch.

**Merlinku:** Ayi woni. Po'iki! Kanahku uhkkosu?

**Chrisku:** Mili uhkkosu.

**Merlinku:** Hon. Tamuhkinɛt milin?

**Chrisku:** Aha. Tamuhkini kɔta.

**Merlinku:** Kanahku sakukata?

**Aiyannahchi:** Tehk'elukayi sakukata.

**Merlinku:** Tehk'elukayi, kanahku uhkkosu?

**Aiyannahchi:** Tehk'elukayi kayi.

**Merlinku:** Lapuhch.

## Lutamashu

It is common for languages to have more or fewer color terms than English does. As you probably noticed from the **yoluyana**, there are some color words in Tunica that describe more than one color in English. For example, the word **ɔshta** can mean 'green', 'blue', or 'purple'. The same is true for the color **kayi**, which can mean 'yellow', 'golden', 'orange', or 'brown' in English. The Tunica words below show the variety of hues that **ɔshta** and **kayi** can describe.

| | |
|---|---|
| **yaka ɔshta** | *little blue heron* |
| **chuhki ɔshta** | *live oak ('evergreen oak')* |
| **hahka ɔshta** | *blue corn* |
| | |
| **hahka kayi** | *yellow corn* |
| **laspikayi** | *gold ('yellow metal')* |
| **tehk'elukayi** | *orange (fruit)* |
| **ala kayi** | *brown thrasher* |

Tunica also has basic color terms that English lacks. **Risa** in Tunica means 'multi-colored, variegated, dappled, checkered, or having a mix of colors'. **Kɛra** means 'speckled, spotted, or mottled'.

To describe even more specific shades of colors, you can add the ending **-nahku**, meaning 'like; similar to', onto the end of a noun. For example, **ɔshta shimilanahku** means '**ɔshta** like a blue jay', and **kayi elu tɔrahtanahku** means '**kayi** like an orange'.

The word for 'color' is **kosu**. However, notice that when you are asking what color something is, you say **kanahku uhkkosu?** which is literally 'what is its color?'. There is an **uhk-** on **kosu**, and this means 'its'. Without **uhk-**, **kanahku kosu** would mean 'which color'. We will learn more about **uhk-** and how to possess things in Chapter 11.

## Hinu 1

**10.1.1. Luhchi pirɛtaki:**
Translate the following sentences.

***Example:*** *Tamuhkini kɔta.* **The smoke is gray.**

1. Tarihku ɔshta. ______
2. Meli uhkkosu. ______
3. Mili kosuhkinahku. ______
4. Taminu risa lɔtaku. ______
5. Tashimila ɔshta haraku. ______

**10.1.2. Luhchi pirɛtaki:**
Translate the following sentences.

***Example:*** *Cows are spotted.* **Yanishi nuhchisinima kɛra.**

1. Are cats white? ______
2. I ate the yellow banana. ______
3. That blue jay is blue like a pond. ______
4. What color is this? ______
5. The bark is striped. ______

**10.1.3. Halɛtaki** (Draw it):
Draw the following images.

| Tachehkini kayi | Tashimila ɔshta |
|---|---|
| Takosuhki mili | Tamuhkini kɔta |
| Taminu risa | Tehk'elu kayi kayi |
| Tayanishi nuhchi kɛra | Tashimila wosu |

# Taka Halani

*Adjectives*

## Yoluyana

| | | | |
|---|---|---|---|
| **hashita** | *light* | **romana** | *heavy* |
| **hayi** | *old* | **nisa** | *new* |
| **hɛntohku** | *small* | **tika** | *big* |
| **kochu** | *short* | **yuru** | *tall; long* |
| **lamihta** | *soft* | **ra** | *hard* |
| **rukasa** | *ugly* | **tashle** | *beautiful* |
| **pɛlka** | *flat* | **yɔla** | *empty* |
| **hinahkushkan** | *but; nevertheless* | | |

## Yanalepini

**Augustinku:** Kanahku ontisa?
**Alicehchi:** Merlinku, Henryku ontisa.
**Augustinku:** Kaku tayuruku?
**Alicehchi:** Merlinku yuru.
**Augustinku:** Henryku takochukun?
**Alicehchi:** Hon. Henryku kochu.

**Chrisku:** Hirihkɔratahina romanan?
**Merlinku:** Aha. Hɛrihkɔratahina hashita.
**Chrisku:** Hinahkushkan tarihkɔratahina tika!
**Merlinku:** Tarihkɔratahina yɔla.

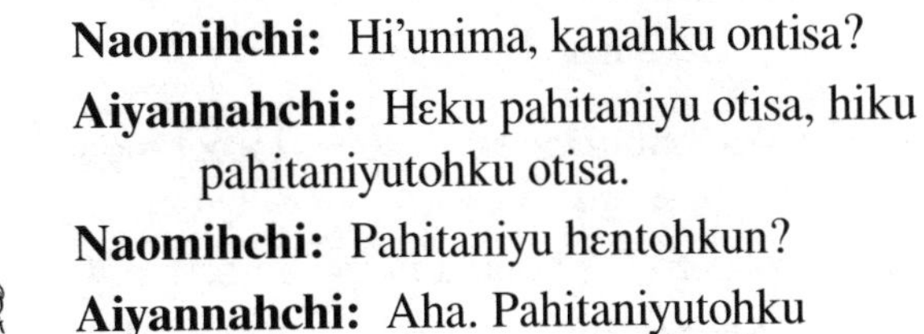

**Naomihchi:** Hi'unima, kanahku ontisa?
**Aiyannahchi:** Hɛku pahitaniyu otisa, hiku pahitaniyutohku otisa.
**Naomihchi:** Pahitaniyu hɛntohkun?
**Aiyannahchi:** Aha. Pahitaniyutohku hɛntohku.
**Naomihchi:** Hɛpahitaniyutohku nisan?
**Aiyannahchi:** Hon.
**Naomihchi:** Hipahitaniyɔt nisan?
**Aiyannahchi:** Aha, hepahitaniyu hayi.

**Alicehchi:** Hiyanishi nuhchi tashle!
**Merlinku:** Hon. Hiyanishi nuhchi tashle, meli, lamihta.
**Alicehchi:** Hɛ'ukitamashu ra, pɛlka.
**Merlinku:** Rukasa! Uhkkosu kayi.
**Alicehchi:** Hon. Lap'ɔhɔ.

## Lutamashu

**Taka halani** is the word in Tunica for adjective. **Taka halani** are words that describe nouns, like 'a *red* turtle' or 'the *small* book'. Some words that are adjectives in English are actually **taya wana** (stative verbs) in Tunica (e.g. **-yashi** 'to be angry'; **-yahpa** 'to be hungry').

**Taka halani** can be used in two ways: with a noun as part of a phrase (like 'the red house'), or, with a noun subject, act as a whole sentence ('the house is red'). When **taka halani** and nouns appear together to form a whole sentence, **taka halani** simply follow the noun. We saw this in the previous section with **kosu**, where **tarihku ɔshta** meant 'the tree is green'. As we saw in the **yanalepini** in this section, this sort of pattern applies to all **taka halani**, not just **kosu**.

**Tarowinahina pɛlka.**
The notebook is flat.

**Tanuhchi tashle.**
The woman is beautiful.

When **taka halani** are part of a larger sentence, they can be followed by gender-number endings. This indicates that they go with the noun. While the gender-number ending can appear on both the noun and the adjective, it is more common that the ending only appears on the **taka halani**, the last word in the phrase.

**Toni yuruku lɔtawi.**
The tall man ran.

**Elu kayi yuru kayisinima sakuni.**
I ate yellow bananas.

However, you may have noticed earlier in this chapter that it is not always the case that a phrase like 'yellow banana' takes a gender-number ending. In **hinu** 10.1.1, we saw the sentence **Taminu risa lɔtaku**. This is because gender-number endings are generally omitted when the noun being described is not a human. This means that **taminu risa** can mean either 'The cat is multi-colored' or 'the multi-colored cat'. When there is a verb in the sentence (like in **taminu risa lɔtaku**), **taminu risa** means 'the multi-colored cat'. When there is no verb (just **taminu risa**), it means 'the cat is multi-colored'.

You saw in the **lutamashu** in the last section that the suffix **-nahku** can be put on nouns to specify the exact color you're talking about. You can use **-nahku** on nouns with any **taka halani** to modify its quality. For example, **lamihta sanahku** means 'soft like the dog', and **hashita muhkininahku** means 'light as smoke'.

Sometimes the adjective can become a noun, meaning something like 'the one who is _____'. For instance, **yuru** 'tall; long' can become **tayuru(ku)** 'the tall one; the one that is tall/long' and **kochu** 'short' can become **takochu(hchi)** 'the one who is short; the short one'. For examples in context, see the first **yanalepini** in this section, on page 148.

## Hinu 2

**10.2.1. Luhchi pirɛtaki:**
Translate the following into English.

***Example:*** *Kanahku kuwatohku rukasa?* **Which bird is ugly?**

1. Tarihku tika patawi. ____________________
2. Taminu lamihta pitaku. ____________________
3. Tasa yuru yanishinahku. ____________________
4. Takosuhki mili sakuki. ____________________
5. Tashimila tashle rapuku. ____________________

**10.2.2. Luhchi pirɛtaki:**
Translate the following into Tunica.

***Example:*** *The bench is flat.* ***Tukitamashu pɛlka.***

1. The short man is running. ____________________
2. The table is new like the chair. ____________________
3. This classroom is empty. ____________________
4. Which cats are small? ____________________
5. What color is the orange? ____________________

**10.2.3. Molɔtaki:**

Fill in the blanks in each question with the best **taka halani** given in that question.

***Example:***

| | | | | |
|---|---|---|---|---|
| *tewali/romantohku* | *kuwatohku* | ***tewali*** | *yanishi nuhchi* | ***romantohku*** |
| 1. kochu/yuru | tihika | ____________ | ashutayi | ____________ |
| 2. romana/hashita | yanishi | ____________ | muhkini | ____________ |
| 3. tika/hɛntohku | kosuhki | ____________ | yanishi | ____________ |
| 4. pɛlka/tashle | rowina | ____________ | nuhchi | ____________ |
| 5. lamihta/ra | rihku | ____________ | minu | ____________ |
| 6. nisa/hayi | pahitaniyu | ____________ | rihku | ____________ |

**10.2.4. Atehpɛtaki:**

Match each word on the left to its opposite meaning on the right.

| | |
|---|---|
| 1. _____ rukasa | a. ra |
| 2. _____ lamihta | b. yuru |
| 3. _____ tika | c. nisa |
| 4. _____ kochu | d. hɛntohku |
| 5. _____ hayi | e. tashle |

## Tetimili: Kaya Tarushtaku tarku hotushi uhki

*Why Rabbit lives along the edge of the woods*

**Tarushtaku** 'Rabbit' has always been known to be a trickster. One day he decided he would become a player of **puna** 'stickball'. The problem was he did not have **puna** or **punatarahpani**. He thought about it, "I know what I will do. I will go to **tahal'ukini** and I will ask for **punatarahpani** and **puna**." **Tarushtaku** thought to himself. **Tarushtaku** knew he would be the best player of **punatarahpani** in **tahal'ukini** and **tarku kichu**. **Tarushtaku** proudly said "**Hotu** will see me and **hotu** will say, **'Ko'o! Lapu!'**"

First, **Tarushtaku** went to the house of **Tayoronishi** to ask for his **punatarahpani**. Then **Tarushtaku** went to the house of **Tayoroni nuhchi** and asked for her **puna**. Knowing the trickster ways of **Tarushtaku**, both **Tayoronishi** and **Tayoroni nuhchi** refused the requests of **Tarushtaku. Tarushtaku** sat quietly along the edge of **tarku** planning how he would acquire **puna** and **punatarahpani**. Today, you will still find **Tarushtaku** along the edge of **tarku** waiting for his chance to play **punatarahpani**.

### Tetimili yoluyana

| | | | |
|---|---|---|---|
| **rushta** | *rabbit* | **Tayoroni nuhchi** | *Tunica woman* |
| **Tayoronishi** | *Tunica man* | | |

### Tetimili wiralepini

1. In this story, we hear how **Tarushtaku** wants to play stickball, but doesn't get the chance because people are suspicious of his wily ways. Write two sentences in Tunica that we might see if **Tarushtaku** did convince people to play stickball with him!

# Chapter 11: Eht'ira

## *Clothes*

**TOPICS:**

# Alienable possession

## Yoluyana

| | | | |
|---|---|---|---|
| **lapu** | *to buy* | **tahch'i tapo** | *sunglasses* |
| **rahpu** | *to put on (coat, stockings, etc.)* | **tapo** | *glasses* |
| **rahpuntira** | *coat* | **tawohku** | *hat* |
| **rahpuntira yuru** | *overcoat* | **tira** | *dress* |
| **ritalapu** | *store; market* | **tirahalu** | *underwear* |
| **shuhpali** | *pants* | **tiratamihku** | *headband* |
| **shuhpali kochu** | *shorts* | **tiratasaru** | *belt* |
| **tahch'i** | *sun* | **weht'ira** | *your (ms) clothes* |

## Yanalepini

**Diamondhchi:** Aiyanna, hihktira tashle! Hihktiratamihku ihkelu. Hihktiratamihku, kata lap'ɔ?

**Aiyannahchi:** Ihktiratamihku ritalapushi lapuni. Hihktahch'i tapo, kata lap'ɔ?

**Diamondhchi:** Hɛtahch'i tapo tahal'ukini kichu wenini.

**Aiyannahchi:** Lapuhch!

**Naomihchi:** James! Kaya weht'ir'aha?

**Jamesku:** Erus'aha.

**Naomihchi:** Weht'ira tewali rahp'iki!
Sahkuhta wihktirahalu,
wihkshuhpali, wihktiratasaru tap'iki,
ilihta wihktapo, wihktawohku,
wihkrahpuntira tap'iki!

**Jamesku:** Ihkwan'aha.

**Naomi:** Hinyatihch yɔlakani.

**Merlinku:** Kaya shuhpali kochu
rahpuntir'ama wihkara?

**Jamesku:** Ihksipi. Hinahkushkan,
ihkshuhpali kochu ihkelu.

**Merlinku:** Ihkrahpuntira yuru chu'iki!
Ihksip'ɛhɛ.

**Jamesku:** Tikahch!

## Lutamashu

Most things in the world do not inherently belong to someone. Objects like chairs, tables, trees, butterflies, and food do not necessarily have to be a person's; one can say **Hiku chehkini** 'That is a chair' or **Hɛku minu** 'This is a cat'. However, it is also possible to own chairs and cats. This is known as possession.

In Tunica there are two ways in which one can express ownership of something. Possession can be inalienable or alienable. First, alienable nouns are objects that you may or may not have a relationship to. For example, you could own that chair, making it 'your chair', or you could have no relationship to it whatsoever. Maybe you've never seen that chair before in your life. These kinds of objects take alienable possession.

Possession in Tunica is indicated with a prefix. So 'my chair' is **ihkchehkini**, composed of the prefix **ihk-** + **chehkini**. Check out the other alienable prefixes in the chart on the next page. Just like with verb endings that tell you who is doing the action, possessive prefixes can be first person (my, our), second person (your), or third person (his, her, their), masculine or feminine, and singular, dual or plural. You have actually seen these prefixes before; they are the same prefixes that are used with **taya wana** (Chapter 8).

| | | SINGULAR | | DUAL | | PLURAL | |
|---|---|---|---|---|---|---|---|
| *1st person* | | **ihk-** | *my* | **ink-** | *our* | **ink-** | *our* |
| *2nd person* | *feminine* | **hihk-** | *your* | **hink-** | *your* | **hink-** | *your* |
| | *masculine* | **wihk-** | *your* | **wink-** | *your* | **wink-** | *your* |
| *3rd person* | *feminine* | **tihk-** | *her* | **sink-** | *their* | **sink-** | *their* |
| | *masculine* | **uhk-** | *his* | **unk-** | *their* | **sihk-** | *their* |

In addition to pets and furniture and other types of inanimate objects, we commonly possess our clothing. The clothing items in the **yoluyana** above are alienably possessed, meaning 1) you don't have to possess them (**rahpuntira** is a perfectly good word on its own), and 2) if you do possess them, they take the prefixes above (**ihkrahpuntira** 'my coat'). This is not the case for all articles of clothing, as we will learn in the next section.

## Hinu 1

**11.1.1. Luhchi pirɛtaki:**
Translate the following into Tunica.

***Example:*** *their (mp) glasses* **sihktapo**

1. my pants
2. our *(d)* coats
3. our *(p)* dresses
4. her headband
5. their *(md)* overcoats
6. their *(mp)* shorts
7. the two men's sunglasses
8. the two women's hats
9. our belts
10. his underwear

**11.1.2. Chu'ɔki:**
Choose the correct English translation of the following Tunica statements.

***Example:*** *ihktiratamihku*
***a. my headband*** *b. her dress* *c. your belt*

1. sinkrahpuntira
   a. their *(mp)* pants b. their *(fp)* belts c. their *(fp)* coats
2. wihktirahalu
   a. your *(ms)* underwear b. your *(ms)* sunglasses c. your *(ms)* hat
3. inktawohku
   a. my pants b. my dress c. our hats
4. uhktapo
   a. their *(md)* hat b. his glasses c. her overcoat
5. tihkshuhpali kochu
   a. her pants b. her shorts c. her sunglasses

# Tetimili: Tawohku

*Hats*

Sesostrie Youchigant talked to Mary Haas about a variety of subjects, including clothing. Here, he describes how to make hats.

**Tɛchara pohtutahch, pɔhtahkantani.**
When they would cut palmetto leaves, they would boil them, they say.

**Lapulehe pɔht'antahch, chutaman hɔwashi uhkrawukatani.**
When (the leaves) were well boiled, they would take them and put them outside, they say.

**Hinyatihch, lawu ili ahak'ihch enihku hɔwashi uhkyɔlakatani.**
They would leave them outside for two or three nights, they say.

**Lawu tamuhki panutihch, tɛcharahchi rɔwa yakatɛni.**
When the dew passed through them, the palmetto (leaves) would turn white, they say.

**Hinyatihch, pasa ishutahch, wilakatani.**
Then they would split (the leaves), peel them, and weave them together, they say.

**Hinyatihch, tawohku mashukatani.**
They would make hats (out of them), they say.

Haas, *Tunica Texts*, text 36C, p. 162

## Tetimili wiralepini

1. Here Sesostrie Youchigant describes how hats are made out of palmetto leaves. Is there a traditional craft you enjoy doing? Is there a different Tunica craft or activity you would like to know?

2. As a project, write a short set of instructions on how to make a craft in Tunica. It can be as complicated as a palmetto hat or as simple as a popsicle stick **ri** 'house'!

# Inalienable possession

## Yoluyana

| | | | |
|---|---|---|---|
| **-alawɛchatapahchu** | *earring* | **-ehtiwahkuni** | *breechcloth* |
| **-ashkalahpi** | *shoes* | **-eruhtamihku** | *shawl* |
| **-ashkalahpit'ɛ** | *boots* | **-esintamihku** | *bonnet* |
| **-ashkarahpuni** | *stockings* | **-hkenirahpuni** | *glove* |
| **-ashkarahpuni kochu** | *socks* | **-hkenitamuri** | *ring* |
| **-astayitira** | *skirt* | **taka** | *thing* |
| **-ehniyutamihku** | *shirt* | **wantaha** | *a long time ago* |

## Yanalepini

**Taworuniku:** Wantaha tonisɛma seht'ira sahu sihkara. Tanuhchisinima sensintamihku, sinkenirahpuni, sɛnshkarahpuni, sɛnstayitira, senruhtamihku sinkara. Tonisɛma sihktawohku, sɛshkalahpit'ɛ, sihkenirahpuni sihkara.

**Taworuhchi:** Tonisɛma sehtiwahkuni sihkaran?

**Taworuniku:** Hon. Wantaha inkonisɛma sehtiwahkuni sihkara.

**Taworuhchi:** Eruhtamihku ihkara. Nihkirhipush chuyakakani.

**Taworuniku:** Lapuhch.

**Rosehchi:** Ritalapush yuk'inaki!
**Chrisku:** Kanahku lap'ɔk'ahcha?
**Rosehchi:** Ihkenitamuri,
ɛlawɛchatapahchu lapunik'ahcha.
Taka lap'ik'ahchan?
**Chrisku:** Hon, ehniyutamihku,
ɛshkarahpuni kochu lapunik'ahcha.
Ɛshkalahpi weninihch,
am'inak'ahcha.
**Rosehchi:** Lapu.

## Lutamashu

Unlike with alienable possession, inalienable possession is used for objects that you have an undeniable relationship with. Things which are inalienably possessed in Tunica include your family members, body parts, and any compound words that include family terms or body parts. In Tunica, these words *must always be possessed*. This is different from English, where you can say '*a mother* knows best' or 'there is *a hair* in my soup'. However, in Tunica you have to specify whose mother knows best or that someone's hair is in your soup.

The difference between alienable and inalienable possession is not only about which nouns have to be possessed. Inalienable nouns take a slightly different set of prefixes than the alienable set you learned in the previous section. Whereas all of the alienable prefixes end in **-hk** (singular) or **-k** (dual/plural), the inalienable prefixes do not have this ending, and instead end either in a vowel or **-n-**, which marks the dual/plural. You have also already seen these prefixes used with **taya wana** that start with the letter **e** (Chapter 8).

| | | SINGULAR | | DUAL | | PLURAL | |
|---|---|---|---|---|---|---|---|
| *1st person* | | **i-** | *my* | **in-** | *our* | **in-** | *our* |
| *2nd person* | *feminine* | **hi-** | *your* | **hin-** | *your* | **hin-** | *your* |
| | *masculine* | **wi-** | *your* | **win-** | *your* | **win-** | *your* |
| *3rd person* | *feminine* | **ti-** | *her* | **sin-** | *their* | **sin-** | *their* |
| | *masculine* | **u-** | *his* | **un-** | *their* | **si-** | *their* |

Recall that the third person masculine dual and plural forms are also used for mixed groups, groups that include a man and a woman: **un-** 'their' (two men or one man and one woman), and **si-** 'their' (several men or men and women).

Because some clothing items are alienably possessed and some are inalienably possessed, you will need to memorize which clothes belong to which category. For example, while **tira** 'dress' becomes **ihk-** + **tira** = **ihktira** 'my dress', **-eht'ira** 'clothes' becomes **i-** + **-eht'ira** = **eht'ira** 'my clothes'. While this may seem confusing, it helps to know that many pieces of clothing base their names on the parts of the body they cover (see Chapter 12). These clothes where the word starts with a body part (like **-ashkarahpuni**, which is **-ashka** 'leg' + **-rahpuni** 'pulled on') are inalienably possessed because body parts are inalienably possessed.

Since many inalienably possessed words in Tunica start with a vowel, it is also important to pay attention to the sound changes that happen when two vowels meet at the beginning of a word. For inalienable prefixes, the only vowel combinations you will need to remember are those that start with **i** and **u**. As an example, here is a full set of possessed forms for **eht'ira** 'my clothes'.

| | | SINGULAR | | DUAL | | PLURAL | |
|---|---|---|---|---|---|---|---|
| *1st person* | | **eht'ira** | *my clothes* | **ent'ira** | *our clothes* | **ent'ira** | *our clothes* |
| *2nd person* | *feminine* | **heht'ira** | *your clothes* | **hent'ira** | *your clothes* | **hent'ira** | *your clothes* |
| | *masculine* | **weht'ira** | *your clothes* | **went'ira** | *your clothes* | **went'ira** | *your clothes* |
| *3rd person* | *feminine* | **teht'ira** | *her clothes* | **sent'ira** | *their clothes* | **sent'ira** | *their clothes* |
| | *masculine* | **oht'ira** | *his clothes* | **ont'ira** | *their clothes* | **seht'ira** | *their clothes* |

Notice that **in-** + **-eht'ira** in the chart above does *not* become **enht'ira**, but is actually **ent'ira**. This is the same process that we saw in Chapter 8 with **-eht'ira** (which is the same word, it's just that it can be used as both a noun and a verb) and **-ehtini**, where **h** is lost after **n**.

## Hinu 2

### 11.2.1. Luhchi pirɛtaki:

Translate the following into English.

***Example:*** *hɛlawɛchatapahchu* ***your (fs) earring***

1. eht'ira ______
2. sɛnshkalahpit'ɛ ______
3. hɛnshkalahpi ______
4. tihkenitamuri ______
5. sihkenirahpuni ______
6. hesintamihku ______
7. hɛnstayitira ______
8. sehtiwahkuni ______
9. ehniyutamihku ______
10. hɛshkarahpuni kochu ______

### 11.2.2. Luhchi pirɛtaki:

Translate the following into Tunica.

***Example:*** *their (mp) clothes* ***seht'ira***

1. my skirt ______
2. his breechcloth ______
3. your *(ms)* socks ______
4. your *(fs)* stockings ______
5. your *(md)* gloves ______
6. your *(fp)* earrings ______
7. your *(mp)* boots ______
8. our rings ______
9. her bonnet ______
10. their *(fd)* shoes ______

### 11.2.3. Molɔtaki:

Fill in the blanks using the information given in the other columns. Some of the nouns require inalienable possessors, while others are independent nouns and require alienable possessors.

***Example:***

| | | | | |
|---|---|---|---|---|
| | *hat* | ***tawohku*** | ***tihktawohku*** | *her hat* |
| | | UNPOSSESSED | POSSESSED | TRANSLATION |
| 1. | *skirt* | -astayitira | ɛstayitira | ___________ |
| 2. | *glasses* | tapo | ___________ | his glasses |
| 3. | *coat* | rahpuntira | tihkrahpuntira | ___________ |
| 4. | *ring* | -hkenitamuri | wihkenitamuri | ___________ |
| 5. | *bonnet* | ___________ | sensintamihku | ___________ |
| 6. | *belt* | ___________ | ___________ | their *(mp)* belts |
| 7. | *boots* | -ashkalahpit'ɛ | ___________ | your *(fd)* boots |
| 8. | *gloves* | ___________ | winkenirahpuni | ___________ |
| 9. | *dress* | ___________ | ___________ | your *(fs)* dress |
| 10. | *shawl* | -eruhtamihku | ___________ | their *(fp)* ___________ |

# Tetimili: Personal adornment

The ways Tunica people dress has changed quite a bit over time. Older ways of dressing and adorning have been communicated to us through our ancestors and are also detailed in Western historical records.

Prior to European contact, Tunica and Biloxi people wore few clothes or personal adornments when carrying out everyday activities in warm weather. Men wore **sehtiwahkuni**, usually made of deerskin, which were passed between the legs and tucked up under **sihktiratasaru** in front and in back, with a considerable length to spare at either end. **Sihktiratasaru** were usually made of woven buffalo hair, skin, or of beaded cord. Women wore **sɛnstayitira**, short, fringed, wraparound skirts woven of plant fiber (mulberry cloth). Married women were covered from the waist to the knees and children dressed simply before reaching puberty. In cold seasons, men and women wore **seruhtamihku** woven of cloth, bark, or fur. Women sometimes wore mantles of feathers like those of the men.

Men covered the upper parts of their bodies with a garment or garments made of the **tahkishi** 'hides' of various animals, such as **nokushi** 'bear', **ya** 'deer' (particularly **tayashi** 'buck'), **hikuwa** 'panther', **chomu** 'wildcat', **kiwa** 'beaver', **nuhki** 'otter', **yishi** 'raccoon', **chiya** 'squirrel', and **yanishikashi** 'buffalo'. Some of these were made long and were worn by elders or others in cool weather. The women processed and sewed animal skins to create such clothing, as well as **sɛshkalahpi tahkishi** 'leather moccasins' and **sɛshkarahpuni** 'stockings/leggings'. **Sɛshkarahpuni** were worn during cold weather or to protect their legs from the underbrush. The lower portions of leggings were tucked under the rims of moccasins and the upper ends were usually fastened to the belt by means of straps.

Personal adornment included tattooing (men and women), teeth blackening (women), many kinds of jewelry, and various hairstyles. Tunica people would paint their faces when going to a dance. Shirts were not necessary, but men and women both wore **seruhtamihku** of **yɛhtat'ɛ uhkyuhtari** 'turkey feathers' or **sesintamihku lalahkihihkut'ɛ uhktahkishi** 'muskrat skin bonnets' in cooler weather. **Yanishikashi uhktahkishi** 'buffalo hides', **say'ɔhta** 'beads', **laspi tapahchu** 'metal ornaments' and other accessories were worn for personal embellishment as necklaces, bracelets, armbands, and **sihkenitamuri** 'rings'. They were also worn as **sɛlawɛchatapahchu** 'ear plugs' and as nose plugs. Both men and women usually wore their hair long. Most of the time they went bare-headed, but warriors sometimes wore porcupine roaches (headdresses).

Tunica and Biloxi people began to alter their style of dress soon after their first encounters with Europeans. Glass beads, metal jewelry and ornaments, and European-style clothing became common trade items among the Tunica in the mid-18th century. Mantles and other garments were made out of European cloth. Gorgets, brooches, bracelets, head and hatbands, and other pieces were hammered cold from European silver coins and polished with ochre.

Today, traditional Tunica-Biloxi women's dresses are made by hand. **Sinktira** consist of a bodice with a fitted waist and a long, full skirt trimmed with ruffles and embellished with rickrack or bias tape. Loosely fitted with the hemline just above the ankle, dresses are usually made in solid red, white, or blue broadcloth. A white or a contrasting color apron, trimmed in the color of the dress, completes the woman's traditional outfit. Men wear long, tailored, fringed hunting jackets and pants made of cloth. Another older style for men includes a breechcloth apron worn over full-length buckskin leggings resembling the cutoff legs of trousers sewn some six inches from the edges and supported by a belt and garters below the knee. Simple moccasins are still worn by both women and men. Tunica-Biloxi traditional regalia and clothing are worn at powwows and special occasions with post-contact style jewelry and beadwork that reflect patterns of pantribal designs.

## Tetimili yoluyana

| | | | |
|---|---|---|---|
| **chiya** | *squirrel* | **nuhki** | *otter* |
| **chomu** | *wildcat* | **say'ɔhta** | *bead* |
| **hikuwa** | *panther* | **ya** | *deer* |
| **kiwa** | *beaver* | **yanishikashi** | *buffalo* |
| **lalahkihihkut'ɛ** | *muskrat* | **yɛhtat'ɛ** | *turkey* |
| **laspi tapahchu** | *metal ornaments* | **yishi** | *raccoon* |
| **nokushi** | *bear* | **yuhtari** | *feather* |

## Tetimili wiralepini

1. Pick three articles of clothing in this **tetimili** that are inalienably possessed. What are they and who is possessing them (e.g., 'more than two women' or 'feminine plural')?

2. Draw a picture of a person wearing three of the articles of clothing mentioned in the **tetimili** and list what they are wearing in Tunica.

# Chapter 12: Ɛnstayi

## *Our bodies*

**TOPICS:**

# Ɛnstayi

*Our bodies*

## Yoluyana

| | | | |
|---|---|---|---|
| **-alakashi** | *hair* | **-esini** | *head* |
| **-alawɛcha** | *ear* | **-esintalu** | *brain* |
| **-ashka** | *foot; toe* | **-eyu** | *arm* |
| **-ashkatɛrashki** | *leg* | **-hkeni** | *hand; finger* |
| **-ashkat'ɛ** | *big toe* | **-lu** | *tongue* |
| **-astayi** | *body* | **-ni** | *tooth; teeth* |
| **-chihki** | *belly* | **-rishi** | *nose* |
| **-china** | *knee* | **-shira** | *back* |
| **-ehniyu** | *heart* | **-shohu** | *mouth* |
| **-ehniyutirishi** | *chest* | **-shtahpu** | *face* |
| **-ehp'ira** | *shoulder* | **-shtosu** | *eye* |
| **-epushka** | *lungs* | **yasha ihkyakati** | *it hurts (me)* |

## Yanalepini

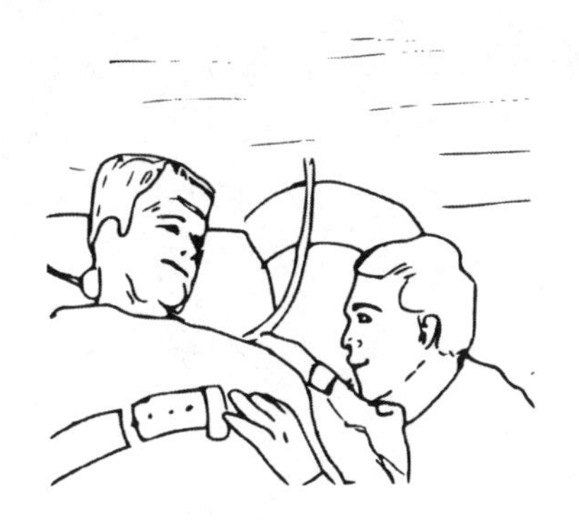

**Frankensteinku:** Oniku mashukani. Ohniyu, uchihki, oyu, ɔshka, osini, ohniyutirishi mekani.

**Igorku:** Hon, Frankenstein.

**Frankensteinku:** Sahkuhta, osini. Ushtosu, ɔlawɛcha, urishi, ushohu wen'iki!

**Igorku:** Ko'o! Hɛku ushtahpu ulu'ɔma. Ɔlakashi mekin?

**Frankensteinku:** Hon. Ɔstayi mash'inaki! Ɔshka, ɔshkatɛrashk'ɛma tap'iki!

**Igorku:** Ɔshkat'ɛ tapikani!

**Frankensteinku:** Lapuhch. Uni po'in?

**Igorku:** Aha. Hinahkushkan opushka wenini!

**Frankensteinku:** Lapuhch. Opushka chuyak'iki!

**Igorku:** Kanahku hɛku?

**Frankensteinku:** Hiku osintalu.

**Igorku:** Kata ukiku?

**Frankensteinku:** Osintalu osini kichu ukiku.

**Frankensteinku, Igorku:** Hot'ina!

**Jayku:** Hɛma lapun?

**Kayhchi:** Aha, lap'ɔhɔ. Patani.

**Jayku:** Lap'ɔhɔ! Wah'an?

**Kayhchi:** Aha. Hinahkushkan ishira, ehp'ira, ihkeni, ichina yasha ihkyakati.

**Jayku:** Sara. Ihkeni yasha ihkyakati. Lawumihta rahpanihch, patani.

**Kayhchi:** Sara.

## Lutamashu

Just like the inalienably possessed clothing items we learned in Chapter 11, body parts in Tunica take the inalienable set of prefixes. This means that body parts cannot be discussed without being possessed, like they are a part of a specific person's body.

Here's an example of a possessive paradigm for **-shtosu** 'eye'.

| | | SINGULAR | | DUAL | | PLURAL | |
|---|---|---|---|---|---|---|---|
| *1st person* | | **ishtosu** | *my eye(s)* | **inshtosu** | *our eye(s)* | **inshtosu** | *our eye(s)* |
| *2nd person* | *feminine* | **hishtosu** | *your eye(s)* | **hinshtosu** | *your eye(s)* | **hinshtosu** | *your eye(s)* |
| | *masculine* | **wishtosu** | *your eye(s)* | **winshtosu** | *your eye(s)* | **winshtosu** | *your eye(s)* |
| *3rd person* | *feminine* | **tishtoshu** | *her eye(s)* | **sinshtosu** | *their eye(s)* | **sinshtosu** | *their eyes* |
| | *masculine* | **ushtosu** | *his eye(s)* | **unshtosu** | *their eye(s)* | **sishtosu** | *their eye(s)* |

Compare this with the paradigm for **-eyu** 'arm':

| | | SINGULAR | | DUAL | | PLURAL | |
|---|---|---|---|---|---|---|---|
| *1st person* | | **eyu** | *my arm(s)* | **enyu** | *our arm(s)* | **enyu** | *our arm(s)* |
| *2nd person* | *feminine* | **heyu** | *your arm(s)* | **henyu** | *your arm(s)* | **henyu** | *your arm(s)* |
| | *masculine* | **weyu** | *your arm(s)* | **wenyu** | *your arm(s)* | **wenyu** | *your arm(s)* |
| *3rd person* | *feminine* | **teyu** | *her arm(s)* | **senyu** | *their arm(s)* | **senyu** | *their arm(s)* |
| | *masculine* | **oyu** | *his arm(s)* | **onyu** | *their arm(s)* | **seyu** | *their arm(s)* |

Notice the difference when the body part begins with **e**. When Tunica words for body parts start with a vowel, it is important to pay attention to the vowel blending rules discussed in Chapter 3. For example, if we wanted to say 'my head', we would say **esini** (**i** + **-esini** = **esini**), or for 'his head', we would say **osini** (**u** + **-esini** = **osini**).

Remember that the prefix only indicates the number of people possessing the thing, not the number of things themselves. To talk explicitly about a specific number of eyes, you can use either numbers or the gender-number endings. If there is no gender-number ending, the number of eyes is inferred from context.

## Hinu 1

**12.1.1. Luhchi pirɛtaki:**
Translate the following into Tunica. Use the charts above if you need help.

***Example:*** *your (ms) knee* **wichina**

1. her hand ____________
2. your *(fs)* head ____________
3. my belly ____________
4. his hair ____________
5. my arm ____________
6. our *(d)* noses ____________
7. their *(mp)* hearts ____________
8. our eyes ____________
9. your *(fd)* feet ____________
10. your *(md)* ears ____________
11. his tongue ____________
12. their *(fp)* big toes ____________

### 12.1.2. Luhchi pirɛtaki:

Translate the following into English.

***Example:*** *winkeni* ***your (md/p) fingers***

1. hinshtahpu
2. ɔnshka
3. hishira
4. wesini
5. irishi
6. tɛstayi
7. ohniyutirishi
8. enyu
9. sichihki
10. senspushka

### 12.1.3. Esini, ehp'ira, ichina, ɛshkat'ɛ

Many of you may be familiar with the classic children's song 'head, shoulders, knees, and toes'. By singing this song translated into Tunica, you can practice inalienable possession and body parts and have fun doing it! The Tunica version has several verses to highlight how the words change when you're talking about different people.

Here is a version of the song in Tunica and English:

| | |
|---|---|
| **esini, ehp'ira, ichina, ɛshkat'ɛ** | *head, shoulders, knees, and toes* |
| **esini, ehp'ira, ichina, ɛshkat'ɛ** | *head, shoulders, knees, and toes* |
| **ishtosu, ɛlawɛcha, ishohu, irishi** | *eyes and ears and mouth and nose* |
| **esini, ehp'ira, ichina, ɛshkat'ɛ** | *head, shoulders, knees, and toes* |

In Tunica, you can sing the song differently when referring to different people. Here are some of the many ways you can sing it. Practice singing this with a group of friends and you'll have your inalienable possession down pat in no time!

**About oneself**

| | |
|---|---|
| **esini** | *my head* |
| **ehp'ira** | *my shoulders* |
| **ichina** | *my knees* |
| **ɛshkat'ɛ** | *my big toes* |
| **ishtosu** | *my eyes* |
| **ɛlawɛcha** | *my ears* |
| **ishohu** | *my mouth* |
| **irishi** | *my nose* |

**To a woman**

| | |
|---|---|
| **hesini** | *your head* |
| **hehp'ira** | *your shoulders* |
| **hichina** | *your knees* |
| **hɛshkat'ɛ** | *your big toes* |
| **hishtosu** | *your eyes* |
| **hɛlawɛcha** | *your ears* |
| **hishohu** | *your mouth* |
| **hirishi** | *your nose* |

**To a man**

| | |
|---|---|
| **wesini** | *your head* |
| **wehp'ira** | *your shoulders* |
| **wichina** | *your knees* |
| **wɛshkat'ɛ** | *your big toes* |
| **wishtosu** | *your eyes* |
| **wɛlawɛcha** | *your ears* |
| **wishohu** | *your mouth* |
| **wirishi** | *your nose* |

**About a woman**

| | |
|---|---|
| **tesini** | *her head* |
| **tehp'ira** | *her shoulders* |
| **tichina** | *her knees* |
| **tɛshkat'ɛ** | *her big toes* |
| **tishtosu** | *her eyes* |
| **tɛlawɛcha** | *her ears* |
| **tishohu** | *her mouth* |
| **tirishi** | *her nose* |

**About a man**

| | |
|---|---|
| **osini** | *his head* |
| **ohp'ira** | *his shoulders* |
| **uchina** | *his knees* |
| **ɔshkat'ɛ** | *his big toes* |
| **ushtosu** | *his eyes* |
| **ɔlawɛcha** | *his ears* |
| **ushohu** | *his mouth* |
| **urishi** | *his nose* |

## Ir'itiki!

*Let's get dressed!*

### Yoluyana

| | | | |
|---|---|---|---|
| **ira** | *to wear; to dress* | **yama** | *to dress in finery; to put on regalia* |
| **lahpi** | *to put on or wear shoes* | **pali** | *to take off shoes* |
| **mihku** | *to wear a headwrapping (bandana, headdress, headband); to wear on the head* | **kimu** | *to take off a headwrapping (bandana, headdress, headband)* |
| **pahchu** | *to put on jewelry, glasses* | **chapu** | *to take off jewelry, glasses* |
| **rahpu** | *to put on (coat, stockings, etc.)* | **paru** | *to take off coats, stockings* |
| **saru** | *to belt* | **rasu** | *to unbelt* |
| **wohku** | *to put on a hat* | **kowu** | *to take off a hat* |

### Yanalepini

**Alicehchi:** Heni Dave! Ak'iki! Wihkrahpuntira yuru par'iki!

**Daveku:** Tikahch. Ihktawohku kowukani.

**Alicehchi:** Heni, Aiyanna! Ak'aki! Hɛshkalahpi pal'ɛki!

**Aiyannahchi:** Lapu! Ɛshkalahpi kochu irakani. Yɔlanihch, ɛshkalahpi lahpinik'ahcha.

**Chrisku:** Kanahku mihkuka, Rose?

**Rosehchi:** Ihktiratamihku mihkukani.

**Chrisku:** Tapo pahch'ɔn?

**Rosehchi:** Hon.

**Chrisku:** Rapukahch, hihktapo pahchukan?

**Rosehchi:** Aha! Rapukanihch, ihktiratamihku kimukani, ihktapo chapukani.

**Chrisku:** Lapuhch.

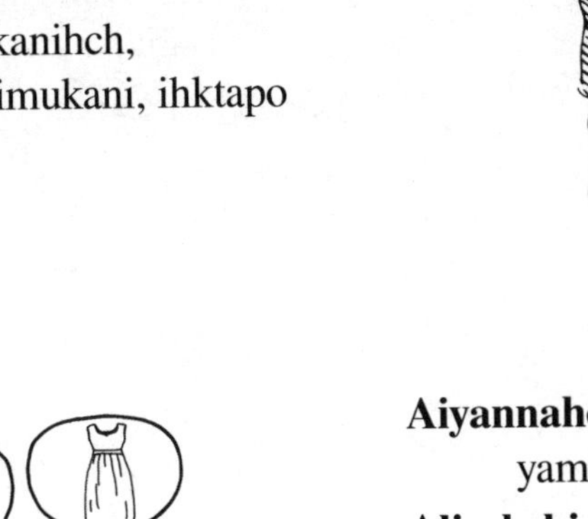

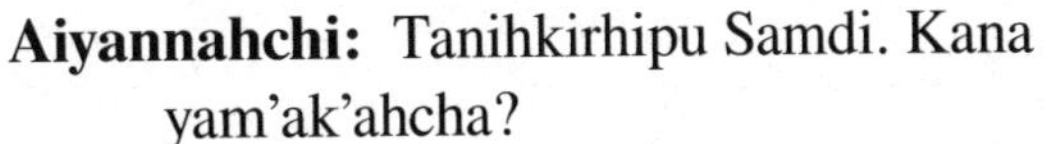

**Aiyannahchi:** Tanihkirhipu Samdi. Kana yam'ak'ahcha?

**Alicehchi:** Ihktira nisa yamanik'ahcha!

**Aiyannahchi:** Hihktira nisa, kanahku uhkkosu?

**Alicehchi:** Ɔshta. Hɛmat, kana yam'ak'ahcha?

**Aiyannahchi:** Ɛstayitira rɔwa yamanik'ahcha.

**Alicehchi:** Tashle panu!

**Merlinku:** Wohkukani.

**Chrisku:** Kanahku tawohku?

**Merlinku:** Ihktawohku tika wohkukani.

**Chrisku:** Sarakihch, kowukin?

**Merlinku:** Hon! Sarakanihch, kowukani.

**Chrisku:** Lapuhch.

**Aiyannahchi:** Ichihki tika panu! Ihktiratasaru rasukani.

**Alicehchi:** Saku namu sak'ɔn?

**Aiyannahchi:** Hon! Lawushi namu sakuni. Ihktiratasaru saruni. Hinahkushkan hahchi rasukani.

**Alicehchi:** Lapuhch.

**Naomihchi:** Dave, Genesis, kanahku irahkwina?

**Daveku, Genesishchi:** Shuhpali kochu irahkina.

**Naomihchi:** Aha. Shuhpali yuru rahpawinaki! Wɛnshkalahpi lahpihkwinan?

**Daveku, Genesishchi:** Aha...

**Naomihchi:** Wɛnshkalahpi lahpiwinaki!

**Daveku, Genesishchi:** Hon, sara...

## Lutamashu

Now that we know the words for body parts and for clothes, we can talk about wearing things. Tunica is a lot more specific than English is when it comes to putting on and taking off clothing. For example, the verb 'to put on a hat' (**wohku**) is completely different from the word 'to put on shoes' (**lahpi**). The **yoluyana** above contains some common verbs that we use to talk about getting dressed.

Notice that the verbs for taking off clothing are related to the verbs for putting the clothing on. The consonants are switched, while the vowels stay the same. For example, **mihku** 'to wear a head-wrapping' is the opposite of **kimu** 'to take off a head wrapping', and the **m** and the **k** have switched places. The **h** disappears in this case because Tunica words can't start with an **hk**.

Many of these verbs carry the idea of the clothing to which they refer. Since the idea of the clothing is already contained within the verb, you don't have to say the article of clothing again when you talk about wearing it. For example, you can simply say **wohkuni** 'I put on a hat', rather than **tawohku wohkuni** (although both are fine). All of these verbs use the same set of endings and rules that we learned in Chapters 2 and 3.

## Hinu 2

**12.2.1. Molɔtaki:**
In each sentence, replace the verb for putting on an object of clothing with the verb for taking it off.

***Example:*** *Uhkentamuri pahchuku.* ***Uhkentamuri chapuku.***

| | | |
|---|---|---|
| 1. | Ihktawohku wohkuni. | Ihktawohku ____________. |
| 2. | Daveku uhktahch'i tapo pahchuwi. | Daveku uhktahch'i tapo ____________. |
| 3. | Inima inktiratamihku mihk'iti. | Inima inktiratamihku ____________. |
| 4. | Wɛnshkalahpi lahpiwitiki! | Wɛnshkalahpi ____________! |
| 5. | Diamondhchi teruhkitapahchu pahchuti. | Diamondhchi teruhkitapahchu ____________. |
| 6. | Samuelku uhkrahpuntira rahpuwi. | Samuelku uhkrahpuntira ____________. |
| 7. | Lisahchi, Aiyannahchi sɛnshkarahpuni rahpusina. | Lisahchi, Aiyannahchi sɛnshkarahpuni ____________. |
| 8. | Buddyku ɔlawɛchatapahchu pahchuku. | Buddyku ɔlawɛchatapahchu ____________. |
| 9. | Hihkenrahpuni rahp'ɔki! | Hihkenrahpuni ____________! |
| 10. | Kaydenku uhktiratasaru saruwi. | Kaydenku uhktiratasaru ____________. |

### 12.2.2. Atehpɛtaki:

Match the following verbs to the items of clothing to which they apply.

***Example:*** **a** *chapuni* *a. ihktapo*

| | | | |
|---|---|---|---|
| 1. _____ kowuni | | a. | ihktiratasaru |
| 2. _____ mihkuni | | b. | ihkrahpuntira |
| 3. _____ saruni | | c. | ɛshkalahpi |
| 4. _____ palini | | d. | ihktiratamihku |
| 5. _____ paruni | | e. | ihktawohku |

### 12.2.3. Pakɛtaki:

Read the prompt, then tell Henry to adjust his clothing to solve the problem.

***Example:*** *Henryku tasahchuni kichu pitawi.* ***Henry, wɛshkalahpi pal'iki!***

1. Henryku uhksipi.

_______________

2. Henryku lapuya pok'ɔhɔ.

_______________

3. Henryku nihkirhipushi hipuku.

_______________

4. Henryku namu sakuwi. Uchihki tika panu.

_______________

### 12.2.4. Kanahku irahkwiti?

What are you wearing? Answer in complete sentences using color terms and the appropriate verb. Find a partner and ask them what he/she is wearing.

***Example:*** *Kanahku iraki/iraka?* ***Ɛlawɛchatapahchu kayi pahchukani.***

## Tetimili: Tachuhchuhinaku uhktawohku

*The redheaded woodpecker's hat*

This story is an adaptation of a traditional Mayan story. It is especially popular among the Kaqchikel, Tz'utujil, and K'iche', but is known throughout the Mayan highlands of Guatemala and Mexico. In the US, the woodpecker is regarded as a symbol of determination and caring. The staccato beats of its woodpecking are mirrored in drumming. Woodpecker topknots, the **tawohku**, of this story are used in dance regalia, especially in the Southwest and California.

The hummingbird appears in many other stories in South, Central, and North America. Incan stories tell how the hummingbird became a divine messenger. The Aztecs regarded the hummingbird as an avatar of the sun. *Huitzilopochtli* 'Hummingbird on the left' was the Aztec god of war, who wore a bracelet of hummingbird feathers on his left wrist. In North America, the hummingbird is often associated with tobacco and is a powerful spirit animal. A Cherokee tale relates the story of a young woman courted by Hummingbird and Crane. She chooses Hummingbird for his beauty, despite his having lost the race around the world staged to determine who the successful suitor would be.

Longer versions of this story reveal how other animals in the world came to have the attributes we associate with them today.

**Wantaha, nisarahchi nisaraku unkmahkani.**
Long ago, a young woman and a young man fell in love, they say.

**Tanisarahchi tesikɔt, tihkkipani uhkwan'ahani.**
As for the woman's father, he did not want to marry her off, they say.

**Tanisarahchi ɔmakahchɛni.**
The young woman was a sorceress, they say.

**Ɔmakaku tesikupa.**
Her father was a sorcerer, too.

**Tanisaraku tɛnakɔlakuwatohku uhkpiran'akɛni.**
She turned the young man into a hummingbird, they say.

**Tesiku hiyawihch, tɛnakɔlakuwatohku tihktira kichu uhkpihun'akɛni.**
Whenever her father would approach, she would hide the hummingbird in her dress, they say.

**Tahch'a kashku panutihch, tanisarahchi shɔwa yatɛni.**
After a few months passed, the young woman got pregnant, they say.

**Hinyatihch, tesiku orusatihch, uhkyashɛni.**
When her father found out, he was angry, they say.

**Tanisarahchi tanisarak'ɔma atehpi lɔt'uwanani.**
The young woman and the young man ran away together, they say.

**Tarku kichu lɔt'uwanani.**
They ran into the forest, they say.

**Hinahkushkan, tesiku pahita unkweni haliwi.**
But the father sent lightning to find them.

**Rihku heluni kichu pihupo'unani.**
They tried to hide in a hollow tree, they say.

**Hinahkushkan, tichihki tika rikini.**
But her belly was too big.

**Hinyatihch, tapahita tihkpatawihch, tipusa tihkpir'akɛni.**
The lightning struck her and she turned into dust, they say.

**Tanisaraku uhkhɛkani.**
The young man was distraught.

**Ɔnchayihchi tihkyayini uhkwana.**
He wanted to save his wife.

**Hinyatihch, tanisaraku ɔmaka sahu me'uwahch, lapu tihkyawik uhkwir'uta.**
So the young man sought another sorcerer and asked him to fix her.

**Tɔmakaku, "Wɛnchayihchi tehniyu wen'iki!" uhknikɔni.**
The sorcerer told him, "Find your wife's heart!" they say.

**"Uhkwen'ik'ihch, wɛnchayi nisa kaliwitak'ahcha," uhknikɔni.**
He said to him, "If you find it, you will make a new wife," they say.

**Tanisaraku ay'ɛhɛ mehkunani. Hinahkushkan, tehniyu weni uhkshtuk'ɔhɔ.**
The young man searched long and hard. Despite this, he couldn't find her heart.

**Hinyatihch, tachuhchuhinaku, "Erusa kata tehniyu urahch," uhknikɔni.**
The redheaded woodpecker said to him, "I know where your wife's heart is," they say.

**Tanisaraku, "Kata ura?" uhkwir'uta.**
"Where?" asked the young man.

**Tachuhchuhinaku, "Tawohku mili tashle wihkara," nikɔni.**
The redheaded woodpecker said, "You have a beautiful red hat," they say.

**Tachuhchuhinaku, "Wihktawohku ihkyuw'ik'ihch, wihkyananik'ahcha," uhknikɔni.**
The redheadedwoodpecker told him, "Give me your hat and I will tell you," they say.

**Hinyatihch, tanisaraku uhktawohku uhkyuwawihch, tachuhchuhinaku uhksh'ɛpa.**
So, when the young man gave him his hat, the redheaded woodpecker was pleased.

**Hinyatihch, tanisaraku mehkunahch, ɔnchayihchi tehniyu weniwɛni.**
Then, when the young man searched, he found his wife's heart, they say.

**Hinyatihch, tɔmakaku hatika lapu tihkyawi.**
Then the sorcerer made her whole again.

**Hishtahahki, tachuhchuhinaku osinihta tanisaraku uhktawohku wohkukɔni.**
To this day the redheaded woodpecker wears the young man's hat on his head, they say.

## Tetimili yoluyana

| | | | |
|---|---|---|---|
| **chuchuhina** | *redheaded woodpecker* | **pahita** | *lightning* |
| **ɔmaka** | *sorcerer; sorceress* | **tɛnakɔlakuwatohku** | *hummingbird* |

## Tetimili wiralepini

1. Can you find three body parts in this story? What are they and who do they belong to?

2. Do you have any family stories that involve help from an unexpected place? Tell us about it here!

# Chapter 13: Ɛhɛli

*My family*

**TOPICS:**

# Inalienable possession

## Yoluyana

| | | | |
|---|---|---|---|
| **-ahali** | *family* | **-hchatohku** | *grandchild* |
| **-anchayi** | *wife* | **-hchi** | *father's sister (paternal aunt)* |
| **-ehku** | *child (kin or animals)* | **-ki** | *mother's brother (maternal uncle)* |
| **-esi** | *father* | **-mila** | *daughter; son* |
| **-eti** | *friend; family* | **ɔka** | *child (general)* |
| **-gachi** | *mother* | **-shayi** | *husband* |
| **-hcha** | *grandparent* | **tostohku** | *baby* |
| **kuhpa** | *to meet; to come together* | | |

## Yanalepini

*Aiyannahchi Chrisku uhkri yukati. Ɔhɔli akuhpata.*

**Aiyannahchi:** Kanahku otisa?

**Chrisku:** Anthonyku otisa. Ihchaku.

**Aiyannahchi:** Wigachihchi tesikun?

**Chrisku:** Hon.

**Aiyannahchi:** Ma uhchatohkukun?

**Chrisku:** Hon.

**Aiyannahchi:** Tihchɛt, kanahku tetisa?

**Chrisku:** Hihchi ihchahchi. Claudiahchi tetisa.

**Aiyannahchi:** Tihchi Anthonyku ɔnchayihchin?

**Chrisku:** Hon. Anthonyku tishayiku. Aiyanna, hɛku ikiku Daveku.

**Aiyannahchi:** Heni! Eti ma lapun?

**Daveku:** Lapu, tikahch. Yukatihch lapuhch!
**Aiyannahchi:** Tikahch!
**Chrisku:** Igachi, Esi, hɛhchi etihchi, Aiyannahchi tetisa.
**Ugachihchi:** Heni! Imilaku otihchin?
**Aiyannahchi:** Hon, enti'unima.

**Rosehchi:** Ihchihchi tostohku tihkwana.
**Alicehchi:** Tehku tihkarahch, lapuhch. Enkusɛma shimitak'ahcha!
**Rosehchi:** Mi'ɔkasɛma po'ɔki! Sihksh'ɛpa. Ɛnhɛli tashle panu!

## Lutamashu

We learned in Chapter 11 that in Tunica there are two types of possession: alienable and inalienable. Family and family members are inalienable, and therefore must always be possessed (your family relationships are a part of you). The family terms listed in the **yoluyana** take the same set of inalienable prefixes as body parts (Chapter 12). Here are some examples:

| | | |
|---|---|---|
| **i + -ehku** | **ehku** | *'my child'* |
| **wi + -anchayi** | **wɛnchayi** | *'your (ms) wife'* |
| **u + -esi** | **osi** | *'his father'* |
| **in + -hchi** | **inchi** | *'our paternal aunt'* |
| **un + -eti** | **onti** | *'their (md) friend'* |
| **si + -hcha** | **sihcha** | *'their grandparent'* |

Because many family terms begin with vowels, vowel blending rules apply (see Chapter 3). Since family terms begin in either **a** or **e** and the inalienable prefixes end in **i** or **u**, the only combinations you'll need for family terms are listed on the next page.

| | |
|---|---|
| **i + a = ɛ** | **u + a = ɔ** |
| **i + e = e** | **u + e = o** |

Remember that vowels blend over **n**'s (so **enti** 'our friend', *not* **ineti**), and that **h** is lost after **n** (so **sincha** 'their *(f)* grandparent', *not* **sinhcha**). Additionally, the word **-ahali** is special. Just like when you add **-aha** to a word that ends in an **i** and the vowels both change to **ɛ** (**-ɛhɛ**), both the vowels at the beginning of **-ahali** always change. Here are some examples with **-ahali**:

| | | |
|---|---|---|
| **i + -ahali** | **ɛhɛli** | *'my family'* |
| **u + -ahali** | **ɔhɔli** | *'his family'* |

**Tostohku** 'baby' and **ɔka** 'child' describe infants and children without indicating any family ties, so they use the alienable prefixes. If you want to talk about someone's child, use **-ehku**, which takes an inalienable prefix.

With respect to family terms, notice that Tunica has different words for aunts and uncles depending on whose siblings they are. So you call your uncles on your mother's side **iku**, and your aunts on your father's side **ihchi**. We will learn in the next section what you would call your father's brothers and your mother's sisters.

Also, **-hcha** is simply 'grandparent" and **-mila** is simply 'son/daughter'. However, unless you are talking directly to the person, you would still indicate gender through gender-number endings. So 'my grandfather' is **ihchaku** and 'my grandmother' is **ihchahchi**, and 'my daughter' is **imilahchi** while 'my son' is **imilaku**.

Kinship is very important to Tunica people. When family members spoke to each other in Tunica, and even in other languages like French and English, they often used the kinship term instead of a name. So they might say **Igachi, sehi lapu!** 'Mother, good morning!' or **Imila, sar'inaki!** 'My child, let us pray!'. When family members are addressed by their names, the kinship term is still used alongside the name, as in **Ihchi, Letitia, eti hɛma lapun?** 'My [paternal] aunt, Letitia, how are you?'. While this sounds weirdly formal when you translate it to English, this is the normal way to address your family members in Tunica.

## Hinu 1

### 13.1.1. Molɔtaki:

Add the appropriate inalienable prefix and gender-number ending to get the indicated meaning.

**Example:** __**i**__ shayi __**ku**__ *my husband*

1. _____hchatohku_________ *your (ms) many granddaughters*
2. _____gachi_________ *our mother*
3. _____hchi_________ *my two paternal aunts*
4. _____mila_________ *her two daughters*
5. _____(e)si_________ *his father*
6. _____ki_________ *their (fp) maternal uncles*
7. _____(e)[h]ku_________ *your (md) children (fp)*
8. _____[h]cha_________ *your (fp) grandmother*
9. _____(a)nchayi_________ *their (mp) wives*
10. _____shayi_________ *her husband*

### 13.1.2. Molɔtaki:

Fill in the blank with the pieces joined together to form the words indicated, then translate.

***Example:***

| | TUNICA WORD | TRANSLATION |
|---|---|---|
| *hi- + hcha + -hchi* | ***hihchahchi*** | ***your (fs) grandmother*** |
| 1. wi- + mila + -ku | ___ | ___ |
| 2. win- + eti + -hchi | ___ | ___ |
| 3. hin- + ahali + -sɛma | ___ | ___ |
| 4. u- + esi + -ku | ___ | ___ |
| 5. ti- + hchi + -sinima | ___ | ___ |
| 6. i- + hchatohku + -ku | ___ | ___ |
| 7. sin- + shayi + -sɛma | ___ | ___ |
| 8. ta- + tostohku + -ku | ___ | ___ |
| 9. un- + ahali | ___ | ___ |
| 10. ta- + ɔka + -sinima | ___ | ___ |

### 13.1.3. Luhchi pirɛtaki:

Translate the following sentences into Tunica.

***Example:*** *Her husband swims.* **Tishayiku woyuku.**

1. Your *(fp)* grandfather is named Bill. ______
2. His wife sings. ______
3. My dad runs. ______
4. Your *(fs)* mom is pretty. ______
5. Her daughter is four years old. ______
6. Their *(mp)* family fights. ______
7. Our three maternal uncles are eating. ______
8. Your *(mp)* two granddaughters walk. ______
9. Their *(fp)* friend *(f)* is sleeping. ______
10. Their *(md)* three sons play. ______

# Age and gender

## Yoluyana

| | |
|---|---|
| **-ahaya** | *opposite-gender sibling* |
| **-ahayasahu** | *opposite-gender cousin* |
| **-ehukuma** | *younger same-gender sibling* |
| **-esit'ɛ** | *father's older brother (older paternal uncle)* |
| **-esitohku** | *father's younger brother (younger paternal uncle)* |
| **-gachit'ɛ** | *mother's older sister (older maternal aunt)* |
| **-gachitohku** | *mother's younger sister (younger maternal aunt)* |
| **-hta** | *same-gender sibling* |
| **-htasahu** | *same-gender cousin* |
| **-htat'ɛ** | *older same-gender sibling* |

## Yanalepini

**Rosehchi:** Hɛma Jeremyku ɔhɔyahchin?
**Aiyannahchi:** Hon.
**Rosehchi:** Hehukumahchi hihkaran?
**Aiyannahchi:** Hon. Silviahchi tetisa.
**Rosehchi:** Silviahchi etihchi! Hɛmat tihtat'ɛhchi.
**Aiyannahchi:** Hon! Intasinima.

**Merlinku:** Jimku werusan?

**Chrisku:** Hon, Jimku esitohkuku.

**Merlinku:** Ahh. Umilaku Bobbyku otisa. Hinyatihch Bobbyku wihtasahukun?

**Chrisku:** Hon. Bobbyku ohukuma Justonku otisa. Ihtasahukupa Justonku.

**Merlinku:** Wɛhɛyasahuhchi wihkaran?

**Chrisku:** Hon, Emmahchi tetisa. Tigachihchi igachit'ɛhchi.

**Merlinku:** Tikahch.

**Augustinku:** Hesit'ɛ inkrish yukaku?

**Alicehchi:** Hon! Wigachitohkuhchi winkrishi ukikati?

**Augustinku:** Aha, yɔlati. Hahchi ihtasahuku uhkrishi ukikati.

**Alicehchi:** Lapuhch.

## Lutamashu

Tunica is often more specific than English when it comes to what you call your family members. In Tunica, the relative age and gender of a person are part of their relationship to you and the other members of your family. Most notably, relative age is important, but only within one's own gender. So a boy would refer to his older brother with one term, **ihtat'ɛku**, and his younger brother with another, **ehukumaku**. A girl would use the same roots to refer to her older sister **ihtat'ɛhchi** and her younger sister **ehukumahchi**. This is also true for your aunts and uncles: you would refer to your father's older brother as **esit'ɛku**, while his younger brother is **esitohkuku**. Likewise, you would refer to your mother's older sister as **igachit'ɛhchi** and her younger sister as **igachitohkuhchi**. These terms reveal another interesting fact about Tunica kinship: your mother's sisters are your 'little' and 'big' mothers, and your father's brothers are your 'little' and 'big' fathers.

The relationship is not the same with your mother's brothers, your father's sisters, or your opposite-gender siblings and cousins. The words for 'mother's brother' and 'father's sister' that we learned in the previous section are not based on **-esi** and **-gachi**; they are totally different. Also, your opposite-gender siblings are all called the same thing (**-ahaya**), regardless of their age.

The last thing to notice is that the word for 'cousin' is simply the word for sibling (same- or opposite-gender) plus **sahu** 'other'. So your cousins are literally your 'other siblings'.

Because the Tunica kinship system is a little more complicated, the following examples will help you figure out what you should call your siblings.

| | |
|---|---|
| **ɛhɛyahchi** | *my sister (said by a boy)* |
| **ɛhɛyaku** | *my brother (said by a girl)* |
| | |
| **ihtat'ɛhchi** | *my older sister (said by a girl)* |
| **ihtat'ɛku** | *my older brother (said by a boy)* |
| | |
| **ehukumahchi** | *my younger sister (said by a girl)* |
| **ehukumaku** | *my younger brother (said by a boy)* |

Notice that the word **-ahaya** is just like **-ahali**; in both words, the first two **a**'s change when you add the inalienable prefix.

## Hinu 2

**13.2.1. Halɛtaki:**

In the space provided, draw your immediate family tree (parents, siblings, children). Show each person's name. Then label each one with their relationship to you (**igachihchi**, **esiku**, etc.) in Tunica, as though you are talking about them.

**13.2.2. Sɛhɛli Hanson:**

The family chart below shows Molly and Ted Hanson and their daughters, Carla and Gwen. Carla is older than Gwen. In this exercise, write the Tunica family term they would use to *directly* address each other.

***Example:*** *What does Ted call Molly?* ***ɛnchayi***

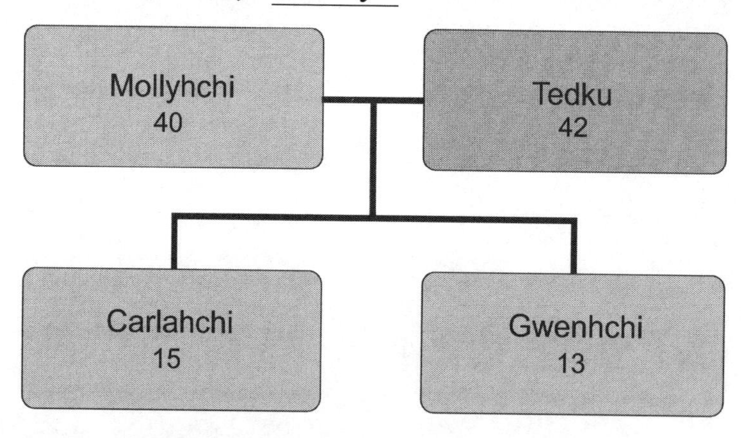


1. What does Molly call Carla & Gwen? ___________

2. What does Carla call Gwen? ___________

3. What does Gwen call Carla? ___________

4. What does Carla call Molly? ___________

5. What does Gwen call Ted? ___________

**13.2.3. Sɛhɛli Gregson:**

In this exercise, use the term they would use to talk *about* each other. Carol and Don are the parents. Their children are Richard, who is 22, Suki, who is 20, and Tom, who is 18.

***Example:*** *What does Carol call Don?* **ishayiku**

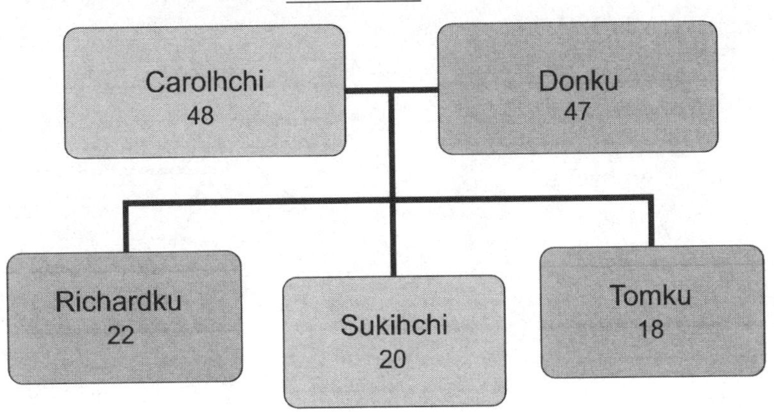


1. What does Suki call Richard? ____________
2. What does Richard call Suki? ____________
3. What does Suki call Tom? ____________
4. What does Richard call Tom? ____________
5. What does Tom call Suki? ____________
6. What does Tom call Richard? ____________

### 13.2.4. Luhchi pirɛtaki:

Fill in the blank with the proper terms for the following. Pay close attention to who is talking.

***Example:*** *his maternal uncle* **ukiku**

1. my brother *(said by a girl)* ____________________
2. my sister *(said by a boy)* ____________________
3. my older sister *(said by a girl)* ____________________
4. my older brother *(said by a boy)* ____________________
5. my younger brother *(said by a boy)* ____________________

### 13.2.5. Luhchi pirɛtaki:

Translate the following phrases into English.

***Example:*** *tihtat'ɛhchi* **her older sister**

1. sɛhɛyahchi

   ________________________________________

2. tɛhɛyasahusɛma

   ________________________________________

3. winchasinima

   ________________________________________

4. sintat'ɛhchi

   ________________________________________

5. hihtasahuhchi

   ________________________________________

### 13.2.6. Family Game

On a sheet of paper, write out family vocabulary terms in the first person singular, as well as **ima**. Tear or cut out the terms and place the slips of paper in a hat (or other suitable container). Thoroughly mix the paper slips, then have each person draw a single one. Each person will either be a family member of the person who draws **ima** or will be **ima**. The number of family terms that are used should be the same as the number participating in the game, to ensure that someone always draws **ima**. Unused terms can be rotated in during the next round of the game. **Ima** will have to ask the other players if they are a specific family member, and they will have to reply either **hon** or **aha**. The round is complete when **ima** has correctly identified all of his/her family members.

# Tetimili: Ɛhɛli

*Family*

Tunica society used to be matrilineal. This means that we traced kinship mostly through the mother's side of the family. Thus, you would consider your mother's relatives to be closer to you than your father's relatives.

Today like most Americans, we consider ourselves to be equally related to our mother's family and to our father's. Most Tunica children take their father's surname rather than their mother's. So Sosthene Youchigant's son Sesotrie was called Sesostrie Youchigant; Sesostrie Youchigant's father's sisters were Celena Youchigant and Marie Youchigant.

In matrilineal times, the family land and home belonged to the mother, who passed them down to her daughters. Today all children tend to share in the family inheritance.

Sesostrie Youchigant related some of his family history to Mary Haas. He states:

**Esiku igachihchi tihkyɔla am'uhki.**
My father left my mother and went away.

**Ihta ili inihki. Inima tostohku.**
We were two brothers. We were small.

**Kanahku yoyani ya'inashtuk'ɔhɔ.**
We could not do any work.

**Inima tostohku rikini.**
We were too small.

**Hinyatihch, ingachihchi taroptini hat'ɛna hahka tapati.**
Then, our mother planted cotton and corn.

**Hinahku inkran'aki tika amari.**
In that way, she supported us until we were big enough.

**Hinyatihch, inima yoyani ya'inihki.**
Then, we worked.

**Tihikatɛpan taroptini hatɛna hahka tapahkina.**
Every year, we planted cotton and corn.

Adapted from Haas, *Tunica Texts*, text 29:a, p. 150

## Tetimili yoluyana

| | | | |
|---|---|---|---|
| **hahka** | *corn* | **roptini** | *cotton* |
| **rikini** | *too (much)* | **tapa** | *to plant; to farm; a farm* |

## Tetimili wiralepini

1. In this story, we learned a bit about how Sesostrie Youchigant grew up and how Tunica families were organized. What are your thoughts on this? Does anything sound familiar? Anything different?

2. Write a few sentences in Tunica about a family from the perspective of a member, like we saw with Sesotrie Youchigant's story here. It can be your own family, a friend's, or even about a family you made up! Be sure to use the family terms you learned in this chapter.

# Chapter 14: Tetisinima

## *Direction Words*

**TOPICS:**

## Hɛhchi, hihchi, mihchi

*This here, that there, and that over yonder*

### Yoluyana

| | |
|---|---|
| **hɛhchi** | *here* |
| **hihchi** | *there* |
| **kafi** | *coffee* |
| **kal'ura** | *it is (standing)* |
| **kotitayuki** | *kitchen* |
| **kɔra** | *car* |
| **kɔrashi** | *garage* |
| **lapuya aka** | *welcome (verb)* |
| **mihchi** | *over there* |
| **nɛhtali** | *bed* |
| **rikafi** | *café; coffee shop* |
| **ritarohinapo** | *library* |
| **ritahɛra** | *police station* |
| **ritarapu** | *hotel* |
| **ritasaku** | *restaurant* |
| **rɔhpant** | *beside; next to; near; close by* |
| **teti** | *road; path; trail; way* |
| **tishuhɔhka** | *window* |
| **titihki** | *bayou; canal; stream* |
| **wolushi** | *restroom* |
| **woyushi** | *pool* |

## Yanalepini

**Aiyannahchi:** Heni! Lapuya ak'iki!
Rosehchɛt yukatin?

**Chrisku:** Hon. Hihchi Rosehchi ukikati.
Kata hihkwolushi kal'ura?

**Aiyannahchi:** Hihchi tawolushi kal'ura.

**Chrisku:** Tikahch.

**Rosehchi:** Heni! Ihkyahpa. Saku
hihkaran?

**Aiyannahchi:** Hon! Lapuya ak'aki! Hinto!
Mihchi kotitayuki kal'ura. Kanahku
chu'ɔki! Sak'ɔki!

**Rosehchi:** Tikahch!

*Augustinku yukaku.*

**Augustinku:** Heni! Hihkkɔrashi wenin'ɛhɛ. Kata ihkkɔra yɔlakani?

**Aiyannahchi:** Mihchi ihkkɔrashi kal'ura. Tohkuhch, mihchi kɔrashi kichu hihkkɔra
yɔl'itan!

**Augustinku:** Lapuhch.

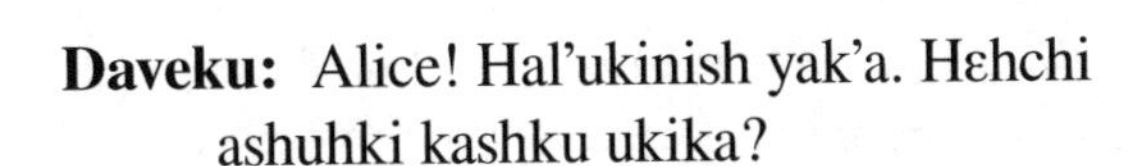

**Daveku:** Alice! Hal'ukinish yak'a. Hɛhchi
ashuhki kashku ukika?

**Alicehchi:** Hɛhchi ashuhki tayihku
ukikani. Mihchi miritarapushi
rapukani.

**Daveku:** Taritarapu hihkelun?

**Alicehchi:** Hon. Mihchi tanɛhtali lamihta,
tatishuhɔhka tika. Ritasaku, rikafi
uhkara.

**Daveku:** Woyushipa uhkaran?

**Alicehchi:** Aha. Hinahkushkan hihchi
tatitihki kichu woyukani. Kata
taritarohinapo kal'ura?

**Daveku:** Hɛteti yuru chu'ɔki!
Taritarohinapo ritahɛra rɔhpant
po'ɔk'ahcha.

**Alicehchi:** Tikahch!

## Lutamashu

In Chapter 9 we learned about the following prefixes:

| | |
|---|---|
| **hɛ-** | here, this, these |
| **hi-** | there, that, those |
| **mi-** | way over there, that one way over there, those way over there |

We learned that you can use these with gender-number endings to describe things and people. For example, **hɛhchi** could be used to talk about 'this girl right here', or to say **Hɛku taworuku** 'this *(ms)* is a student'. Another use for **hɛ-**, **hi-**, and **mi-** is to describe location. When used with the feminine gender-number ending **-hchi**, you can describe three degrees of distance:

| | |
|---|---|
| **hɛhchi** | here |
| **hihchi** | there |
| **mihchi** | way over there |

These words always take the feminine when describing locations. Typically, these words appear at the beginning of the sentence before the subject. Take a look at the following examples:

**Hɛhchi ima pitani.**
I walked here.

**Hihchi teht'ira lapukati.**
She buys her clothes there.

**Mihchi puna wiyawi.**
He threw a ball way over there.

As you saw in the **yanalepini**, when we are talking about the location of buildings, we add another word to the end of the sentence: **kal'ura**. **Kal'ura** means 'it is' or 'it exists', and also indicates that the object being discussed is 'standing'. Just like in English, in Tunica we consider buildings to be standing. This is why discussing the location of buildings involves **kal'ura**, as shown in the examples below.

**Hihchi ihkkotitayuki kal'ura.**
My kitchen is there.

**Mihchi inkkɔrashi kal'ura.**
Our garage is way over there.

**Hɛhchi ritahɛra kal'uran?**
Is the police station here?

## Hinu 1

**14.1.1. Luhchi pirɛtaki:**
Translate the following sentences into Tunica.

***Example:*** *Where is the restaurant?* ***Kata taritasaku kal'ura?***

1. I swim in the pool here. ____________
2. We entered the hotel way over there. ____________
3. The garage is there. ____________
4. Let's go way over there. ____________
5. During the powwow we dance there. ____________

**14.1.2. Luhchi pirɛtaki:**
Translate the following sentences into English.

***Example:*** *Mihchi eruhksiti.* ***They (fp) are laughing over there.***

1. Hɛhchi tawolushi lapun? ____________
2. Hihchi rikafi kal'ura. ____________
3. Mihchi po'ɔki! ____________
4. Hɛhchi esiku taritahɛrashi yoyani yawi. ____________
5. Mihchi titihki woyukati. ____________
6. Hihchi wantaha tahkishi irata. ____________

**14.1.3. Hin'aki:**

Using **hɛhchi**, **hihchi**, and **mihchi**, write 3 original sentences from your own life with each, for a total of 9 sentences.

***Example:*** ***Hɛhchi worukani.*** ('I study here.')

1. ______________________________
2. ______________________________
3. ______________________________
4. ______________________________
5. ______________________________
6. ______________________________
7. ______________________________
8. ______________________________
9. ______________________________

# Kata?

*Where?*

## Yoluyana

| | |
|---|---|
| **ahkihta** | *in back of; behind* |
| **ahkishi** | *in back of; behind* |
| **atehini** | *around; about* |
| **haluhta** | *beneath; under; at the bottom* |
| **halushi** | *below; down; underneath* |
| **hɔwahta** | *outside of* |
| **hɔwashi** | *outdoors; outside of; outside* |
| **katotu** | *everywhere* |
| **mayihta** | *on the other side of* |
| **tirishi** | *right side; on the right; in front of* |

## Yanalepini

**Chrisku:** Ihkminu lewi!

**Alicehchi:** Wihkri halushi me'in?

**Chrisku:** Hon. Hihchi ihkminu wenin'ɛhɛ.

**Alicehchi:** Wihkhalanipahi ahkihta me'in?

**Chrisku:** Hon. Hihchi ihkminu wenin'ɛhɛ.

**Alicehchi:** Tatishuhɔhka tirishi me'in? Tanɛhtali mayihta me'in? Tawolushi kichu me'in?

**Chrisku:** Katotu meni. Ihkminu lewi!

**Alicehchi:** Po'iki! Mihchi wihkminu pokani. Tateti rɔhpant rapuku.

**Chrisku:** Ko'o! Ihkminu lek'ɔhɔ!

**Naomihchi:** Merlin, hɔwashtihki am'iki! Hɛ'ɛsh ashuhki lapu.

**Merlinku:** Hon, amikani. Hal'ukini atehini lɔtanik'ahcha. Hinyatihch, rihku haluhta ukinik'ahcha.

**Naomihchi:** Lapuhch. Imapa hɔwashtihki amikani. Inkri ahkishi yoyani yanik'ahcha.

**Merlinku:** Tari hɔwahta yoyani yahkinahch, lapuhch.

**Naomihchi:** Hon. Hinto!

## Lutamashu

Earlier, we learned that **-sh** means 'to; toward', **-shi** means 'at', and **-hta** means 'on'. In this section we will learn several more ways to express location and direction in Tunica.

In English we have prepositions, such as *in* or *under*, which come before the object being related to. So in the sentence 'in the house', *in* comes before *the house*. However, Tunica uses postpositions or **ahkihtaku** to express relationships between things, which means that direction words come after the noun. As we have seen in earlier chapters, to say 'in the house' in Tunica, we'd say **tari kichu**, literally 'the house in'.

This is true for all **ahkihtaku** in Tunica. Notice how the **ahkihtaku kichu**, **haluhta**, and **hayihta** all come immediately after their respective nouns:

> **Chrisku takotitayuki *kichu* sakuku.**
> Chris is eating *in* the kitchen.
>
> **Tanɛhtali *hayihta* rapukani.**
> I sleep *on* the bed.

Typically, a phrase with an **ahkihtaku** comes after the subject and before the main verb. So in the first example above, the **ahkihtaku** phrase **kotitayuki kichu** comes after **Kaydenku**, but before **sakuku**. If the sentence also contains an object noun, then the **ahkihtaku** phrase comes between the subject and the object. See the position of **kosuhki** in the following sentence:

> **Chrisku takotitayuki kichu *kosuhki* sakuku.**
> Chris is eating *crawfish* in the kitchen.

Almost all words for directions and locations are **ahkihtaku** in Tunica. We will learn most of them in this chapter. Remember that they all behave in the sentence just like **kichu**.

Earlier we learned **hayihta** means 'on' and **hayishi** means 'above'. Some **ahkihtaku** have common variations like this; they can end with either **-hta** or **-shi**. The difference between many of the forms is subtle and for the most part they are interchangeable. The following words are commonly seen with **-hta** or **-shi**:

**hayihta** on; over
**hayishi** up; above

**haluhta** beneath; under; at the bottom
**halushi** below; down; underneath

**ahkihta** in back of; behind
**ahkishi** in back; behind

**hɔwahta** outside of
**hɔwashi** outdoors; outside of; outside

## Hinu 2

**14.2.1. Akuhpɛtaki** (Group together)**:**
In the following sentences, underline the **ahkihtaku**, and draw parentheses around the **ahkihtaku** phrase (the **ahkihtaku** and the noun it comes after). Then, rewrite the sentence without the **ahkihtaku** phrase.

***Example:*** *Ima (ihkri kichu) pitani.* ***Ima pitani.***

1. Kanahku tahalanipahi hayishi poka?

2. Igachihchi kotitayuki kichu yoyani yakati.

3. Tasa taritasaku ahkishi sakuku.

4. Tatishuhɔhka mayihta ukini.

5. Lisahchi tayi tirishi ukikati.

**14.2.2. Luhchi pirɛtaki:**
Translate the following Tunica sentences into English.

***Example:*** *Tanuhchisinima taritahɛra hɔwahta eruhksiti.*
***The women are laughing outside of the police station.***

1. Ɔkasinima namu taworunihchi akurani lɔtahksiti.

2. Tatitihki mayihta woy'iki!

3. Ritarohinapo hɔwashi luhchi Yoroni worukati.

4. Wetiku uhktawohku haluhta ɔlakashi uhkaran?

 ______________________________________

5. Tarku kichu yaluhki mekata.

 ______________________________________

**14.2.3. Luhchi pirɛtaki:**
Translate the following sentences from English into Tunica.

***Example:*** *We two ate outside of the coffee shop.* **Tarikafi hɔwahta sak'ina.**

1. She is sleeping under a tree.

 ______________________________________

2. I ran around the store.

 ______________________________________

3. The children are playing outside the school.

 ______________________________________

4. His father is walking on the other side of the bayou.

 ______________________________________

5. My dog sleeps outside the house.

 ______________________________________

# Spatial relationships

## Yoluyana

| | | | |
|---|---|---|---|
| **akurani** | *around; surrounding* | **mayisahu** | *left side; on the left* |
| **atehpi** | *together; joined together; side-by-side* | **ruhkini** | *in front* |
| **atɛhkala** | *in the middle; in between* | **sehi lapu** | *good morning* |
| **hishtahahki** | *still; always* | **ura** | *it is (lying down)* |

## Yanalepini

*Taritaworunishi ashuhki sahkuhta.*

**Taworunihchi:** Sehi lapu, hotu!

**Taworusɛma:** Sehi lapu, Taworuni!

**Taworunihchi:** Hotu, ukiwitiki!

*Tawor'unima wachihkuna.*

**Taworunihchi:** Hapawinaki! Kaya wachihkwina?

**Chrisku:** Genesishchi rɔhpant ukikan'ɛhɛ.

**Samuelku:** Imapa, Genesishchi rɔhpant ukikan'ɛhɛ.

**Taworunihchi:** Chris, hɛhchi uk'iki! Samuel, hihchi uk'iki! Genesis, kata Chrisku, Samuelku ukihkunahch, hɛma atɛhkala uk'ɛtan, tohkuhch.

**Genesishchi:** Aha. Ihkwan'aha. Imat, kata Diamondhchi, Summerhchi ukihksinahch, ima atɛhkala ukinik'ahcha.

**Lisahchi:** Taworuni, imat kata Chrisku, Samuelku ukihkunahch, ima atɛhkala ukinik'ahcha.

**Taworunihchi:** Ko'o! Tikahch, Lisa. Kata Chrisku, Samuelku ukihkunahch, hɛma atɛhkala uk'ɛki! Genesis, kata Diamondhchi, Summerhchi ukihksinahch, hɛma atɛhkala uk'ɛk'ahcha.

*Hotu ukita.*

**Alicehchi:** Hɛritalapu tika panu! Kana ihktaka weninik'ahcha?

**Chrisku:** Kanahku meka?

**Alicehchi:** Tahina mekani.

**Chrisku:** Tahina rowinahina atehpi ura.

**Alicehchi:** Kata rowinahina ura?

**Chrisku:** Kata tanahchuni ura, atɛhkala rowinahina wen'ɛk'ahcha.

**Alicehchi:** Tikahch. Kata chehkini weninik'ahcha?

**Chrisku:** Tachehkinisinima tarihkɔra akurani wen'ɛk'ahcha.

**Alicehchi:** Tarihkɔra rowinara ruhkini kal'uran?

**Chrisku:** Aha. Tarihkɔra rowinara mayisahu kal'ura.

**Alicehchi:** Hishtahahki tarihkɔra pokan'ɛhɛ.

**Chrisku:** Kata tahalanipahisinima, tapahitaniyusinima pokahch, tarihkɔra atɛhkala kal'ura.

**Alicehchi:** Tikahch, hahchi tarihkɔra pokani.

## Lutamashu

While in the previous section we learned about people going and doing things in different places, this section deals with the location of something in relation to something else, e.g., how to say 'the pens are next to the notebooks' or 'Carla is sitting between Bill and Darrell'.

First, the **ahkihtaku atɛhkala** works a little differently than 'between' in English. To use **atɛhkala** you have to first locate the two things, people, or places, that will serve as the reference points, and then place the object with respect to them. So if you want to say 'I am eating between where Jack and Mary are singing', you first mention where Jack and Mary are (and what they're doing): **kata Jackku Maryhchi harahkunahch** 'where Jack and Mary are singing'. Then you say that you are eating between them: **ima atɛhkala sakukani**. So the complete sentence is **Kata Jackku, Maryhchi harahkunahch, ima atɛhkala sakukani.** The suffix **-hch** sets off the location of the two reference points, telling us who or what the action or person lies between. Here are a few more examples.

> **Chrisku sa'unima uhkara. Kata tasa'unima shimihkunahch, puna atɛhkala wiyawi.**
> Chris has two dogs. He threw a ball between them where the dogs were playing.
>
> **Nokush'unima nɛhtali hayihta rapuhkuna. Kata tanokush'unima rapuhkunahch, Goldilockshchi atɛhkala rapukati.**
> Two bears are sleeping on beds. Goldilocks is sleeping between where the bears are sleeping.
>
> **Tigachihchi, tesiku hipuhkuna. Kata hipuhkunahch, Trudyhchi atɛhkala hipukati.**
> Her mother and father are dancing. Trudy is dancing between them.

Additionally, sometimes we want to talk about the location of two objects, where one is behind the other, in front of the other, beside the other, etc. For example, in the **yanalepini**, the table was to the left of the whiteboard. In Tunica, this is expressed **Tarihkɔra rowinara mayisahu kal'ura**. To say that an object is behind/in front of/etc. another object, we use the verb **ura** for things that lie flat and **kal'ura** for things that stand up straight. Here are a few more examples:

> **Saku tarihkɔra hayihta ura.**
> Food is on the table.
>
> **Tihkrowina taritarohinapo kichu ura.**
> Her book is in the library.
>
> **Tashuhkitawirani tatishuhɔhka tirishi ura.**
> The clock is to the right of the window.

Finally, **tirishi** and **mayisahu** can also be used as **taka halani** 'adjectives', particularly when describing body parts. For example, in Chapter 12 we learned **-hniyutirishi** 'chest', which is literally '[what's] in front of the heart'. Also, you can add **tirishi** or **mayisahu** to body parts to mean 'right X' or 'left X' respectively. Some common right and left body parts are listed on the following page.

| | | | |
|---|---|---|---|
| **-alawɛcha mayisahu** | *left ear* | **-alawɛcha tirishi** | *right ear* |
| **-ashka mayisahu** | *left foot* | **-ashka tirishi** | *right foot* |
| **-ashkatɛrashki mayisahu** | *left leg* | **-ashkatɛrashki tirishi** | *right leg* |
| **-china mayisahu** | *left knee* | **-china tirishi** | *right knee* |
| **-ehp'ira mayisahu** | *left shoulder* | **-ehp'ira tirishi** | *right shoulder* |
| **-eyu mayisahu** | *left arm* | **-eyu tirishi** | *right arm* |
| **-hkeni mayisahu** | *left hand* | **-hkeni tirishi** | *right hand* |
| **-shtosu mayisahu** | *left eye* | **-shtosu tirishi** | *right eye* |

## Hinu 3

**14.3.1. Atehpɛtaki:**

Using **atɛhkala**, join the following two sentences so that the second action takes place between the two objects or people mentioned in the first sentence.

***Example:*** *Aiyannahchi Alicehchi pitahksina. Sinksa pitaku.*
***Kata Aiyannahchi, Alicehchi pitahksinahch, sinksa atɛhkala pitaku.***

1. Daveku, Samuelku lɔtahkuna. Rosehchi lɔtakati.

   ______________________________

2. Buddyku, Samuelku wachihkuna. Unkminu wahaku.

   ______________________________

3. Harryku, Summerhchi woyuhkuna. Diamondhchi woyukati.

   ______________________________

4. Ima, Samuelku sarahkina. Imilahchi sarakati.

   ______________________________

5. Aiyannahchi, Chrisku, Henryku shimikata. Sihksa wɛsaku.

   ______________________________

### 14.3.2. Luhchi pirɛtaki:

Translate the following sentences into natural-sounding English.

***Example:*** *Tanɛhtali tarihkɔra rɔhpant ura.* ***The bed is next to the table.***

1. Taritarapu ruhkini har'iti.

   ______

2. Wihktahch'i tapo takɔra kichu ura.

   ______

3. Hɔwashi ura.

   ______

4. Kata inima rapuhkitihch, inksapa atɛhkala rapuku.

   ______

5. Kata ɛshkalahpi ura?

   ______

### 14.3.3. Luhchi pirɛtaki:

Translate the following sentences into natural-sounding Tunica.

***Example:*** *The dog is walking in front of the house.* ***Tasa tari tirishi pitaku.***

1. The book is next to the desk.

   ______

2. My sock is on the bench.

   ______

3. The road is to the left of the police station.

   ______

4. My clothes are underneath the cat.

   ______

5. He and I are working; you (fs) are playing between us.

   ______

## Tasapashi, tihikashi, pikatishi, lekatishi

*North, south, east, and west*

### Yoluyana

| | | | |
|---|---|---|---|
| **hali hipu** | *powwow grounds* | **riwantaha** | *museum* |
| **haliwɛka** | *cemetery* | **-shtihki** | *toward* |
| **lekatishi** | *west* | **tasapashi** | *north* |
| **onimahoni** | *American Indian; Native American* | **tetirihku** | *nature trail* |
| **pikatishi** | *east* | **tihikashi** | *south* |
| **risep'ɛhɛ** | *health center* | **tonimahoni hal'ukini** | *reservation; Native American village* |
| **Ritetimili** | *Cultural & Educational Resources Center (CERC)* | **tɔhashi** | *casino* |

### Yanalepini

*Augustinku tonimahoni hal'ukini Tayoronihku-Halayihkush yukaku. Hinahkushkan, leku.*

**Augustinku:** Hɛhchi taritarohinapo kal'uran?

**Naomihchi:** Aha. Hɛku tatɔhashi. Taritarohinapo hɛhchi rɔhpant kal'ura.

**Augustinku:** Taritarohinapo tariwantaha tihikashi kal'uran?

**Naomihchi:** Aha. Taritarohinapo Ritetimili kichu kal'ura. Tariwantahapa Ritetimili kichu kal'ura.

**Augustinku:** Kana Ritetimilish yukakani?

**Naomihchi:** Tetirihku hayihta tasapashtihki pit'iki!

**Augustinku:** Hɛhchi yakanihch, haliwɛka poni.

**Naomihchi:** Hon. Haliwɛka hɛntohku, risep'ɛhɛ rɔhpant ura. Tahali hipu haliwɛka pikatishi ura. Tateti tika lekatishi ura.

## Lutamashu

If you look at the list of directional words above, you will notice the ending **-shi** which appears on cardinal directions (north, south, east, and west) and means 'at'. The cardinal direction words can themselves be broken down. North is **ta** 'the' + **sapa** 'cold' + **shi** 'at', literally 'at the cold', while south is **tihika** 'summer' + **shi** 'at', literally 'at the summer'. West is **le** 'disappear' + **kati** 'she (habitual)' + **shi** 'at', literally 'where she disappears', referring to the setting sun. Finally, the word for east is composed of **pi** 'emerge' + **kati** 'she (habitual)' + **shi** 'at', literally 'where she emerges', referring to the rising sun. The cardinal directions play an important role in several rituals, such as the **nihkirhipu** grand entry where dancers enter from **pikatishi** (where the sun rises) and proceed in a clockwise direction (**tihikashi**, **lekatishi**, **tasapashi**, then back to **pikatishi**).

Unlike the **ahkihtaku**, cardinal directions can be used on their own as well as with a noun.

> **Tariwantaha *tasapashi* kal'ura.**
> The museum is to the *north*.
>
> **Tarisep'ɛhɛ haliwɛka *tasapashi* kal'ura.**
> The health center is *north* of the cemetery.

For each direction, the **-shi** 'at' form alternates with **-shtihki** 'toward' to mean 'toward the north', 'toward the south', etc. **-shtihki** can also also be used on other words like **tirishi** and **mayisahu** to indicate movement toward a direction. Look for cardinal directions and **-shtihki** in the following examples:

> **Tonimahonisɛma *lekatishtihki* pitata.**
> Native Americans walked *westward*.
>
> **Sɛma hali hipu *pikatishi tihikashtihki* hipukata.**
> They dance from the east of the powwow grounds to the south.
>
> ***Tirishtihki* hinahkiti.**
> We write to the right.

Just as in the previous lessons, the location of buildings is expressed with **kal'ura**, while the location of other non-living objects use **ura**. **Ura** is also used with roads, as shown in the last line of the **yanalepini**, as well as the powwow grounds and the cemetery, since they are flat spaces rather than buildings.

## Hinu 4

**14.4.1. Luhchi pirɛtaki:**
Translate the following sentences into English.

***Example:*** *Lekatishtihki lɔtahkuna.* **They (md) run west.**

1. Tasapashi ura. ______
2. Haliwɛka Taritetimili pikatishi ura. ______
3. Tahch'i lekatishtihki hilakati. ______
4. Riwantaha tihikashi mashuta. ______

**14.4.2. Luhchi pirɛtaki:**
Translate the following sentences into Tunica.

***Example:*** *The police station is east of the road.* **Tarihɛra tateti pikatishi kal'ura.**

1. You *(fs)* walk south on the long trail. ______
2. You *(md)* look to the north. ______
3. The health center is north of the casino. ______
4. The CERC is west of the powwow grounds. ______

### 14.4.3. Chu'ɔki:

Choose the direction where the following things and places are with respect to the Tunica Reservation in Marksville, Louisiana.

***Example:*** *Nokushi kayi*

***a. Lekatishi*** *b. Tihikashi* *c. Pikatishi*

1. Baton Rouge
   a. Tasapashi b. Lekatishi c. Tihikashi
2. Atlantic Ocean
   a. Tihikashi b. Pikatishi c. Lekatishi
3. Pacific Ocean
   a. Pikatishi b. Tasapashi c. Lekatishi
4. Arkansas
   a. Lekatishi b. Tasapashi c. Tihikashi
5. New Orleans
   a. Tasapashi b. Pikatishi c. Tihikashi

## Tetimili: Wantaha, hahchi, hishtahahki

*A long time ago, now, still*

**Wantaha, hahchi, hishtahahki** speaks for itself. If one is old enough to remember the old houses and the old dirt roads, one also remembers the elders and the stories they passed on. Just as nature and natural settings still thrive on the land, like the doe and her fawn at the tree line, so too, the Tunica-Biloxi people, language and culture thrive.

**Wantaha teti halitipusa urani.**
A long time ago, there was a dirt road, it is said.

**Hahchi teti nisa, ri nisa mashukata.**
Now, they build new houses and roads.

**Wantaha latihch, tahch'a hayishihchi tawɛhanitahkɛni.**
A long time ago, at night, the moon above was the only light, it is said.

**Hahchi tawɛhani nisa hayihta likahksiti.**
Now the modern lights shine above.

**Hishtahahki ya nuhchi tihkyatohk'ɔma tarku hotushi kal'urana.**
A doe and her fawn still stand at the edge of the woods.

**Hishtahahki latihch, chushisinima rihku kichu ukihksiti.**
Still at night, owls perch in trees.

**Hishtahahki latihch, nɛrasɛma katotu teti hayihta pitakatani.**
Still at night, spirits walk everywhere on the road, it is said.

**Chomusinima tonimahoni hal'ukini ahkishi lɔtahksiti.**
Bobcats run behind the reservation.

**Tala tarku kichu mishtihkitohku kal'ura.**
Further into the woods, the cane is standing.

**Tonisɛma Tawatoruwishipɛta kichu nini namu wohkukata.**
The people catch many fish in the Coulée des Grues.

**Sehitihch, tonisɛma tarku kichu wɛr'ɔnta.**
In the morning, people hunt in the woods.

**Tahch'ahipu yukatihch, nihkirhipu yuwakatahch, tahipusɛma tahali hipushi rasht'ɛ wɛsa hipukata.**
In May, when they give a powwow, the dancers jump and dance with great effort at the powwow grounds.

**Hishtahahki ɛstamilisinima tahali hipu hayihta narahksiti.**
Still red-tailed hawks fly above the dance grounds.

**Nihkirhipushi, akurani hotushi takunkuri tapɛkasɛma sihkkunkuri rasht'ɛ pɛkakata.**
When it is powwow, at the edge of the dance circle, the drummers strongly beat their drums.

**Hahchi hɛhchi inimat onimahonisɛma, hishtahahki hɛhali hayihta ɔ'ɔn'iti.**
Now here, we, Indian people, on our part, we still exist on this land.

## Tetimili yoluyana

| | | | |
|---|---|---|---|
| **chushi** | *owl* | **nɛra** | *spirit; ghost* |
| **ɛstamili** | *red-tailed hawk* | **Tawatoruwishipɛta** | *Coulée des Grues* |

## Tetimili wiralepini

1. In this **tetimili** we heard a story comparing the past and the present. Pick a set of lines from the story discussing something from the past, something that happens still, and something that happens now. Have you experienced or heard about what's described here?

2. Take a moment and write your own three line story discussing something that happens now, something that still happens, and something that once happened. This can be based off of your real life or something you imagine. Don't forget to make sure your verb endings match whether something is ongoing or completed!

# Chapter 15: Taya nahchu hatika

## *Transitive verbs again*

**TOPICS:**

# Transitive verbs with objects

## Yoluyana

| | | | |
|---|---|---|---|
| **chuhpa** | *to kiss* | **ni** | *to tell; to say* |
| **heni** | *to greet* | **niyupo** | *to remember* |
| **hεra** | *to watch* | **sehitihch** | *at dawn; when the sun rises/rose* |
| **kaha** | *to meet; to come upon; to come across* | **tama** | *to be with; to live with; to accompany* |
| **kipa** | *to marry* | **yayi** | *to take care of; to save; to be saved* |
| **lawu yuru** | *all night long* | | |

## Yanalepini

**Alicehchi:** Merlin, imilasinima sinkmekani. Hε'εsh sinkkah'in?

**Merlinku:** Aha. Hε'εsh sinkkahan'εhε. Tarku kichu sinkme'εn? Hihchi shimihksiti.

**Alicehchi:** Aha, tarku kichu sinkmen'εhε. Hihchi yukanik'ahcha. Tikahch.

**Merlinku:** Sinkweninihch, ihkni'εki!

**Alicehchi:** Wihkninik'ahcha. Tikahch.

*Sehitihch:*

**Merlinku:** Himilasinima sinkwen'εn?

**Alicehchi:** Hon, imilasinima sinkwenini.

**Merlinku:** Kata?

**Alicehchi:** Tarku kichu shimihksiti.

**Merlinku:** Sinkwen'ε. Ihksh'εpa. Himilasinima sinkyay'εki!

**Jayku:** Kay, ka'ash akah'inahch, niyupo'an?

**Kayhchi:** Hon, niyupokani. Wihkkahanihch, wihkhenini. Lawu yuru yanahkina. Hinyatihch, sehitihch tahch'i hɛr'ina.

**Jayku:** Hon. Hihktamakanihch, ihksh'ɛpa. Alice, ihkkip'ak'ahchan?

**Kayhchi:** Hon, Jay! Wihkkipanik'ahcha. Imapa ihksh'ɛpa. Ihkchuhp'iki!

*Tihkchuhpaku.*

**Jayku:** Inkashuhki hotu atam'inak'ahcha.

## Lutamashu

As we saw in Chapter 5, transitive verbs are verbs that can take an object (e.g., "I eat *cake*"). In this example, *eat* is a transitive verb and *cake* is its object.

Transitive verbs must be marked for subject in the same way as intransitive verbs. However, transitive verbs may also indicate their object. If the object is a person, such as "I hit you" or "You bite me," then the object must be marked on the verb. Objects of transitive verbs are marked with the same set of prefixes we learned in Chapters 8 and 11, which are also used to indicate alienable possession and the subjects of stative verbs:

| | | SINGULAR | | DUAL | | PLURAL | |
|---|---|---|---|---|---|---|---|
| *1st person* | | **ihk-** | *me* | **ink-** | *us two* | **ink-** | *us* |
| *2nd person* | *feminine* | **hihk-** | *you* | **hink-** | *you two* | **hink-** | *you all* |
| | *masculine* | **wihk-** | *you* | **wink-** | *you two* | **wink-** | *you all* |
| *3rd person* | *feminine* | **tihk-** | *her* | **sink-** | *them two* | **sink-** | *them* |
| | *masculine* | **uhk-** | *him* | **unk-** | *them two* | **sihk-** | *them* |

Look at the verbs in the following examples. Because the object is a person, the verbs take object prefixes.

> **Uhkheniku.**
> He is greeting him.
>
> **Uhtat'ɛ uhkhɛraku.**
> He is watching his older brother.
> *or* His older brother is watching him.
>
> **Ugachihchi tihkyayiku.**
> He is caring for his mother.

However, if the object is *not* a person, adding the object marker is not required, as you have seen with all the transitive verbs before this chapter. As we see in the following examples, the non-human objects (*ball*, *corn*, and *chair*) are all clearly stated in the sentence, but are not marked on the verb itself.

> **Tapuna wiyakani.**
> I am throwing the ball.
>
> **Chehkini mashuki.**
> You *(ms)* are making a chair.
>
> **Elu kayi yuru sakukati.**
> She is eating a banana.

However, if the object noun isn't present in the same sentence, then it is more common to use object marking, even if the noun is not human. For example, if we are talking about buying a hat, after I mention the hat the first time, usually the hat will just be referred to as "it," rather than saying "the hat" every time. Tunica does the same thing using these object prefixes. This scenario in Tunica might go something like this:

> **Summerhchi:** Tawohku lapuni.
> **Buddyku:** Lapuhch! Kata uhklap'ɔ?
> **Summerhchi:** Nikirhipushi uhklapuni.

After the first mention, **tawohku** was indicated by **uhk-**, rather than having to say "**tawohku**" every time.

## Hinu 1

**15.1.1. Luhchi pirɛtaki:**
Provide the English translations for the following Tunica sentences.

***Example:*** *Wihkhenini.* ***I greeted you (ms).***

1. Ushtahpu niyupokati. ____________________
2. Kuwatohku hɛraka. ____________________
3. Tihchahchi tihkyayikati. ____________________
4. Ɛhɛli sihktamakani. ____________________
5. Taworuniku uhktaworusɛma sihkkahawi. ____________________
6. Tanuhchi tihkniwi. ____________________
7. Uhchatohkusɛma sihkchuhpawi. ____________________
8. Hotu hihknini. ____________________
9. Halanipahi hɛrakati. ____________________
10. Sinkniyupokani. ____________________

**15.1.2. Luhchi pirɛtaki:**

Provide Tunica translations for the following English sentences.

***Example:*** *His mother kissed him.* **Wigachihchi uhkchuhpati.**

1. She is meeting her friend. ______________________
2. I married my husband. ______________________
3. Those two *(m)* don't remember him. ______________________
4. I took care of his younger brother. ______________________
5. She kissed her younger sister. ______________________
6. *(2fs)* Tell me! ______________________
7. We will meet our new chief tomorrow. ______________________
8. They *(f)* greeted each other. ______________________
9. We are accompanying them. ______________________
10. Do you *(ms)* remember me? ______________________

**15.1.3. Arhilani:**

Here's a story in Tunica about a family's morning activities. Add the correct object prefixes to the transitive verbs *if they need it.* If not, leave the space blank. There may be multiple possible answers in some cases.

***Example:*** *ɔnchayihchi* **tihk** *chuhpawi*

Ima ɛhɛli tamakani. Sehitihch, esiku igachihchi _____heniku, _____chuhpaku. Igachihchi "sehi lapu!" _____nikati. Igachihchi, ɛsik'ɔma _____yayihkuna. Sehitich, ihksaku _____sakukani. Hɔwashi, kuwatohku _____pokani. _____niyupokani. Lawushi, _____kahani. Lawu yuru harawi. Sehinta, hatika _____po'ik'ahcha.

# Word order

## Yoluyana

| | | | |
|---|---|---|---|
| **-ashkalahpi chɛra** | *dance moccasins* | **mohtu** | *to wrap* |
| **awɛhɛ** | *nothing* | **satohku** | *puppy* |
| **-eruhkitapahchu** | *necklace* | **takayuwa** | *gift* |
| **hali** | *to send* | **tawista** | *candy; sweets* |
| **Ingras'ashuhki** | *Christmas* | **yuwa** | *to give* |

## Yanalepini

**Henryku:** Kata amika?

**Alicehchi:** Taritalapush yukakani.

**Henryku:** Kanahku ihkchuyak'ak'ahcha?

**Alicehchi:** Kanahku wihkwana?

**Henryku:** Satohku ihkchuyak'aki!

**Alicehchi:** Satohkusinima hiritalapushi sihkaha.

**Henryku:** O, hinyatihch ehukuma ihkchuyak'aki!

**Alicehchi:** Onisɛma sihklapuhkit'ɛhɛ.

**Henryku:** Tawista sihkaran? Tawista ihkchuyak'aki!

**Alicehchi:** Hon. Tawista wihkchuyakanik'ahcha.

**Chrisku:** Kanahku yaka?
**Rosehchi:** Ingras'ashuhki yukakati. Takayuwa mohtukani.
**Chrisku:** Lapuhch. Kanahku higachihchi tihkyuw'ak'ahcha?
**Rosehchi:** Teruhtamihku tihklapuni.
**Chrisku:** Hɛhɛyat, kanahku uhklap'ɔk'ahcha?
**Rosehchi:** Awɛhɛ. Oruhkitapahchu uhkmashuni.
**Chrisku:** Ko'o! Hesiku kanahku uhkyuw'ak'ahcha?
**Rosehchi:** Puna uhkyuwanik'ahcha. Uhkpuna hayi. Ashuhkitɛpan tasa puna wiyaku.
**Chrisku:** Kanahku hiku?
**Rosehchi:** Ikiku uhktakayuwa. Sehinta uhkhalinik'ahcha. Ɛshkalahpi chɛra tashle ihkyuwawi.
**Chrisku:** Imat, kanahku ihkyuw'ak'ahcha?
**Rosehchi:** Wihkninik'ahch'aha. Ingras'ashuhki sehitihch, po'ik'ahcha. Kanahku ihkyuw'ik'ahcha?
**Chrisku:** Ehniyu.

## Lutamashu

As we saw in Chapter 5, Tunica uses Subject-Object-Verb word order. But what happens when you use a verb like **yuwa** 'give' where there is an agent (the person doing the giving, which is in subject position), a patient (the thing being given, which in English is usually a direct object), and a recipient (the person receiving the gift, which in English is often an indirect object)? In Tunica, the order is as follows:

AGENT – RECIPIENT – PATIENT – VERB

So to say 'Merlin gave Tina a ball', you would write **Merlinku Tinahchi puna tihkyuwawi**. Notice that the recipient, **Tinahchi**, is what is marked on the verb with **tihk-**. This is because

Tina is a person, and people are what usually get marked on the verb, regardless of whether they are a patient or a recipient.

Keep in mind that word order and verb prefixes and endings will tell you who is doing what to whom. So **Billku Alicehchi minu tihkyuwawi** means that it's Bill that gave Alice a cat, whereas **Alicehchi Billku minu uhkyuwati** means that it was *Alice* who gave *Bill* a cat.

## Hinu 2

**15.2.1. Atehpɛtaki:**
In each question, the words make a complete Tunica sentence, but they are in the wrong order. Re-write the words in the correct order on the line below so that it matches the English meaning.

***Example:*** *Harry met Sally.*
*tihkkahawi Sallyhchi Harryku*
***Harryku Sallyhchi tihkkahawi.***

1. Constance threw the ball to Carmen.
   Carmenhchi tapuna tihkwiyati Constancehchi

   ______________________________

2. Donovan brought his sister clothes.
   tihkchuyakawi Donovanku ɔhɔyahchi teht'ira

   ______________________________

3. Bill gave his mother a necklace.
   teruhkitapahchu Billku tihkyuwawi ugachihchi

   ______________________________

4. Dave will give his wife a present on Christmas morning.
   sehitihch Ingras'ashuhki Daveku takayuwa ɔnchayhchi tihkyuwawik'ahcha

   ______________________________

5. Andrew bought candy for his son.
   tawista uhklapuwi Andrewku umilaku

   ______________________________

### 15.2.2. Luhchi pirɛtaki:

Translate the following sentences. Pay attention to word order!

***Example:*** *Aiyannahchi Genesishchi tihkpoti.* **Aiyanna saw Genesis.**

1. Lisahchi Diamondhchi puna tihkwiyati. ______________________
2. Clydeku ugachihchi minu tihkyuwawi. ______________________
3. Naomihchi Merlinku uhkkahati. ______________________
4. Minervahchi tesiku sa tihklapuwi. ______________________
5. Collinku ɔnchayihchi teruhkitapahchu tihkhaliwi. ______________________

### 15.2.3. Luhchi pirɛtaki:

Translate the following sentences. Pay attention to word order!

***Example:*** *Carrie wrapped your (fs) gift.* **Carriehchi hihktakayuwa mohtuti.**

1. Courtney threw a ball to Sullivan. ______________________
2. Samuel gave food to the birds. ______________________
3. She brought them *(mp)* candy. ______________________
4. He bought his daughter dance moccasins. ______________________
5. The teacher gave her students many gifts. ______________________

# Tetimili: Hahka uhkkalin'uhkɛni

*The origin of corn*

In many Native traditions, objects of importance tend to have origin stories. These origin stories usually depict how the object came to be and how it became important. For instance, the story below describes how corn came to be for the Tunica people. But the story is also a good example of how sometimes the stories can be "lost" in translation. In the following story, you will see the word **lɔpatɛra**. At present we can only speculate about what **lɔpatɛra** could be, since it was not identified at the time of recording. All we know is that it is a plant that deer like to eat, which makes sense in the context of this story.

**Uhayiku toniku tayaku unkkalin'uhkɛni.**
The Old Man created man and deer, they say.

**Hinyatihch, tahahkaku talɔpatɛraku unkkalin'uhkɛni.**
Then he created corn and lɔpatɛra vine, they say.

**Hinyatihch, unkyanalepihkutani.**
He spoke to the two of them, they say.

**Kaku tahahkaku uhksakuw'ihch, uwi onɛni.**
Whichever would eat the corn would become a person, they say.

**Kaku talɔpatɛraku uhksakuw'ihch, ya uhkpiratik'ahchani.**
Whichever ate the lɔpatɛra would turn into a deer, they say.

**Hinyatihch, tayaku tahalihta patawihch, wahakɔni.**
Then the deer fell to the ground and wept, they say.

**Hinyatihch, hakaliwihch, yanakɔni.**
Then when he arose, he spoke, they say.

**"Ihksakuw'ihch, ɔmaka imanahku yaw'ihch, ihksakuwik'ahcha," nikɔni.**
"(The man who would) eat me should become a sorcerer like me and he shall eat me," he said.

**Hinyatihch, toniku uhkwahkawihch, uhksak'uhkɛni.**
Then the man broke off and ate the corn.

**Uhkrishi yukawihch, tahahkaku uhksak'uhkɛni.**
When he got home he ate the corn, they say.

**Hinyatihch, tayaku tarku kichu ak'uwani.**
The deer went off into the woods, they say.

## Tetimili yoluyana

| | | | |
|---|---|---|---|
| **kali** | *to stand* | **rapa** | *to kill* |
| **lɔpatɛra** | *unidentified vine that deer like to eat* | **wahka** | *to break off* |

## Tetimili wiralepini

1. Write a few sentences to end the story. How is the deer's life in the forest? How is man's life in the village? Your time and place words from Chapter 14 will come in handy here.

2. Clearly our relationship with corn has been very important and continues to be important today. What are some foods you like to eat that contain corn? Give your answers in Tunica if you can!

# Chapter 16: Atɛhtaya

*Embedding*

**TOPICS:**

## -wana, -sh'ɛpa

*want to, like to*

### Yoluyana

| | | | |
|---|---|---|---|
| **ala** | *cane* | **-sh'ɛpa** | *to like to; to enjoy* |
| **eksha tɛrashki** | *pine needles* | **titiht'ɛ** | *river* |
| **kɔsa** | *to scrape (scales or hide)* | **wila** | *to braid; to weave* |
| **lɔhka** | *basket* | **wohku** | *to go fishing; to catch fish* |
| **nahtali** | *bank (of a river); shore* | **yoyani** | *work* |
| **nini** | *fish* | | |

### Yanalepini

**Merlinku:** Kanahku ya hihkwana?

**Aiyannahchi:** Lɔhka wila ihkwana.

**Merlinku:** Ala hihkaran?

**Aiyannahchi:** Aha. Eksha tɛrashki ihkara. Lɔhka wila wihkwanan?

**Merlinku:** Aha. Imat wohku ihkwana. Hihkwanan?

**Aiyannahchi:** Hon. Tikahch. Nahtali hayihta ukikanihch, lɔhka wilanik'ahcha.

**Merlinku:** Chehkini chuyaka hihkwanan?

**Aiyannahchi:** Aha. Nahtali hayihta uki ihksh'ɛpa.

**Merlinku:** Imapa. Yuk'inaki!

*Titiht'ɛsh yuk'una. Merlinku nini wohkuku.*

**Merlinku:** Hɛnini chu'ɔki! Uhkkɔs'aki!

**Aiyannahchi:** Aha, uhkkɔsa ihkwan'aha. Mahat ya'iki!

**Merlinku:** Nini saku hihkwanan?

**Aiyannahchi:** Hon. Nini saku ihksh'ɛpa.

**Merlinku:** Hinyatihch uhkkɔs'aki!

**Rosehchi:** Igachi, etisinima sinkpo ihkwana!

**Tigachihchi:** Hihkyoyani hot'ɔn?

**Rosehchi:** Hon!

**Tigachihchi:** Kata yukitik'ahcha?

**Rosehchi:** Taritalapu yuk'itik'ahcha. Tirasinima nisa lapu inkwana.

**Tigachihchi:** Lapuhch. Hetisinimapa hihkpo sinksh'ɛpa.

**Rosehchi:** Tikahch!

## Lutamashu

Often, when you are talking about things you enjoy, you want to mention activities that you might like to do. In English this can be done with the word 'to' plus the basic form of the verb, as in the sentence, "I like *to read*." Other verbs in English require a different way of changing the second verb: adding an *-ing* ending, as in "We enjoy *walking*," but the result is the same.

If you want to talk about your favorite activities in Tunica, it requires stative verbs, namely **-wana** 'want' or **-sh'ɛpa** 'like, enjoy'. As the main verb of a Tunica sentence is usually the last word of the sentence, the stative verb with its prefix will be last. The other verb appears right before it, with no endings. See the following example sentences:

> **Brianku *hipu* uhksh'ɛpa.**
> Brian likes to dance. *or* Brian likes dancing.
>
> **Hɛma *woru* hihkwanan?**
> Do you *(fs)* want to study?
>
> ***Hihkyayi* ihkwana.**
> I want to take care of you *(fs)*.

If the second verb is a **taya nahchu**, then it keeps its object prefix, but still loses its subject ending (like **hihkyayi**). Here are a couple additional examples of this type of sentence:

> **Uhkkɔsa ihkwan'aha.**
> I don't want to scale it.
>
> **Wihkpo sihksh'ɛpa.**
> They *(mp)* enjoy seeing you *(ms)*.

## Hinu 1

### 16.1.1. Ey'ɔki:

Circle the complements of **-wana** and **-sh'ɛpa**, the verbs with no endings.

***Example:*** *Tasa meli* **lɔta** *uhkwana.*

1. Buddyku, Henryku shimi unkwana.
2. Alicehchi wila tihksh'ɛpa.
3. Clydeku, Rosehchi, ima eru inkwana.
4. Hɛma hipu hihkwanan?
5. Takuwatohku ɔshta hara uhksh'ɛpa.
6. Ima waha ihksh'ɛp'aha.

### 16.1.2. Molɔtaki:

Fill in the blanks with bare forms of verbs of your choosing.

***Example:*** *Ugachihchi* **lɔta** *tihksh'ɛpa.*

1. Ma __________ wihkwana.
2. Genesishchi, Chrisku, Samuelku __________ sihksh'ɛpa.
3. Winima __________ winkwana.
4. Takuwatohkusinima __________ sinkwana.
5. Taworuku __________ uhksh'ɛpa.
6. Inima hotu __________ inksh'ɛpa.

## -wan

*in order to*

### Yoluyana

| | | | |
|---|---|---|---|
| **hokokura** | *elderberry* | **rayi** | *mulberry* |
| **humameli** | *blackberry* | **-wan** | *in order to* |
| **Ispani** | *Spanish* | **Yoroni** | *Tunica person; Tunica people* |
| **luhchi** | *language* | **yuki** | *to prepare food* |
| **mari** | *to gather (things)* | | |

### Yanalepini

**Merlinku:** Kata amiki?

**Chrisku:** Saku mariwan amikani.

**Merlinku:** Kanahku mar'ik'ahcha?

**Chrisku:** Rayi, hokokura, humameli yukiwan marinik'ahcha.

**Merlinku:** Ko'o! Rayi ihkelu. Wihkrish wihksaku sakuwan yukanik'ahcha.

**Chrisku:** Hinto!

**Aiyannahchi:** Kaya luhchi Yoroni woruhkiti?

**Naomihchi:** Kaya luhchi Ispani woruhkiti?

**Aiyannahchi:** Tihkyanawan woruhkiti.

**Naomihchi:** Luhchi Yoronipa yanawan woruhkiti. Luhchi Yoroni yanawan, woruhkiti ashuhkitɛpan. Inima Tayoronisinima, inkluhchi yan'itik'ahcha.

**Aiyannahchi:** Lapuhch.

## Lutamashu

The ending **-wan** means 'in order to'. For example, in the dialogue above, Naomi asks, **Kaya luhchi Ispani woruhkiti?** 'Why do we study Spanish?' and Aiyanna replies, **Tihkyanawan woruhkiti.** 'We study it in order to speak it.' There are a few important things to notice about how **-wan** is used here. First, notice that **-wan** replaces the usual endings of the verb **yana** 'to speak', giving us **tihkyanawan** 'in order to speak it'. Second, notice that the verb expressing the purpose comes first (**tihkyanawan**) and the main verb expressing what is being done for that purpose comes second (**woruhkiti**). Unlike the verb that **-wan** attaches to, this second verb takes the usual endings. We can see more examples using **-wan** in the following sentences:

**Naomihchi ala lɔhka mashuwan tihkara.**
Naomi has cane (in order) to make baskets.

**Ukiwan yakakani.**
I am coming (in order) to stay.

**Tihkweniwan yɔlawi.**
He left (in order) to find her.

## Hinu 2

**16.2.1. Luhchi pirɛtaki:**
Translate the following sentences from English to Tunica.

***Example:*** *I am reading in order to learn.* **Woruwan rohina pokani.**

1. I prepared food in order to eat. ________________
2. She is gathering pine needles in order to weave baskets. ________________
3. They *(md)* are leaving in order to gather elderberries. ________________
4. I went to the river in order to catch fish. ________________
5. We *(p)* study in order to speak Tunica. ________________

### 16.2.2. Molɔtaki:

Use **-wan** to answer the following questions, using the phrase suggested in parentheses.

***Example:*** *Kaya wor'ɔ? (rohina po)* **Woruwan rohina pokani.**

1. Kaya tahali hipush yukaki? (hipu) ______
2. Kaya rahpahkiti? (pala) ______
3. Kaya tonisɛma yukikata? (saku) ______
4. Kaya tasasinima lɔtahksiti? (minu tapi) ______
5. Kaya rahpuntira rahpuka? (hɔwashtihki ami) ______
6. Kaya yɔl'a? (ihkrishi ami) ______
7. Kaya tahina lapuwi? (hina) ______
8. Kaya tihkri yɔlati? (yoyani ya) ______
9. Kaya humameli maruhkiti? (yuki) ______
10. Kaya wohkuta? (nini kɔsa) ______

## -shkan

*but*

### Yoluyana

| | | | |
|---|---|---|---|
| **ahkishisɛma** | *the rest; remainder (of people)* | **nira** | *to steal* |
| **akuhpani** | *together* | **rapa** | *to kill* |
| **Halayihku** | *Biloxi person/people; Biloxi tribe* | **Shihkalpalkaku** | *Natchez person/people; Natchez tribe* |
| **hihkutohku** | *mouse* | **-shkan** | *but; nevertheless; however* |
| **hinahkutan** | *maybe* | **-shruka** | *to be afraid* |
| **laka** | *to live (3fp/3mp)* | **Tayoroniku** | *the Tunica people; the Tunica tribe* |

### Yanalepini

**Rosehchi:** Hɛ'ɛsh ihkri kichu hihkutohk'unima poni.

**Naomihchi:** Hihkshrukan?

**Rosehchi:** Aha. Unkponishkan, ihkshruk'aha. Hinahkushkan hihkutohkusinima ihkri kichu laka. Lap'ɔhɔ.

**Naomihchi:** Kaya?

**Rosehchi:** Ihksaku nirasiti.

**Naomihchi:** Kanahku ya'ak'ahcha? Sinkrap'akahcha?

**Rosehchi:** Hihkutohkusinima ihkel'ɔhɔshkan, sinkrapa ihkwan'aha.

**Naomihchi:** Hinahkutan sinktap'ɛk'ahcha.

**Rosehchi:** Hinyatihch…?

**Naomihchi:** Naomihchi tihkri rɔhpant sinkyɔl'ak'ahcha. Tihchi minusinima tihkara.

**Rosehchi:** Hinahkushkan tihkminusinima tahihkutokusinima rapasitik'ahcha!

**Chrisku:** Tayoroniku Quizquizshi lakahch, kaku inkchɔhaku?

**Naomihchi:** Cahura Joligoku inkchɔhaku.

**Chrisku:** Kaya Quizquiz yɔl'iti?

**Naomihchi:** Wantaha Tashihkalpalkaku Cahura Joligoku uhkkaha uhkwana. Cahura Joligoku saku, nɛhtali sihkyuwawi. Hinahkushkan lawushi Tashihkalpalkaku yakawi. Tashihkalpalkaku Cahura Joligoku uhkrapawi.

Inkchɔhaku uhkrapatashkan ɔnchayihchi, umilaku unkrapat'aha. Tashihkalpalkaku inkonisɛma namu sihkrapawi. Hinahkushkan ahkishisɛma yɔlata. Quizquiz yɔl'itihch, tihikashtihki am'iti. Inkri yɔl'itishkan ri nisasinima mash'iti. Hahchi Tayoroniku Tahalayihk'ɔma akuhpani laka.

## Lutamashu

We learned **hinahkushkan** 'but, however, nevertheless' in Chapter 10. **Hinahkushkan** is used at the beginning of a sentence or a phrase to mean 'but, however'. For instance, to say "But Mom, I don't want to!" you'd say, **Hinahkushkan igachi, ihkwan'aha!**

In this section we learn a shorter form, **-shkan**, that means the same thing. The difference between **hinahkushkan** and **-shkan** is that **-shkan** is used to mean 'but' when it's in the middle of a sentence. For example, in the **yanalepini** we saw **Unkponi*shkan*, ihkshruk'aha** 'I saw them *(md)*, but I wasn't afraid'. Here **-shkan** is used because this is only one sentence. Although in English *but* usually comes after a comma (*I'm here, but you're not*), **-shkan** must be attached to another word. So in the previous example, **-shkan** was attached to **unkponi** 'I saw them *(md)*'. While it may look a little strange at first, **-shkan** always comes before the comma (or that natural pause where a comma would be). Here are a couple more examples.

**Uhksakunishkan, ihkwan'aha.**
I ate it, but I didn't want to.

**Kanahku tihkni ihkwanashkan, yɔlati.**
I wanted to tell her something, but she left.

## Hinu 3

**16.3.1. Atehpɛtaki:**
Join each of the pairs of sentences with **hinahkushkan**.

***Example:*** *Calvinku hɔwashi amiwi. Shimiw'ɛhɛ.*
***Calvinku hɔwashi amiwi. Hinahkushkan shimiw'ɛhɛ.***

1. Ritalapu amini. Kanahku lapun'ɛhɛ.

 ______________________________

2. Rosehchi hihkutohku poti. Tihkshruk'aha.

 ______________________________

3. Sakunik'ahcha. Ihkyahp'aha.

 ______________________________

4. Wahakati. Tihksh'ɛpa.

 ______________________________

5. Uhkpowitiki! Uhktap'ɛhɛtan!

 ______________________________

**16.3.2. Atehpɛtaki:**
Using the sentences you made in Hinu 16.3.1, rework them to use **-shkan** rather than **hinahkushkan**.

***Example:*** *Calvinku hɔwashi yukawi. Shimiw'ɛhɛ.*
***Calvinku hɔwashi yukawishkan shimiw'ɛhɛ.***

1. ______________________________
2. ______________________________
3. ______________________________
4. ______________________________
5. ______________________________

## Tetimili: Lɔhka

*Basketry*

Basket-making has long been a part of Tunica culture. Elisabeth Pierite explains her family's history of basket-making:

**Ɛhɛli lɔhka wila inksh'ɛpa.**
My family enjoys making baskets.

**Ihchat'ɛhchi tihika namu lɔhka wil'aki.**
My great-grandmother has made baskets for many years.

**Wantaha hɛhɛli lɔhka laspi chuwan pal'ɔnta.**
Years ago, her family sold baskets as a part of their income.

**Ihchat'ɛhchi tihchi, tigachihichi, tihtat'ɛhchi sinkri yɔlasitashi; hal'ukinish sihklɔhka tolu paluwan pitana'ara, inkniti.**
My great-grandmother told us that she, her mother, and her older sister would walk from their home to town with a bundle of baskets to sell.

**Hɛ'ɛsh, tihklɔhka riwantaha kichu mewitik'ahcha.**
Today, you will find baskets that my great-grandmother has made in museums.

**Kana inkonisɛma lɔhka mashukata?**
How do our people make baskets?

**Hɛ'ɛsh, lɔhka eksha tɛrashki mashuhkiti.**
Today, we make pine needle baskets.

**Hinahkushkan wantaha eksha tɛrashki chu'it'ɛhɛ.**
But we didn't always use pine needles.

**Wantaha, inkonisɛma ala chuta.**
Years ago, our people used cane.

**Kana inkonisɛma lɔhka ala mashuta?**
How did our people make cane baskets?

**Inkonisɛma tala kichu amina'ara; ala sama pohtuta.**
Our people would go to canebrake and cut cane that was ready for harvest.

**Ala, lɔhka mashuwan, ishu kiyuna'ara.**
They split and peeled cane to make baskets.

**Hinyatihch, ala hɔwashi sihuniwan uk'ɛnta.**
Afterwards, they placed the cane outside to dry.

**Tahch'i ala hotu sih'ɔtahch, lɔkha mashutashtuku.**
When the sun dried the cane completely, it was ready to weave baskets.

**Sahkuhta, ala meruta. Alatolu mashuta.**
First, they gathered the cane. They made cane bundles.

**Hinyatihch, ɔshkachehkini kichu talatolu, rut'ɛ el'ɔma rawuta. Pɔht'anta.**
Next, they placed the bundled cane and walnuts in a vat. They boiled them.

**Ala meli yakati.**
The cane would turn black.

**Ɔshkachehkini kichu ala yusaw'ama pohtatahch, ala kayi yakati.**
If they boiled cane in the vat with sugar maple, the cane would turn yellow.

**Ɔshkachehkini kichu ala hisaw'ama pohtatahch, ala mili yakati.**
If they boiled cane in the vat, with bloodroot, the cane would turn red.

**Lɔhka wilata.**
They wove baskets.

## Tetimili yoluyana

| | | | |
|---|---|---|---|
| **ala kichu** | *canebrake* | **ɔshkachehkini** | *iron pot* |
| **-hchat'ɛ** | *great-grandparent* | **rut'ɛ elu** | *walnut* |
| **hisawa** | *bloodroot* | **yusawa** | *southern sugar maple* |

## Tetimili wiralepini

1. There is one example of **hinahkushkan** in this **tetimili**. Can you find it? Now, rewrite it below using **-shkan**.

2. Do you have a tradition of making baskets or other objects in your family? Describe the process of making that object below in English, but using as many Tunica words as you can.

3. Reading comprehension: if you wanted to use natural dyes to make a black and yellow cane basket, what materials would you use? Answer in Tunica!

# Chapter 17: Saku

## *Food*

**TOPICS:**

## Taya korini ili

*Class II verbs (habitual)*

### Yoluyana

| | | | |
|---|---|---|---|
| **chiya** | *squirrel* | **-tahki** | *only; nothing but* |
| **hahka** | *corn* | **taya korini ili** | *class II verb* |
| **heru (II)** | *to steam* | **taya korini sahku** | *class I verb* |
| **ishu (II)** | *to shuck (corn); to strip (cane)* | **tishuma** | *meat* |
| **iyushɛla** | *possum* | **tomu** | *to pound; to mash* |
| **kotitapa** | *vegetables* | **wɛra (II)** | *to hunt* |
| **kuwa** | *duck* | **wi (II)** | *to listen* |
| **molu (II)** | *to fill* | **wira (II)** | *to ask a question; to count* |
| **pala** | *to trap* | **wishita'eri** | *pitcher; water jug* |
| **rɔhpa (II)** | *to roast* | **woru (II)** | *to teach* |
| **rushta** | *rabbit* | **ya** | *deer* |
| **sama (II)** | *to cook; to bake* | **yɛhtat'ɛ** | *turkey* |
| **suhpi** | *supper* | **yit'ɛ** | *potato* |

## Yanalepini

**Augustinku:** Suhpi samahkatani.

**Naomihchi:** Ko'o! Kanahku samahkwita?

**Augustinku:** Ya uhktishuma rɔhpahkatani. Kanahku sahu saku inkwana?

**Naomihchi:** Hahka, yit'ɛ, kotitapa wihkwanan?

**Augustinku:** Hon. Tahahka ishuhkhɛtan?

**Naomihchi:** Hon. Tayit'ɛpa tomunik'ahcha. Kotitapapa heruhkatani. Kanahku kɔra wihkwana?

**Augustinku:** Wishitahki. Wishita'eri moluhkatani.

**Naomihchi:** Ko'o! Ihkyahpa.

**Merlinku:** Hɛ'ɛsh imilasinima pala sinkworuhkatani.

**Naomihchi:** Kanahku palawitik'ahcha?

**Merlinku:** Rushta, chiya, iyushɛla pal'itik'ahcha. Imilasinimapa ya, yɛhtat'ɛ, kuwa wɛrahksinta.

**Naomihchi:** Lapuhch.

**Merlinku:** Kanahku yaka hɛ'ɛsh?

**Naomihchi:** Hɛ'ɛsh ehkusɛma lɔhka wila sihkworuhkatani.

**Merlinku:** Hehkusɛma hihkwihkantan?

**Naomihchi:** Hon, ihkwihkanta. Hishtahahki ihkwirahkanta.

**Merlinku:** Lapuhch. Hot'itihch, akuhpani sak'itiki!

**Naomihchi:** Lapu! Ayi wonik'ahcha.

## Lutamashu

In this set of **yanalepini**, many of the verbs use a different set of endings. That is because these verbs belong to a different class than the ones we have learned so far. Up until this chapter, the action verbs we have introduced are called **taya korini sahku**, or Class I verbs. Most of the verbs introduced in this chapter are **taya korini ili**, or Class II verbs.

Like **taya korini sahku**, **taya korini ili** use an ending to indicate the person (1st, 2nd, 3rd) and number (singular, dual, plural) of the subject. However, these **taya korini ili** endings are different. The habitual forms of the **taya korini ili** endings are given below.

| | | SINGULAR | DUAL | PLURAL |
|---|---|---|---|---|
| *1st person* | | **-hkatani** | **-hkinta** | **-hkinta** |
| *2nd person* | *feminine* | **-hkhɛta** | **-hkhɛnta** | **-hkhɛnta** |
| | *masculine* | **-hkwita** | **-hkwinta** | **-hkwinta** |
| *3rd person* | *feminine* | **-hkata** | **-hksinta** | **-hksinta** |
| | *masculine* | **-hkuta** | **-hkunta** | **-hkanta** |

Just like with the endings for **taya korini sahku** that you are already familiar with, habitual **taya korini ili** endings begin with **hk**. Compare the dual and plural forms; they are the same except for the 3rd person masculine dual, **-hkunta**, and plural, **-hkanta**. Note that all the dual and plural forms have an **n** before **ta**.

Also like **taya korini sahku**, **taya korini ili** can be **taya nahchu** and have objects. These objects are marked using the same prefixes for **taya nahchu** that we learned in Chapter 15. In fact, we already saw this in the **yanalepini** with words like **ihkwirahkanta** 'they ask me questions'. Here are some more examples of **taya korini ili**:

**Igahchihchi tihkwihkatani.**
I am listening to my mother.

**Robertku yɛhtat'ɛ wɛrahkuta.**
Robert hunts turkeys.

**Suhpi samahksinta.**
They *(fd/p)* are cooking supper.

Some verbs can be either **taya korini sahku** or **taya korini ili**, depending on their meaning. For instance, **woru**, when it means 'to teach', is **taya korini ili**. When it means 'to learn', it is **taya korini sahku**. Compare the following:

> **Luhchi Yoroni worukani.**
> I am learning the Tunica language.
>
> **Ihchahchi luhchi Yoroni ihkworuhkata.**
> My grandmother is teaching me the Tunica language.

From now on, **taya korini ili** will be indicated with **(II)** in the **yoluyana**, as well as in the glossary at the end of the book.

## Hinu 1

**17.1.1. Molɔtaki:**
Fill in the blank with the habitual form of the **taya korini ili** in parentheses. If more than one gender is possible, pick one for your answer.

***Example:*** *Inima kuwa* **samahkinta** *(sama).*

1. Taworuni luhchi Ispani __________________. (woru)
2. Hinima iyushɛla __________________. (wɛra)
3. Rosehchi __________________. (wi)
4. Hɛma yit'ɛ __________________. (sama)
5. Thomasku tishuma __________________. (rɔhpa)
6. Winima wishita'eri __________________. (molu)
7. Ma tashuhki __________________. (wira)
8. Ima igachihchi __________________. (wira)
9. Bertramku kotitapa __________________. (heru)
10. Tɔkasɛma hahka __________________. (ishu)

### 17.1.2. Atehpɛtaki:

Match the **taya korini ili** ending on the right with the **taya korini sahku** ending on the left that has the same person and number.

***Example:*** *a -kani* *a. -hkatani*

1. _____ -ku
2. _____ -hkiti
3. _____ -kati
4. _____ -hkwiti
5. _____ -hksiti
6. _____ -ka
7. _____ -ki
8. _____ -kata
9. _____ -hkuna
10. _____ -hkhina

a. -hksinta
b. -hkwita
c. -hkhɛnta
d. -hkinta
e. -hkunta
f. -hkuta
g. -hkwinta
h. -hkanta
i. -hkata
j. -hkhɛta

# Taya korini ili

*Class II verbs (completive)*

## Yoluyana

| | | | |
|---|---|---|---|
| **hahchu** | *salt* | **kapashi** | *chicken* |
| **hahkamuchi** | *bread* | **kohina** | *cup* |
| **hahkamuchitohkutaya** | *bread dough* | **maka** | *lard; grease; oil; fat* |
| **hahkatomu** | *flour* | **ɔndetishi** | *milk* |
| **hahkatomuyasha** | *yeast* | **pɔhta (II)** | *to boil (something)* |
| **heku (II)** | *to mix in; to stir up* | **suhpi (II)** | *to leave (bread) to rise; to soak* |
| **hishi (II)** | *to sift* | **wishiyimohku** | *tea* |
| **iyut'ɛ** | *pig* | **wista (II)** | *to sweeten; to tame* |

## Yanalepini

**Chrisku:** Merlin, lawushi kanahku sak'i?

**Merlinku:** Lawushi, Annahchi im'ama tishuma sam'inta.

**Chrisku:** Tishuman? Kapashi uhktishuman? Iyut'ɛ uhktishuman?

**Merlinku:** Kapashi uhktishuma.

**Chrisku:** Kanahku sahu samawinta?

**Merlinku:** Hahkapa sam'inta. Namu sak'ina!

**Rosehchi:** Igachi, wishiyimohku ihkwana.

**Alicehchi:** Lapu, wishi pɔhtahtani.

**Rosehchi:** Tohkuhch, ihkkohina molɔtatan.

*Alicehchi tihkkohina moluhkata.*

**Rosehchi:** Tawishiyimohku wistɛtan?

**Alicehchi:** Aha. Hinahkushkan uhkwistahtanik'ahcha.

**Rosehchi:** Tikahch.

**Daveku:** Hahkamuchi samahkwitan?

**Augustinku:** Hon.

**Daveku:** Hahkamuchitohkutaya suhpiwitan?

**Augustinku:** Aha. Hishtahahki tahahkamuchitohkutaya hekuhkatani.

**Daveku:** Kana hahkamuchitohkutaya mashukihch, hɛra ihkwana.

**Augustinku:** Sahkuhta hahkatomu hishihtani. Hinyatihch hahchu, maka, hahkatomuyasha, ɔndetishi hekuhtani. Hinyatihch uhksuhpihtanik'ahcha.

**Daveku:** Ko'o! Taka nisa ihkworuwita.

## Lutamashu

Just like **taya korini sahku**, **taya korini ili** can be completive as well as habitual. The completive forms of the **taya korini ili** endings are provided in the following chart.

| | | SINGULAR | DUAL | PLURAL |
|---|---|---|---|---|
| *1st person* | | **-htani** | **-inta** | **-inta** |
| *2nd person* | *feminine* | **-hɛta** | **-hɛnta** | **-hɛnta** |
| | *masculine* | **-wita** | **-winta** | **-winta** |
| *3rd person* | *feminine* | **-ata** | **-sinta** | **-sinta** |
| | *masculine* | **-uta** | **-unta** | **-anta** |

The completive **taya korini ili** endings are almost the same as the habitual **taya korini ili**, just without the **hk** in front. The exception is the first person singular, which is **-htani** in the completive, *not* **-atani**.

Because many of the completive **taya korini ili** endings begin with a vowel, the vowels blend in the same ways that you saw in Chapter 3. Here are some examples of completive **Taya korini ili** with blended vowels.

**Inima kotitapa pɔht'inta.**
We boiled vegetables.

**Tonisɛma tahahkatomu hish'ɛnta.**
The people sifted the flour.

Also, remember that if an ending that begins with **h** is added to a multi-syllable word that ends in a vowel, the **h** is lost and the vowels blend. This rule applies here to the endings **-hɛta** and **-hɛnta**. Since we have not yet seen vowel combinations where **ɛ** is the second vowel, here are the rules:

**i + ɛ = ɛ** **u + ɛ = ɔ**

**a + ɛ = ɛ** **o + ɛ = ɔ**

The following sentences demonstrate what words with **-hɛnta** and **-hɛta** look like.

**Hɛma tawishiyimohku wistɛta.**
You *(fs)* sweetened the tea.

**Hahka suhpɛnta.**
You *(fd/p)* soaked corn.

**Hinima tayit'ɛ hekɔnta.**
You *(fd/p)* stirred up the potatoes.

As described in Chapter 3, if an ending beginning in a vowel is added to a single-syllable word like **wi** 'to listen', the second vowel will blend, but the first vowel is not lost. Additionally, if **-hɛta** or **-hɛnta** is added to a single-syllable verb, then the **h** stays and the vowels don't blend.

**Sihkwihɛta.**
You *(fs)* listened to them.

**Uhkwi'ɛta.**
She listened to him.

Just like for **taya korini sahku**, the completive forms of **taya korini ili** are used to make the **taya waka** and future forms as well. As always, the **taya waka** forms take **-ki** or **-tan** and the future forms take **-k'ahcha**, as in the following examples.

**Takapashi rɔhpawintaki!**
You *(md)* roast the chicken!

**Tanuhchisinima hahkamuchi samasintak'ahcha.**
The women will make bread.

## Hinu 2

**17.2.1. Luhchi pirɛtaki:**
Translate the following into Tunica.

***Example:*** *We stirred in the oil.* ***Tamaka hek'inta.***

1. She cooked the deer meat. __________
2. He sifted the corn. __________
3. Roast the pig! *(to a woman)* __________
4. They *(mp)* sweetened the milk. __________
5. We will leave the bread to rise. __________

**17.2.2. Luhchi pirɛtaki:**
Translate the following into English.

***Example:*** *Tahahka ish'uta.* ***He shucked the corn.***

1. Hahkatomuyasha hekuwitan? __________
2. Iyut'ɛ wɛrɛta. __________
3. Wishi pɔhtahtani. __________
4. Wishiyimohku wistɛntaki! __________
5. Wihkkohina moluhtanik'ahcha. __________

**17.2.3. Molɔtaki:**

Change the **taya korini ili** from their completive forms into their habitual forms or vice-versa.

***Example:*** *Gracehchi taworusɛma* sihkwor'ɔta. ***sihkworuhkata***

1. Daveku, Merlinku, Augustinku ya wɛr'anta. ________________
2. Diamondhchi, Alicehchi hahka ishusinta. ________________
3. Hahkamuchi suhpɛnta. ________________
4. Hahkatomu hishɛta. ________________
5. Daveku, Augustinku tatishuma pɔht'unta. ________________
6. Chrisku hahkamuchi samahkuta. ________________
7. Clydeku hahchu hekuhkuta. ________________
8. Genesishchi kotitapa heruhkata. ________________
9. Rosehchi, Alicehchi, Lisahchi hahkamuchi suhpihksinta. ________________
10. Rosehchi, Chrisku, Augustinku wishiyimohku wistahkanta. ________________

# -ni

## Yoluyana

| | |
|---|---|
| **-ani** | *it is said* |
| **arhila (II)** | *to tell a story* |
| **hahkamuchitohkuwista** | *cake; baked sweets* |
| **hahpari (II)** | *to tell a lie* |
| **hichut'ɛ** | *eagle* |
| **huma** | *berry* |
| **humamili** | *strawberry* |
| **maru** | *to return* |
| **paka (II)** | *to reply; to answer* |
| **palu (II)** | *to sell* |
| **pira (II)** | *to become; to turn into* |
| **rahpa (II)** | *to play stickball* |
| **sɛkana** | *pecan* |
| **shihka (II)** | *to help; to assist; to aid* |
| **shihpi (II)** | *to drive (a vehicle)* |
| **shira (II)** | *to strain; to exert oneself* |
| **tehi (II)** | *to go around; to circle* |
| **teshu (II)** | *to eat breakfast* |
| **uru (II)** | *to whoop; to yell; to shout* |

## Yanalepini

**Chrisku:** Ima etisɛm'ama hɔwashi rahpaniwan amihkiti.

**Naomihchi:** Sakuhta teshuwitaki! Shiran'ɛhɛtan!

**Chrisku:** Teshuhtanik'ahcha, shirahtanik'ahch'aha.

**Naomihchi:** Ihkhahpariwitan? Ihkpakawitaki!

**Chrisku:** Aha! Hishtahahki hihkwihkatani.

**Naomihchi:** Lapuhch.

**Rosehchi:** Arhilani wini ihkwana. Tohkuhch, ihkarhilɛtatan.

**Alicehchi:** Ashuhki sahku, Tayoroni chɔhaku hichut'ɛ pir'utani. Hahchi hayishi uruhkuta. Lapuya wihkhɛtahch, kata tehihkutahch, herusa.

**Rosehchi:** Ko'o! Hatika! Arhilani sahu ihkarhilɛtaki!

**Alicehchi:** Hahkamuchitohkuwista samani ihkwana.

**Merlinku:** Ko'o! Hihkshihkahtanik'ahcha.

**Alicehchi:** Huma, sɛkana ihkwana.

**Merlinku:** Taritalapush sinklapuwan shihpihtanik'ahcha. Hihchi huma, sɛkana paluhkanta.

*Merlinku taritalapush shihp'uta, maruwi.*

**Alicehchi:** Sɛkana, huma me'in? Kanahku huma sihkara?

**Merlinku:** Hon. Humamili lapuni.

**Alicehchi:** Lapu, tikahch.

## Lutamashu

In Chapter 16, we learned Tunica uses verbs without any endings ('bare' verbs) to mean "to X," like "I want *to go*," or "she likes *to eat* bread." If you want to use **taya korini ili** in this way, it is necessary to add a **-ni** ending, which indicates that it's Class II. Take a look at the difference again between **woru (I)** 'to learn' and **woru (II)** 'to teach' in the following examples.

**Woru ihkwana.**
I want to learn.

**Woruni ihkwana.**
I want to teach.

The only way that we know that **woru** is supposed to mean 'to teach' in the second example is because of that **-ni** ending. We saw other examples of **-ni** in the **yanalepini** as well, like **Hahkamuchitohkuwista samani ihkwana** 'I want to bake a cake', and **Arhilani wini ihkwana** 'I want to listen to a story.'

These **taya korini ili** with **-ni** are also used in the same ways that bare verbs appear with **taya korini sahku**. To say 'in order to do X', **-wan** (see Chapter 16) gets added to the **-ni** form of **taya korini ili**, like in the following examples:

**Samaniwan maruti.**
She returned in order to bake.

**Wishi pɔhtaniwan chuyakani.**
I brought water in order to boil it.

**-ni** forms of **taya korini ili** are also used to form negative **taya waka**. Recall from Chapter 6 that negative **taya waka** involve adding **-ahatan** to a 'bare' verb, which for **taya korini ili** is the **-ni** form. There is no person or plural marking. Because **-ahatan** is always added to **-ni**, the endings together will always be **-n'ɛhɛtan**.

**Urun'ɛhɛtan!**
Don't shout!

**Hahparin'ɛhɛtan!**
Don't lie!

## Hinu 3

**17.3.1. Molɔtaki:**
Fill in the blank with the correct form of the verb given in parentheses. Consider whether the verb requires an object and what form it should take.

***Example:*** *Clydeku ima* ***ihkwini*** *uhkwana. (wi)*

1. Ima hahkamuchi ________________ ihksh'ɛpa. (sama)
2. Ima ________________ɛhɛtan! (paka)
3. Winima ihkwishiyimohku ________________! (wista)
4. Samuelku, Augustinku yasinima ________________ unkwana. (wɛra)

5. Esiku tishuma ________________wan yɔlawi. (rɔhpa)

6. Ma ________________ wihksh'ɛpan? (teshu)

7. Ayi kuwa ________________wan woni. (rɔhpa)

8. Winima uhkkɔra ________________ɛhɛtan! (shihpi)

9. Ehukumahchi ________________ ihksh'ɛpa. (shihka)

10. Igachitohkuhchi hahka ________________ tihkwana. (tomu)

**17.3.2. Luhchi pirɛtaki:**
Translate the following sentences into English.

***Example:*** *He stopped in order to listen.* ***Winiwan hapawi.***

1. Tahahkamuchitohkutaya kichu hahchu, maka hekuwitaki! ________________

2. Arhilani tihkwana. ________________

3. Tahahkatomu hishin'ɛhɛtan! ________________

4. Hichut'ɛsinima tehini sinksh'ɛpa. ________________

5. Wantaha teshuniwan wɛr'anta. ________________

**17.3.3. Luhchi pirɛtaki:**
Translate the following sentences into Tunica.

***Example:*** *I like to drive my car.* ***Ihkkɔra shihpini ihksh'ɛpa.***

1. Don't steam the vegetables! ______________________
2. He doesn't like to lie. ______________________
3. I enjoy exerting myself. ______________________
4. Don't answer it! *(to a man)* ______________________
5. How do you *(fs)* tame a chicken? ______________________

# Tetimili: Hahka Ɔshta

*Green Corn*

**Hahka Ɔshta** was one of the most important community celebrations for the Tunica-Biloxi people, as it was for most tribes of the southeastern United States. When the first corn ripened, each family harvested three to four ears of corn. This corn was used to prepare corn packets that would be brought to tribal cemeteries to honor deceased relatives and ancestors. Then each family brought the first corn to the cemeteries. The community came together to feast and to dance, to renew ties with family and friends, to forgive transgressions and to mend relationships. Tribal members met at the dance grounds and lit a ceremonial fire, **ayi**. Back in the day when people kept a fire going at home for cooking, for heat, and for heating water for baths and cleaning, the home fires were extinguished and the hearths cleaned out for **Hahka Ɔshta**. Homes were straightened up; trash and junk were discarded. People might also fast and/or take herbal medicines to cleanse their bodies. Everything was made ready for a **sihina** 'clean' start with the new corn.

People would gather at the dance grounds, **tahali hipu**; they would all join in for **punatarahpani** 'stickball games'. At night the dances began, and would carry on all night long. The dances opened with **Osin'ili Hipu**, the Double-Head Dance. The succession of dances continued through the night with animal and social dances such as **Yishi Hipu** 'Raccoon Dance', **Kapashi Hipu** 'Chicken Dance', **Hiki Hipu** 'Quail Dance', and **Tirishichɔha Hipu** 'Chief-Ahead Dance'. At midnight, the lead singer, who was often the chief, began **Lawutɛhkala**

**Hipu** 'Midnight Dance' and **Lawu Ahara Hipu** 'Daybreak Dance'. This was a time for the community to renew itself, to come together and celebrate the bounty of the corn harvest. At the end of the communal celebration, each female head of household would take an ember, **tɛnayi**, from the ceremonial fire with which to re-light the home fire.

The Tunica Tribe was an early ally of the French. The French dubbed this ceremony *Fête du Blé* 'Festival of Wheat', since it reminded them of the celebration in France for the first wheat harvests. As the Tunica people became less agricultural and more involved in wage labor, it became harder to participate in long festivals. The four- to eight-day **Hahka Ɔshta** celebration was reduced to a weekend affair and then gradually to private family celebrations.

The ancestors were and are an important part of the family. To honor them now, we take packets of parched green corn, carefully wrapped in husks, to family graves. Songs are sung to the ancestors, whose spirits (sometimes seen as birds) come to join their descendants in the celebration. The first corn harvest is a time of joy and celebration.

## Tetimili yoluyana

| | | | |
|---|---|---|---|
| **Hahka Ɔshta** | *Green Corn ceremony* | **Osin'ili Hipu** | *Double-Head Dance* |
| **Hiki Hipu** | *Quail Dance* | **sihina** | *clean* |
| **Kapashi Hipu** | *Chicken Dance* | **tɛnayi** | *ember* |
| **Lawu Ahara Hipu** | *Daybreak Dance* | **Tirishichɔha Hipu** | *Chief-Ahead Dance* |
| **Lawutɛhkala Hipu** | *Midnight Dance* | **Yishi Hipu** | *Raccoon Dance* |

## Tetimili wiralepini

1. This isn't the first time we've discussed corn in this textbook! What role does corn play in our culture and stories? Be sure to incorporate other times we've seen it discussed.

2. Pick one of the activities listed here (e.g., **punatarahpani**, **hipu**, cleaning the home, etc.) and write a few sentences as if you are someone participating in these events.

# Chapter 18: Ahkihtaku

## *Postpositions*

**TOPICS:**

## -hchan, -shtuku, -tohku

*must, can, little*

### Yoluyana

| | | | |
|---|---|---|---|
| **am'ilta** | *both* | **hiyu (II)** | *to wake (someone) up* |
| **aparu** | *sky* | **nisara** | *young person* |
| **hahkamuchitohku** | *biscuit* | **ɔndetishitɔrahki** | *ice cream* |
| **hali** | *earth; ground; land* | **-shtuku** | *can; able to* |
| **-hchan** | *must; have to* | **-tohku** | *small; little; young* |

### Yanalepini

**Rosehchi:** Shimi ihkwana! Hɔwashi shim'inaki! Tashuhki tashle, taparu ɔshta.

**Daveku:** Hɔwashi shiminishtuk'ɔhɔ. Yoyani yakani.

**Rosehchi:** Ka'ash shim'inashtukuk'ahcha?

**Daveku:** Sahkuhta ihkyoyani ya hotunihchan.

**Rosehchi:** Lapuhch. Wihkyoyani ya hot'ihch, shim'inashtuku.

**Daveku:** Lapuhch. Shim'inak'ahcha.

**Chrisku:** Ɔndetishitɔrahki sakunishtuk'ɔhɔ.

**Augustinku:** Kanahku? Ɔndetishitɔrahki ihkelu panu! Kaya uhksak'ishtuk'ɔhɔ?

**Chrisku:** Ɔndetishitɔrahki ɔndetishi kichu ura. Ima ɔndetishi sakunishtuk'ɔhɔ.

**Augustinku:** Ihkshpitu. Ima ɔndetishi sakunishtukushkan, ma uhksak'i'ɛhɛhchan. Hɛhahkamuchitohku ɔndetishi kichu ur'aha. Am'ilta uhksak'inashtuku. Ihkyahpa! Sak'inaki!

**Chrisku:** Hon! Hahkamuchitohkusinima sak'inaki!

**Rosehchi:** Hinisaraku uhkpo'ɔn? Satohku tashle uhkara.

**Aiyannahchi:** Hon, uhkpokani. Uhksatohku tahali hayihta rapuku.

**Rosehchi:** Tanisarakupa tashle. Uhkyan'inaki!

**Aiyannahchi:** Inima ya'in'ahahchan. Tasatohku hiyuni inkwan'aha.

**Rosehchi:** Hon. Uhkyan'inahchan.

## Lutamashu

To say "I must (do something)" or "I can (do something)," the endings **-hchan** and **-shtuku** are used. **-shtuku** is used to express one's ability to do something. See the examples below.

**Ima luhchi Yoroni yananishtuku.**
I can speak Tunica.

**Hiputishtuku.**
She can dance.

**-hchan** is used to express that one must or has to do something. This can also be a very strong **taya waka** 'command'.

> **Hɛma yɔl'ahchan!**
> You *(fs)* must leave!

> **Ashuhkitɛpan wishi kɔr'itihchan.**
> We must drink water every day.

In all of the examples above, **-hchan** and **-shtuku** come after the completive endings of the verbs. This same pattern applies for **Taya korini ili** as well.

> **Tihkhiyuwitahchan!**
> You *(ms)* must wake her up!

> **Luhchi Yoroni woruhtanishtuku.**
> I am able to teach Tunica.

In contrast, in order to say *I can't go to the store* or *You must not leave*, **-hchan** and **-shtuku** behave differently from each other. While **-aha** is added after **-shtuku**, it is added before **-hchan**. See the examples below.

> **Hiputishtuk'ɔhɔ.**
> She can't dance.

> **Ashuhkitɛpan kafi kɔr'it'ɛhɛhchan.**
> We mustn't drink coffee every day.

Unlike **-hchan** and **-shtuku**, **-tohku** primarily gets added to nouns and means 'little' or 'young'. We have already seen many words that use **-tohku**, although the meaning is more transparent in some cases than in others. Take a look at the list of words from previous chapters on the following page.

| | | |
|---|---|---|
| **satohku** | 'puppy' | **sa** 'dog' + **-tohku** |
| **palatohku** | 'point, goal' | **pala** 'a win' + **-tohku** |
| **Tahch'asap'aratohku** | 'November' | **tahch'a** 'sun' + **sap'ara** 'winter' + **-tohku** |
| **romantohku** | 'slowly' | **romana** 'heavy' + **-tohku** |
| **wiranitohku** | second | **wirani** 'minute' + **-tohku** |
| **ritaworutohku** | 'classroom' | **ritaworu** 'school' + **-tohku** |
| **pahitaniyutohku** | 'laptop' | **pahitaniyu** 'computer' + **-tohku** |
| **kuwatohku** | 'bird' | **kuwa** 'duck' + **-tohku** |
| **-hchatohku** | 'grandchild' | **-hcha** 'grandparent' + **-tohku** |
| **-gachitohku** | 'younger maternal aunt' | **-gachi** 'mother' + **-tohku** |
| **-esitohku** | 'younger paternal uncle' | **-esi** 'father' + **-tohku** |
| **hahkamuchitohku** | 'biscuit' | **hahkamuchi** 'bread' + **-tohku** |

**-tohku** can be used on any noun. This includes body parts, so **ihkenitohku** is 'my little finger'. Sometimes **-tohku** is not the last part of the word; for example, in **hahkamuchitohkuwista** 'cake', **wista** 'sweet' comes after **hahkamuchitohku** 'little bread'.

Gender number endings also come after **-tohku**; recall from Chapter 13 that 'my mother's younger sister' would be **igachitohkuhchi**.

## Hinu 1

**18.1.1. Pakɛtaki:**

Answer the following **aha/hon** questions for yourself. Include the full form of the verb in your answer.

***Example:*** *Yɔl'ahchan/Yɔl'ihchan?* ***Hon. Yɔlanihchan.***

1. Wor'ɔhchan/Wor'ihchan? ________________
2. Urɔtahchan/Uruwitahchan? ________________
3. Sak'ahchan/Sak'ihchan? ________________
4. Woy'ɔshtukun/Woy'ishtukun? ________________
5. Tɛwali lɔt'ashtukun/lɔt'ishtukun? ________________
6. Wɛrɛtashtukun/Wɛrawitashtukun? ________________

### 18.1.2. Molɔtaki:

Using **-hchan** or **-shtuku**, state what the following people must or can do. Be aware of which statements involve **Taya korini ili**! Whether you should use **-hchan** or **-shtuku** is indicated in parentheses.

***Example:*** *Tachɔh'unima – yama (-hchan)* ***Tachɔh'unima yam'unahchan.***

1. Taworusɛma – wi (-hchan) ________________
2. Tanisarasinima – sama (-shtuku) ________________
3. Ima – yana (-hchan) ________________
4. Ma – lahpi (-hchan) ________________
5. Tɔkasɛma ɔndetishitɔrahki – saku (-shtuku) ________________
6. Winima – shihka (-shtuku) ________________

### 18.1.3. Molɔtaki:

Change the following positive sentences into negative sentences.

***Example:*** *Wɛr'utahchan.* ***Wɛr'ut'ahahchan.***

1. Hahparihtanishtuku. ________________
2. Kotitapa pɔht'atahchan. ________________
3. Sihkhiy'intashtuku. ________________
4. Wihkyit'ɛsinima niranishtuku. ________________
5. Ayi wonihchan. ________________
6. Ritahɛrash yukatahchan. ________________

### 18.1.4. Pirɛtaki:

Add **-tohku** to the following nouns and then translate them.

***Example:***

| PARTS OF WORD | COMBINED WORD | TRANSLATION |
|---|---|---|
| *takohina + -tohku* | ***takohinatohku*** | ***the little cup*** |

| | PARTS OF WORD | COMBINED WORD | TRANSLATION |
|---|---|---|---|
| 1. | minu + -tohku | ______ | ______ |
| 2. | ya + -tohku | ______ | ______ |
| 3. | ihkɔka + -tohku | ______ | ______ |
| 4. | tihklɔhka + -tohku | ______ | ______ |
| 5. | ɔshka + -tohku | ______ | ______ |

## -po-, -hila-, -hapa-

*try, about to, already*

### Yoluyana

| | | | |
|---|---|---|---|
| **-hapa-** | *already; finished* | **taharani** | *fiddle; musician; singer* |
| **hara** | *song* | **tahi (II)** | *to string an instrument* |
| **-hila-** | *about to; almost; nearly; fixin' to* | **tishki** | *broth; soup; stew* |
| **honu** | *to come down (from); to descend; to recede* | **wichi** | *to climb; to mount* |
| **onrɔwahka** | *rice* | **yayi** | *to take care of; to save; to be saved* |
| **-po-** | *to try* | **yunka taharani** | *fiddle strings* |

### Yanalepini

**Alicehchi:** Henry, kanahku yaki?
**Henryku:** Hɛrihku wichipokani. Ihkshihkɛtashtukun?
**Alicehchi:** Hon, wihkshihkapohkatani.
*Henryku tarihku wichiwihch, honuku.*
**Henryku:** Tikahch! Ihkyay'ɛ.
**Alicehchi:** Awɛhɛ. Ma roman'ɛhɛ.

**Naomihchi:** Ima ritalapush yukilakani. Kanahku hihkwana?

**Aiyannahchi:** Yunka taharani nisa ihklap'ɔshtukun? Ihktaharani tahihtanihchan.

**Naomihchi:** Hara nisa hinilakan?

**Aiyannahchi:** Hon. "Tayoroniku Tahalayihkuku Onti Ya'una" arhilahtanik'ahcha.

**Naomihchi:** Lapu, hahchi amikani.

**Aiyannahchi:** Tikahch. Hita!

**Rosehchi:** Ihkyahpa. Kanahku saku inkwana?

**Naomihchi:** Kapashi uhktishuman?

**Merlinku:** Aha. Ima lawushi kapashi uhktishuma sakɔpani.

**Naomihchi:** Yanishi uhktishuma tishkin?

**Rosehchi:** Aha. Rapusahku yanishi uhktishuma tishki sakɔp'iti.

**Naomihchi:** Onrɔwahkan?

**Merlinku:** Aha. Ima kotitapa namu sakupokani.

**Naomihchi:** Onrɔwahka kotitap'aman?

**Merlinku:** Hon, lapuhch.

**Rosehchi:** Sak'itiki!

## Lutamashu

The endings **-po-**, **-hila-**, and **-hapa-** can be added to verbs to provide extra meaning about how and when the action is taking place. **-po-** means 'try to', while **-hila-** adds the meaning 'about to, almost, nearly, fixin' to', and **-hapa-** means 'already, finished'. Unlike **-hchan** and **-shtuku**, **-po-**, **-hila-**, and **-hapa-** come between the verb root and the endings that tell you who is doing the action. Look at the examples on the next page.

-po-: **Rapuponi.**
I tried to sleep.

**Rahpapohkuta.**
He is trying to play stickball.

-hila-: **Sakilaku.**
He is about to eat.

**Mehilati.**
She was about to search.

-hapa-: **Amεpati.**
She has already gone.

**Samap'uta.**
He already cooked. *or* He finished cooking.

Like with **-hat**, **-hiti**, and **-hεta**, the **h** in **-hila-** and **-hapa-** is dropped and the vowels blend together. For example, in **sakilawi**, the **u** of **saku** and the **i** of **hila** join to make **i**, while in **amεpati** the **i** of **ami** joins with the **a** of **hapa** to make **ε**.

If the verb that **-hila-** or **-hapa-** is attaching to is only one syllable (e.g., **ya**, **le**, **me**, **po**), then the **h** is not dropped. Even though the **h** sticks around, the first vowel of **-hapa-** will still change.

**Lehεpani.**
I already got lost.

**Pohɔpani.**
I already saw it.

**Yahapani.**
I already did it.

Because **-hapa-** means 'already', it can only be used with completive endings. However, as in the examples above, **-po-** and **-hila-** can be used with both habitual and completive endings.

These three endings probably look familiar; in previous chapters we saw the verbs **hapa** 'to stop', **hila** 'to move', and **po** 'to see'. **-hila-**, **-hapa-**, and **-po-** most likely came from these verbs, although in the case of **hila** and **po**, clearly there has been a change in meaning. The other difference between these endings and the verbs **hapa**, **hila**, and **po** is that these endings cannot be stressed. See Chapter 0 for more on stress in Tunica.

## Hinu 2

**18.2.1. Molɔtaki:**
Join these pieces together to make the correct verb form.

***Example:*** *hara + -hapa- + -siti* ***harapasiti***

1. mashu + -hila- + -a ____________________
2. kuhpa + -hapa- + -iti ____________________
3. tahi + -po- + -ata ____________________
4. pahchu + -hapa- + -wi ____________________
5. yama + -po- + -ni ____________________
6. hiyu + -hila- + -hkuta ____________________

**18.2.2. Chu'ɔki:**
Choose the correct English translation for the following Tunica sentences.

***Example:*** *Uhkyayipota.*
***a. They tried to save him.***
*b. They were about to save him.*
*c. They already saved him.*

1. Taharani tahɛp'ata.
   a. She finished stringing the fiddle.
   b. She tried to string the fiddle.
   c. She is about to string the fiddle.
2. Ɛhɛli teshil'anta.
   a. My family already ate breakfast.
   b. My family is about to eat breakfast.
   c. My family is trying to eat breakfast.
3. Tanisaraku uhkhiyupohkata.
   a. She already woke up the young man.
   b. She is trying to wake up the young man.
   c. She is about to wake up the young man.

4. Tayɛhtat'ɛ palilawi.
   a. He already trapped the turkey.
   b. He tried to trap the turkey.
   c. He almost trapped the turkey.

5. Tanisarahchi tahahka herɔp'ata.
   a. The young woman tried to steam the corn.
   b. The young woman is about to steam the corn.
   c. The young woman already steamed the corn.

**18.2.3. Chu'ɔki:**

Choose the correct Tunica translation for the following English sentences.

***Example:*** *I am about to cook the rice.*

***a. Tonrɔwahka samilahkatani.***

*b. Tonrɔwahka samapahkatani.*

*c. Tonrɔwahka samapohkatani.*

1. They almost strung it.
   a. Uhktahipo'ɔnta.
   b. Uhktahɛp'anta.
   c. Uhktahil'anta.

2. I tried to roast the duck.
   a. Takuwa tishuma rɔhpapahtani.
   b. Takuwa tishuma rɔhpilahtani.
   c. Takuwa tishuma rɔhpapohtani.

3. We already sold our car.
   a. Inkkɔra palil'inta.
   b. Inkkɔra palɔp'inta.
   c. Inkkɔra palupo'inta.

4. He is trying to climb that tree.
   a. Hirihku wichipoku.
   b. Hirihku wichilaku.
   c. Hirihku wichɛpaku.

5. They finished mixing the bread dough.
   a. Tahahkamuchitohkutaya hekupo'ɔnta.
   b. Tahahkamuchitohkutaya hekɔp'anta.
   c. Tahahkamuchitohkutaya hekil'anta.

# Tetimili: Rihku, yimohku

*Trees and plants*

Southeastern Native Americans obtain many resources from their local environment, including the trees and plants that grow in their territory. The land provides food, medicine, and other useful products. Plants even help the Tunica track time and the seasons, as can be seen in the Tunica word for the month of March: **Komelitahch'a** (lit. 'hackberry month').

Plants also serve religious purposes. The Tunica people were among the Southeastern Native American tribes that used to prepare 'black drink' for ritual consumption. Archaeological evidence has indicated that a primary ingredient of this beverage was **rihk'ɔsht'elutohku** (*Ilex vomitoria*, yaupon holly). This same tree still grows in the area today.

In former times, plants were also used by warriors in battle. One of the sturdiest trees in the region, **rurɔwa** (*Carya tomentosa*, white hickory), provided us with strong weapons known as **tarukɔsa**, which were hickory sticks stripped of bark. **Tarukɔsa** feature prominently in the *Tunica Texts*, used by the Tunica chief and another chief to fight to the death before becoming eagles (Haas, *Tunica Texts*, texts 8A and 8B, p. 72).

Trees and plants continue to play an important role in the lives of many Tunica-Biloxi people, and some younger tribal members have begun relearning uses for native plant species.

## Tetimili yoluyana

| | | | |
|---|---|---|---|
| **rihk'ɔsht'elutohku** | *yaupon holly* | **tarukɔsa** | *hickory sticks stripped of bark* |
| **rurɔwa** | *white hickory* | **yimohku** | *plant; herb* |

## Tetimili wiralepini

1. In this story we learned about different uses our Tunica ancestors had for local plants. Think about the plants around you today: what role do they play in your life? Is there any plant you use to mark seasons as we do with the **komeli**? Any plant you like to eat or drink?

2. Look at the word for yaupon holly: **ruhk'ɔsht'elutohku**. What are the different components of this word? What do they tell you about yaupon holly?

# Chapter 19: Nini sachihkuta!

*It's raining fish!*

**TOPICS:**

## Taya Tahch'i

*Feminine weather verbs*

### Yoluyana

| | | | |
|---|---|---|---|
| **ay'ɛhɛp'aha** | *before long; a short while; not long after* | **sehi** | *to rise (of the sun); morning; dawn* |
| **hemu** | *(the moon) to wax* | **tolu** | *full (moon); round* |
| **kashi** | *truth; true; original; real* | **tɔha (II)** | *(the sun) to pass the meridian* |
| **la** | *to set; to get to be night* | **wɛha** | *to be sunny* |
| **mira** | *to lighten up; to clear up (weather)* | **wɛka** | *(the moon) to wane* |

### Yanalepini

**Aiyannahchi:** Ihkyahpa.
**Chrisku:** Hɔwashi saku hihkwanan?
**Aiyannahchi:** Aha, wɛhakat'ɛhɛ.
**Chrisku:** Hinahkushkan, tɔhahkatahch, miratik'ahcha.
**Aiyannahchi:** Hon, kashi yanaki. Hɔwashi sak'inaki!

**Henryku:** Esi, po'iki! Tahch'a tolu!

**Osiku:** Hon, lawumihta hemuti.

**Henryku:** Ashutayi kashku tahch'a hemukati?

**Osiku:** Tahch'a ashutayi ili hemukati. Hinyatihch, ashuhki enihku tahch'a tolu. Hinyatihch, ashutayi ili wɛkakati.

**Henryku:** Ah, hahchi lapuya erusa.

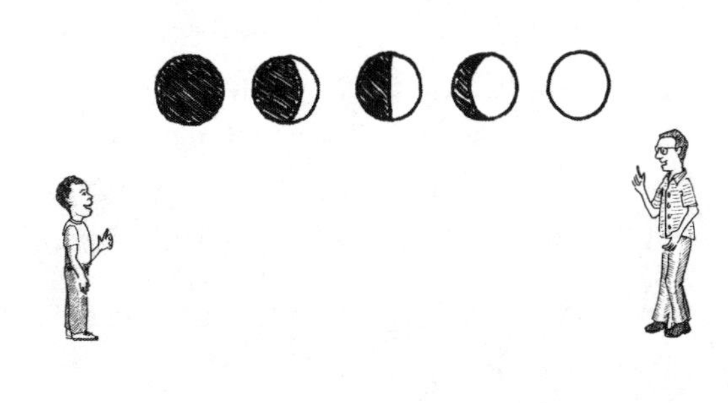

**Rosehchi:** Ima etisɛm'ama woruwan yɔlahkiti.

**Alicehchi:** Hinahkushkan lahapati!

**Rosehchi:** Erusashkan rowina namu po'itihchan.

**Alicehchi:** Hon. Hinahkushkan, sehitihch, taritaworush yuk'ahchan.

**Rosehchi:** Igachi, erusa. Ay'ɛhɛp'aha marunik'ahcha.

**Alicehchi:** Lapuhch.

## Lutamashu

According to traditional Tunica beliefs, weather and celestial phenomena are either caused by or represented by supernatural beings. **Tahch'i** 'the sun' is a young woman; when the sky clears (**mirakati**) or the sun rises (**sehikati**), we have her to thank. **Tahch'a** 'the moon' is also a woman; when we say the moon is waxing (**Tahch'a hemukati**) or waning (**Tahch'a wɛkakati**), we are talking about her. This is why the verbs that relate to the sun or the moon in Tunica always take feminine endings. This means there is no "it" here in Tunica, like in the English *it is sunny*. Instead, we would say **wɛhakati** 'she is shining'. These verbs are therefore called **Taya Tahch'i**.

Because these events are caused by certain beings (not you or me), they will only ever take the 3rd person singular endings. So for **tahch'i** and **tahch'a** weather verbs, they will always end in **-ti** or **-kati** if they are **Taya korini sahku** (e.g., **lati** 'it was night' or **sehikati** 'it is getting light') or **-ata** or **-hkata** if they are **Taya korini ili** (e.g., **tɔh'ata** 'it was afternoon' or **tɔhahkata** 'it is getting to be afternoon').

We have already seen a few examples of **tahch'a** and **tahch'i** weather and time words, which we can now recognize, like **sehitihch** 'at dawn; when the sun rises/rose', which is really **sehi** + **-ti** + **-hch**. Also in Chapter 4 we learned to use verbs like **tihkara** and possessives like **ashutayi tihkashuhki** when talking about days and months. Because months in Tunica are based on **tahch'a**, who is a woman, all the words for days and months involve feminine forms.

## Hinu 1

### 19.1.1. Chu'ɔki:

Choose the best answer in Tunica to describe what someone might be doing or what might be happening given the scenarios below.

***Example:*** *The visible part of the moon is getting smaller and smaller each night.*
***a. wɛkakati*** *b. hemukati* *c. mirakati*

1. The sky is light blue.
   a. wɛhakati b. lakati c. hemukati
2. The streetlights come on.
   a. sehikati b. tɔhahkata c. lakati
3. There is quite a bit of light outside, even though it's nighttime.
   a. mirakati b. tahch'a tolu c. tɔhahkata
4. Roosters are crowing.
   a. sehikati b. wɛkakati c. lakati
5. People are putting away their umbrellas.
   a. tahch'a tolu b. mirakati c. hemukati

**19.1.2. Pakɛtaki:**

Answer the following questions in Tunica to the best of your ability. Please write in complete sentences.

***Example:*** *Hahchi wɛhakatin?* ***Hon, wɛhakati./Aha, wɛhakat'ɛhɛ.***

1. Hahchi tahch'a wɛkakatin? ______________________
2. Ashuhki kashku tahch'a tolu? ______________________
3. Hahchi tɔhahkatan? ______________________
4. Tahch'i, tahch'a nuhchisiniman? ______________________
5. Kanahku wiranit'ɛ tahch'i sehiti? ______________________

# Taya Rahihta

*Masculine weather verbs*

## Yoluyana

| | |
|---|---|
| **huri** | *to blow (wind); wind* |
| **laka** | *to frost* |
| **mira (II)** | *to flash* |
| **mohti (II)** | *to snow* |
| **mɔcha (II)** | *to drizzle* |
| **nalu (II)** | *to hail* |
| **puhti** | *to be foggy* |
| **rahi (II)** | *to thunder* |

| | |
|---|---|
| **Rahihta** | *the Thunder Being* |
| **sachi** | *to rain* |
| **sapi** | *to beat down (rain)* |
| **shahu** | *to patter* |
| **tishi** | *to sleet* |
| **wihu** | *to blow gently (wind)* |
| **yowi (II)** | *to blow circularly (wind)* |

## Yanalepini

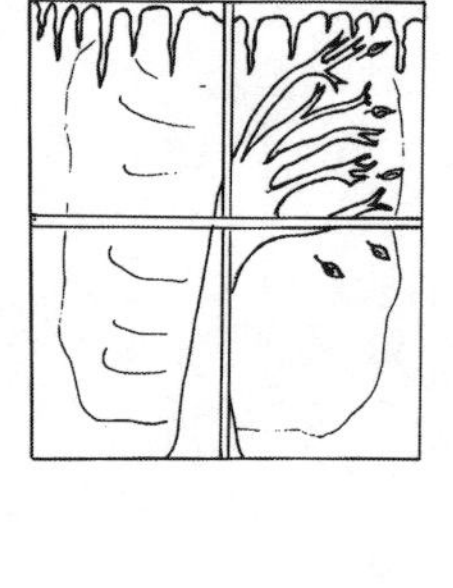

**Aiyannahchi:** Henry, tatishuhɔhka hɔwashi po'iki!

**Henryku:** Tahali po'ɔki! Lakawi!

**Aiyannahchi:** Hon. Huriku, mohtilahkuta.

**Henryku:** Hɛ'ɛsh taritaworush yuk'inahchan?

**Aiyannahchi:** Erus'aha. Naluhkutahch, taritaworush yuk'inak'ahch'aha.

**Henryku:** Lapuhch.

**Chrisku:** Kaya rahpapɛta?
**Rosehchi:** Sachiwi. Hahchi sapiku.
**Chrisku:** Rahihkuta. Taparushi mir'uta.
**Rosehchi:** Mɔchahkutahch, huri wihukuhch, inkrish mar'inashtuku.
**Chrisku:** Hon. Tari kichu uk'inaki!

*Merlinku Naomihchi tahaliwɛkash shihpihkunta.*
**Merlinku:** Shihpihtanishtuk'ɔhɔ.
**Naomihchi:** Kaya?
**Merlinku:** Lapuya ponishtuk'ɔhɔ. Tishiku.
**Naomihchi:** Tishik'ɔhɔ. Puhtiku.
**Merlinku:** Hiku wihɛtashtukun? Takɔra hayihta shahuku.
**Naomihchi:** Hon. Hinahkushkan, tishik'ɔhɔ. Tahuri yowihkuta.
**Merlinku:** Hinyatihch, shihpɛtahchan.

## Lutamashu

As we saw in the **yanalepini**, not all weather words are feminine. There are some weather events which in Tunica are considered to be caused by **Rahihta** (Thunder Being), who is a man. This includes most words for various forms of precipitation (rain, sleet, hail, etc.), as well as the thunder, since that is **Rahihta** personified. We call these verbs **Taya Rahihta**.

Because all of the words in the **yoluyana** above are considered to be caused by a masculine singular entity, they always take masculine singular endings. These include **-ku** and **-wi** for **Taya korini sahku** (e.g., **puhtiwi** 'it was foggy' and **huriku** 'the wind is blowing') and **-uta** and **-hkuta** for **Taya korini ili** (e.g., **nal'uta** 'it was hailing' and **mohtihkuta** 'it is snowing').

This means that when we use verbs related to the weather and time, we need to consider the gender of the supernatural being that is associated with them.

## Hinu 2

**19.2.1. Molɔtaki:**

Label the following weather phenomena as "**Tahch'a**" if they are done by the moon, "**Tahch'i**" if they are done by the sun, and "**Rahihta**" if they are done by the Thunder Being.

***Example:*** *nalu* ***Rahihta***

1. wɛka ________
2. huri ________
3. sapi ________
4. la ________
5. yowi ________
6. hemu ________
7. tɔha ________
8. puhti ________
9. sehi ________
10. mɔcha ________

**19.2.2. Atehpɛtaki:**

In the blanks below, put the letter of the verb with the best way to answer the question (multiple answers may be correct).

***Example:*** *Sachikuhch,* ***a*** *a. worukani.*

1. Miratihch, _____
2. Mohtihkutahch, _____
3. Latihch, _____
4. Naluhkutahch, _____
5. Rahihkut'ahahch, _____
6. Lakakuhch, _____

a. onimohti (snowman) mashukani.
b. woyukani.
c. ri kichu ukikani.
d. ihkrahpuntira yuru rahpukani.
e. hɔwashi shimikani.
f. rapukani.

## Tetimili: Ninisinima taparu kichu hopata

*When fish fell from the sky*

It is apparent that the cultural historical account of **Kosuhk'ariya** 'the Crawfish Shaman', from Etienne Chiki (William Ely Johnson) Gatschet's consultant in 1886, and the 1947 occurrence of the **Ninisinima taparu kichu hopata.** 'When fish fell from the sky – Falling of the fish' in the town of Marksville as reported by Ms. Eleanor Gremillion are not mere myths. The evidence suggests at least two documented occurrences of weather phenomena that occurred in the area, one at least as early as 1886, and another in 1947. It is possible that further instances occurred earlier and more frequently than those for which we have documentation.

**Kosuhk'ariyaku ɔmakaku.**
The Crawfish Shaman was a shaman.

**Kosuhk'ariyaku aparush uhki.**
He lived in the sky.

**Ushtahp'utush kosuyuwishi rah'aki.**
Rainbows were painted on his cheeks.

**Etienne Chikiku Albert Gatschetku uhkyanawi.**
Etienne Chiki (William Eli Johnson) spoke to Albert Gatschet.

**"Kosuhk'ariyaku taninitohku takosuhki shuhpawi," niwi.**
"The Crawfish Shaman sucked up little fish and crawfish," he said.

**Tahalish sinkpat'uta.**
He let them fall to earth.

**Haashchi Gatschetk'ɔma hurikorini taninisinima eri tapiwi, niy'una.**
Haas and Gatschet thought that whirlwinds took and lifted the fish.

**Tahch'awɛra 23, 1947 yukatihch, tonisɛma Marksville kichu hɛku pota.**
On October 23, 1947, the people of Marksville saw this.

**Ashuhkilahoni, nini tikasinima, ninitohkusinima taparu patasiti.**
In the early morning, many fish, big and small, fell from the sky.

**Tawohkusɛma taninisinima wishi Marksville rɔhpant hopisiti, nita.**
Fishermen said the fish came from waters near Marksville.

**Tonisɛma ninisinima sakutashtukɔni.**
The people could eat the fish, it is said.

**Eleanor Gremillionhchi poti:**
Ms. Eleanor Gremillion saw it:

> **"Tihika michu ilitɛya enihku ahak'ihch tihika michu ilitɛya manku ihkyukati.**
> "I was 23 or 24 years old then.
>
> **Hayina ihkri ahkihta ura. Ent'ira uhksowihkatani.**
> I was hanging clothes (on the clothesline) in the backyard.
>
> **Igachi, ihtat'ɛ ent'ira sahchisirana.**
> My mother and my sister were washing clothes.
>
> **Kanahku esini pɛkawi.**
> (I felt) something hit my head.
>
> **Tahali hayihta poni.**
> I looked on the ground.
>
> **Nini tika uhki.**
> It was a big (2½ to 3-pound) fish.
>
> **Ihkri tirishi hayinash yukani. Ninisinima namu patasiti.**
> I went in the front yard, and I saw the same thing. Many fish were falling.
>
> **Taninisinima Joffrionku, Sookie Royku, Brouillettekupa sihkpɛkasiti.**
> (as well as) Mr. Joffrion and Sookie Roy and Mr. Brouillette (on their way to work and school) were being hit by fish too.
>
> **Teliya ihkahashkan hihchi ahkini. Arhilahtanishtuku.**
> I don't have any pictures, but I was in it and I can tell you the story.
>
> **Hɛ'ɛrhilani tonisɛma namu tahal'ukini akurani yan'a'arani."**
> I told this story to many people all over the world."

**Lawushi taninisinima sach'utahch, Ariya Dr. James Nelson Gowanloch tipusayowin-isinima powi.**
Dr. James Nelson Gowanloch (a chief biologist for the Louisiana Department of Wildlife and Fisheries) noticed several dust devils the day before the rain of fish (Hutchins, Ross E. The Day it Rained Bass, 1957).

**Etienne Chikiku Albert Gatschetku hurikorini namu ɔ'ɔnasiti, uhkniwi.**
Etienne Chiki told Albert Gatschet that there were lots of whirlwinds.

**Ɔmakahchi Korintohku tetisahchi hurikorinitohkunahku pokati.**
The sorceress called Korintohku was seen as a "little whirlwind" (Haas, 1953).

**Tonisɛma Marksville kichu Times-Picayune uhktahinaku uhkyanana'ara.**
The people of Marksville spoke with a Times-Picayune writer.

**kapash'ohku, tishuma sakutashtuk'ɔhɔhch, ninisinima patasiti, nita.**
When they can't eat eggs or meat, fish fall, they said (Times-Picayune, October 23, 1947).

**Kosuhk'ariyanahku, Uhayishiku tonisɛma sihkshihkahkuta.**
Like the Crawfish Shaman, The One Above helps people.

**Kosuhk'ariya ninisinima kosuhkisinim'ama shuhp'uta; halihta sinkpat'uta.**
The Crawfish Shaman sucks up fish and crawfish, and lets them fall to earth.

**Kosuhk'ariyaku saku yuwaku.**
The Crawfish Shaman gives food.

## Tetimili yoluyana

| | | | |
|---|---|---|---|
| **hurikorini** | *whirlwind* | **kosuyuwishi** | *rainbow* |
| **Kosuhk'ariya** | *Crawfish Shaman* | **shuhpa (II)** | *to suck (something) up* |

## Tetimili wiralepini

1. In this story we hear about how Crawfish Shaman provided fish to Marksville! What parts of this story stand out to you?

2. What weather verbs do we see in this story? Who is performing them?

# Chapter 20: Yoluyana mash'itiki!

*Let's make words!*

**TOPICS:**

## Yoluyana nisa

*New words*

### Yoluyana

| | |
|---|---|
| **hara (II)** | *to play a musical instrument* |
| **henishi** | *lobby; reception area* |
| **huwa** | *to scrub* |
| **kɛrashi** | *farm* |
| **kunkuri** | *drum* |
| **naka** | *war; battle; warrior; soldier* |
| **shihpari** | *beans* |
| **shulihkitohku** | *squash* |
| **ta-** | *-er (agentive/instrumental)* |
| **taharanishuru** | *flute* |
| **tapa** | *to plant; to farm; a farm* |
| **tatapa** | *farmer* |
| **Uhayishiku** | *The One Above; the Creator* |
| **waka** | *to command; an order* |

### Yanalepini

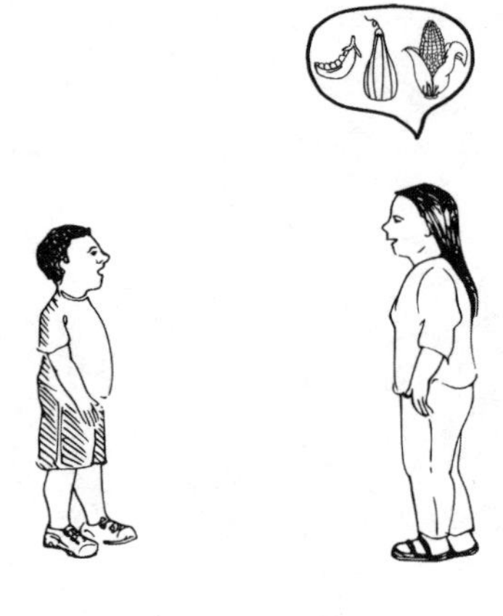

**Chrisku:** Kanahku yaka?

**Alicehchi:** Tapakani.

**Chrisku:** Kanahku tapaka?

**Alicehchi:** "Intasinima enihku" tapakani: hahka, shihpari, shulihkitohku.

**Chrisku:** Hɛma tatapahchin? Kɛrashi hehtinin?

**Alicehchi:** Aha. Ihkri ahkishi tapakani. Lapuya sakuwan tapakani.

**Chrisku:** Lapuhch.

**Aiyannahchi:** Merlin, kanahku yoyani yaki?

**Merlinku:** Ima taharaniku.

**Aiyannahchi:** Kanahku harawita?

**Merlinku:** Taharani, kunkunri, taharanishuru harahkatani. Hara sahku wini hihkwanan?

**Aiyannahchi:** Hon! Ko'o!

**Henryku:** Ma ihktawakakun?

**Daveku:** Hon! Ima wihktawakaku. Heni, nakaku!

**Henryku:** Hɛ'ɛsh naka wachihkitin?

**Daveku:** Aha, hɛ'ɛsh wachihkit'ɛhɛ. Uhayishiku tikahch uhkyuw'itiki!

**Henryku:** Hon. Kanahku wihkwaka?

**Daveku:** Tawolushi tahenish'ɛma huwa wihkwakakani.

**Henryku:** Hon, tawakaku!

## Lutamashu

Every language has ways to add words. Sometimes a word gets borrowed from another language (e.g., *pizza* in English comes from Italian). Other times, speakers of languages create new words, also called neologisms, for new items or concepts. This happens all the time in English, as we add new devices or as young people use the language in new ways. For example, 100 years ago, no one 'googled' anything, 'emailed', or said something was 'cool' if it wasn't literally cold. All languages add new words over time in this way.

There was a period of time between ca. 1920 and 2010 when Tunica was not being spoken every day. When we started speaking it again, we needed new words for many aspects of our modern world that didn't exist before. Here are just a few examples:

| | |
|---|---|
| **tawɛhani yuru** | 'laser' ('long light') |
| **kɔrahaluni** | 'tractor' ('field car') |
| **polunt'ɛ hayi** | 'million' ('old thousand') |
| **aparu muchu** | 'to skydive' ('sky dive') |

We can see that Tunica was also adding new words with the arrival of Europeans and their goods and foods on the North American continent. For example, we have words like **on-rɔwahka** for 'rice' (literally 'white man's corn') and **ahkalayihtatahinu** 'train' (literally 'on-the-level-mover') which Sesostrie Youchigant recorded with Mary Haas in the 1930s.

Now there are new Tunica words being created all the time. Every year, members of **Kuh-pani Yoyani Luhchi Yoroni** 'Tunica Language Working Group' and tribal participants hold sessions in which we create new words as new needs develop. If you participate in one of the tribe's immersion camps, you might get a chance to propose a neologism of your own!

All of the new words that have been added to Tunica have been formed through several regular processes. All of these processes are productive, meaning that if you stick to these ways of making new words, the odds are good that another Tunica speaker will understand you, even if they have never heard that word before.

First, it is a general property of Tunica that most verbs can be used as nouns. This should be familiar from English, since we can say both 'to run' and 'a run', 'to fight' and 'the fight', 'to google' and 'Google', without any change except using 'to' rather than 'a', 'the', or nothing at all. Many Tunica verbs can be used as nouns, either with no change to the word or by adding **-ni** for **Taya korini ili**:

| | | |
|---|---|---|
| **hipu** 'to dance' | → | **hipu** 'a dance' |
| **heni** 'to greet' | → | **heni** 'greetings' |
| **arhila (II)** 'to tell a story' | → | **arhilani** 'a story' |
| **wira (II)** 'to count' | → | **wirani** 'minute; time' |

Another way that verbs can become nouns is by adding **ta-**. We have seen **ta-** when it means 'the, a(n), some', but **ta-** can also be added to verbs to make agentive nouns, meaning the person or thing that performs the action. This **ta-** works like the English ending -er:

swim + *-er* = swimmer, someone who swims

jump + *-er* = jumper, someone who jumps

think + *-er* = thinker, someone who thinks

The Tunica equivalents of 'swimmer', 'jumper', and 'thinker' all use **ta-**:

**ta-** + **woyu** = **tawoyu**, someone who swims

**ta-** + **wɛsa** = **tawɛsa**, someone who jumps

**ta-** + **niyu** = **taniyu**, someone who thinks

If the verb is **Taya korini ili**, a **-ni** is needed at the end of the word as well.

**ta-** + **palu** = **tapaluni**, a seller

**ta-** + **rahpa** = **tarahpani**, a stickball player

**ta-** + **shihpi** = **tashihpini**, a driver

In Chapter 3, we learned that when **ta-** is used to mean 'the' on a word starting with a vowel, that **ta-** becomes **t** like in the word **toni**. However, when **ta-** is used to make an agentive or an instrumental it doesn't reduce to **t**. Instead, it appears as **ta'**. For example, you could make the word 'gambler' by adding the agentive **ta-** to the verb **ɔha** ('to gamble'), giving you **ta'ɔha**.

In addition to indicating the person who does an action, **ta-** is also used to make words for things that do the action. When it is used in this way, **ta-** is called an instrumental, since these types of objects often are tools or instruments.

**ta-** + **hina** = **tahina** 'pencil, pen, marker' (instrument of writing)

**ta-** + **po** = **tapo** 'glasses' (instrument of seeing)

**wishi** + **ta-** + **eri** = **wishita'eri** 'pitcher' (instrument of lifting water)

We have already learned a number of other words that take this **ta-**, some of which are neologisms, while others have always been a part of the Tunica language. Some examples are on the next page.

**ta-** + **nira** = **tanira** 'thief' (someone who steals)

**ta-** + **sahchuni** = **tasahchuni** 'glue' (instrument of attaching)

**pahi** + **ta-** + **niyu** = **pahitaniyu** 'computer' ('electric thinker')

At this point you may be wondering, since **ta-** is both 'the/an/some' and '-er', what happens when you want to say 'the _____ er', like 'the scissors' or 'the commander'? And how can you tell when **ta-** creates an instrumental vs. an agentive? For example, would **tahishi** be 'a sifter' like something used to sift flour, or the person who is doing the sifting? Also, isn't there ambiguity between 'the _____ ' and 'a _____ er', like **taharani** 'the fiddle' vs. **taharani** 'a/the musician'?

In response to the first question, it is not possible to have two **ta-** prefixes on the same word. So, for example, **tawohku** means both 'the hat' and 'a hat', using the same form. As for the second question, sometimes a word can be either agentive or instrumental! For example, **tahina** is usually 'instrument of writing', but 'writer', like the career, would also be **tahina**. The only difference would be that the writer would have a gender-number ending, like **tahinahchi**. To the third question, **taharani** is ambiguous between 'the fiddle' and 'a/the musician'; however, the person will have a gender-number ending to make it clear which is meant.

In addition to **ta-**, we learned in Chapter 7 that **-shi** can be added to nouns to mean 'at'. **-shi** can also be used to make new words, where it gets added to various types of roots to mean 'the place of _____ ', or 'the location where _____ is/happens'. For example, in the **yoluyana** we saw **henishi** 'lobby'. This is literally **heni** 'to greet' + **-shi** 'at', or 'the place of greeting'. We have already learned a few other words with **-shi** in Chapter 14:

| | |
|---|---|
| **kɔra** 'car' | **kɔrashi** 'garage' ('place of cars') |
| **woyu** 'to swim' | **woyushi** 'pool' ('place of swimming') |
| **ɔha** 'to bet; to gamble' | **ɔhashi** 'casino' ('place of gambling') |

The new word made with Verb + **-shi** is always a noun referring to a location or place.

## Hinu 1

**20.1.1. Molɔtaki:**
Make nouns from the following verbs and give the English translation. These nouns don't require a **ta-** prefix.

***Example:***

| *saku* | ***saku*** | ***food*** |
|---|---|---|
| VERB | NOUN | TRANSLATION |
| 1. niyu | ________ | ________ |
| 2. waka | ________ | ________ |
| 3. sara | ________ | ________ |
| 4. wɛra (II) | ________ | ________ |
| 5. uru | ________ | ________ |

**20.1.2. Molɔtaki:**
Using verb roots you know, form words that would mean the following.

***Examples:*** *a marriage* **kipa** *(< kipa 'to marry'); a skydiver* **ta'aparu muchu** *(< aparu muchu 'to skydive')*

1. A memory ________
2. A kiss ________
3. A bedroom ________
4. A mixer (device) ________
5. A helper ________
6. A scrubber ________
7. A stickball area ________
8. A trap ________
9. A hunter ________
10. A track (for running) ________
11. A sweetener ________
12. A lie ________
13. A hunting ground ________
14. A builder ________
15. A dressing room ________

**20.1.3. Molɔtaki:**

Given the words below, figure out what each could mean. If you think it could have more than one meaning, list all of them.

***Example:*** *tahipu* ***a dancer***

1. yoyanishi ____________
2. tahɛra ____________
3. tapita ____________
4. tarapa ____________
5. taworunishi ____________
6. tawohku (fishing) ____________
7. tatomu ____________
8. shimishi ____________
9. tarɔhpani ____________
10. tawini ____________
11. pahitaniyushi ____________
12. tahali (send, dispatch) ____________
13. tapɛka ____________
14. kuhpashi ____________
15. tawila ____________

# Compounding

## Yoluyana

| | | | |
|---|---|---|---|
| **arupo** | *to dream; a dream* | **takashimi** | *toy* |
| **ha (II)** | *to borrow; to lend* | **tapiheni** | *to shake hands* |
| **hɔhkaheluni** | *a hole; a depression* | **wiralepi (II)** | *to ask a question* |
| **huchilami** | *to tan (hides)* | **yanalepi (II)** | *to talk; to speak* |
| **sɛhapo** | *to examine* | | |

## Yanalepini

*Chrisku uhktakashimi shimiku.*

**Henryku:** Wihktakashimi ihkyuw'iki!

**Chrisku:** Aha!

*Henryku takashimi chupoku.*

**Henryku ugachihchi:** Henry! Hap'iki! Uhktakashimi wihkwanan? Sahkuhta uhkwiralepiwitahchan. Chrisku uhkyanalepiwitahchan.

**Henryku:** Chris, shimi ihkwana. Wihktakashimi ihkhawitatan, tohkuhch.

**Chrisku:** Atehpi shimi wihkwanan?

**Henryku:** Hon!

**Henryku ugachihchi:** Lapu! Tapiheniwinaki!

*Henryku Chrisku atapihenihkuna.*

**Aiyannahchi:** Alice, lawumihta arupo'ɔn?

**Alicehchi:** Hon! Ihkarupo kichu, hɔhkaheluni sɛhaponi.

**Aiyannahchi:** Kanahku po'ɔ?

**Alicehchi:** Kosuhkisinima hɔhkaheluni kichu woyuhksiti. Sinktapiponi.

**Aiyannahchi:** Imapa lawumihta aruponi. Ihkarupo kichu, ɛshkalahpi chɛra mashuwan huchilamini.

**Alicehchi:** Ko'o!

## Lutamashu

The third strategy for making new words in Tunica is called compounding. Compounding is when you put two or more words together to make a new word. The kinds of words you are using will determine the order in which they get put together. Here are some examples of compound words in Tunica.

**Noun + Adjective Compounds:**

| | | | |
|---|---|---|---|
| **onimahoni** 'Indian' | from **oni** 'person' | + | **mahoni** 'common, free' |
| **hɔhkaheluni** 'hole, depression' | from **hɔhka** 'hole' | + | **heluni** 'hollowed out' |
| **humameli** 'blackberry' | from **huma** 'berry' | + | **meli** 'black' |
| **elutɔrahta** 'orange' | from **elu** 'fruit' | + | **tɔrahta** 'bitter' |

In compounds with adjectives, the adjective always comes last. The resulting compound is a noun.

**Noun + Noun Compounds:**

In noun + noun combinations, the main noun is second. This is just like in English, where a 'snowball' is a ball made of snow and a 'mailbox' is a box for your mail.

| | | | |
|---|---|---|---|
| **ɔndetishitɔrahki** 'ice cream' | from **ɔndetishi** 'milk' | + | **tɔrahki** 'ice' |
| **wishiyimohku** 'tea' | from **wishi** 'water' | + | **yimohku** 'herb, grass' |

If one of the nouns is formed using **ta-**, then the **ta-** noun is second.

| | | | |
|---|---|---|---|
| **ritasaku** 'restaurant' | from **ri** 'house' | + | **tasaku** 'food' |
| **-hkenitamuri** 'ring' | from **-hkeni** 'hand, finger' | + | **tamuri** 'squeezer' |
| **lutamashu** 'grammar' | from **lu** 'tongue, language' | + | **tamashu** 'maker, builder' |

In all cases, the resulting compound is a noun.

**Noun + Verb Compounds:**

| | | | |
|---|---|---|---|
| **hahkatomu** 'flour' | from **hahka** 'corn' | + | **tomu** 'to pound' |
| **takashimi** 'toy' | from **taka** 'thing' | + | **shimi** 'to play' |
| **pirashu** 'birthday' | from **pira** 'to become' | + | **ashu(hki)** 'day' |

As with the other compounding types, noun-verb compounds are nouns. Although the noun usually precedes the verb, sometimes the verb can come first, like in **pirashu**.

**Verb + Verb Compounds:**

| | | | |
|---|---|---|---|
| **chuyaka** 'to bring' | from **chu** 'to take' | + | **yaka** 'to come back' |
| **tapiheni** 'to shake hands' | from **tapi** 'to grab' | + | **heni** 'to greet' |
| **yanalepi** 'to speak, to talk' | from **yana** 'to speak, to talk' | + | **lepi** 'to explain' |

While it is common for multiple verb roots to appear in the same phrase in Tunica, There are very few verb-verb compounds, where two verb roots regularly occur together and mean more than the sum of their parts. In some of these compounds, one of the two verbs never appears on its own; for example, **lepi** never appears without **yana** or **wira**, and **aru** in **arupo** does not have independent meaning. While most of the time these compounds occur with the verbs in a particular order (it is always **arupo**, never ***po'aru**), some of them can appear infrequently in the opposite order (e.g., **chuyaka** is more common than **yakachu**, although both are possible).

As a final note, just because something is a compound does not mean it is always written as one word. Sometimes a phrase is used to denote a single concept. For example, in English *ice cream* is a single thing; if it were truly a descriptive phrase, it would be *iced cream*. The same thing is true in Tunica, where sometimes several words are used to describe a single thing. Tunica is a very descriptive language, so often names for things are descriptions of them. For example, **elu kayi yuru** means 'banana' because bananas are long yellow fruits. Similarly, **chuhki ɔshta** means 'live oak', which is a specific type of oak tree rather than just any green oak. Whether something is written as one word or many words, the same processes lead to these descriptions becoming new words.

## Hinu 2

**20.2.1. Molɔtaki:**
Identify the pieces of the following compounds. What does each piece mean?

***Example:*** *humamili 'strawberry'* ***huma 'berry' + mili 'red'***

1. kosuwishi 'paint'

 ______________________________

2. Ashuki Tikahchyuwa 'Thanksgiving day'

 ______________________________

3. takayuwa 'gift'

 ______________________________

4. esimeli 'my godfather'

 ______________________________

5. hahkamuchitohkuwista 'cake'

 ______________________________

6. Rapusahku 'Monday'

 ______________________________

7. ritaworutohku 'classroom'

 ______________________________

8. Risep'ɛhɛ 'health center'

 ______________________________

9. laspikayi 'copper, gold'

 ______________________________

10. Tetirihku 'nature trail'

 ______________________________

**20.2.2. Molɔtaki:**

Using the words you have learned thus far, take a guess as to how you might say the following in Tunica. Provide a literal translation as well.

***Example:*** *zombie* ***osintalutasaku ('brain-eater')***

1. construction worker ______________________
2. weather forecast ______________________
3. cucumber ______________________
4. Valentine's Day ______________________
5. fireworks ______________________
6. football ______________________
7. calendar ______________________
8. mail ______________________
9. sweet potato ______________________
10. sundress ______________________

## Tetimili: Luhchi tihkyaru

*Tongue twisters*

Word games, including rhyming songs, puns, and riddles, are pastimes enjoyed by all ages in gatherings of family and friends. Brett C. Nelson created these **luhchi tihkyaru** 'tongue twisters' in Tunica.

**Tanakaku tanahkaku tanaka yaku.**
The warrior wages war on the butterfly.

**Tanahkaku tanakaku tanaka yaku.**
The butterfly wages war on the warrior.

**Tɔmakaku tɔmahkaku tanaka ya uhkmahka.**
The sorcerer loves to wage war on the alligator.

**Tɔmahkaku tɔmakaku uhkmahk'aha.**
The alligator doesn't love the sorcerer.

**Tɔmahkasinima tawishish laka.**
Some alligators live in the water.

**Ɔmahka sahku tawishi holahkaku.**
One alligator peeks out of the water.

**Tɔmahkaku nahka sahku poku.**
The alligator sees one butterfly.

### *Tatahkaku/Tahahkaku (The bat/The corn)*

**Tatahkasinima tamarɔha kichu laka.**
Some bats live in the mountain cave.

**Hahka halunish kal'ura.**
Some corn stands in a field.

**Tahka sahku tamarɔha holahkaku.**
One bat peeks out of the cave.

**Tatahkaku tahahka poku.**
The bat sees the corn.

**Tatahkaku tahahkash naraku.**
The bat flies to the corn.

**Tatahkaku tahahka kashkutohku uhkwahkaku.**
The bat breaks off a little bit of corn.

**Tatahkaku tahahka uhkmariku.**
The bat gathers the corn.

**Tatahkaku tawishi sakaku.**
The bat crosses the water.

**Tahahka tawishi kipataku.**
The corn falls into the water.

## Tetimili yoluyana

| | | | |
|---|---|---|---|
| **nahka** | *butterfly* | **tahka** | *bat (animal)* |
| **ɔmahka** | *alligator* | **tamarɔha** | *mountain cave* |

## Tetimili wiralepini

1. Challenge your friends and family to try out these tongue twisters! Which one is the hardest?

2. What Tunica words that you've learned have you found hard to pronounce? If you'd like, try to make your own tongue twisters out of them!

# Appendices

# Appendix A: Dialogue translations

## TOPICS:

## Chapter 1

**Aiyanna:** Hello! How are you *(fs)*?

**Alice:** Good, and you *(fs)*?

**Aiyanna:** Good thank you. What's your *(fs)* name?

**Alice:** My name is Alice. And you, what is your *(fs)* name?

**Aiyanna:** My name is Aiyanna.

**Alice:** Good.

**Merlin:** Hello! How are you *(ms)*?

**Chris:** Good, and you *(ms)*?

**Merlin:** Good thank you. What's your *(ms)* name?

**Chris:** My name is Chris. And you, what is your *(ms)* name?

**Merlin:** My name is Merlin.

**Chris:** Good.

**Merlin:** How are you *(fs)*?

**Aiyanna:** Good, and you *(ms)*?

**Merlin:** Good thank you. What's your *(fs)* name?

**Aiyanna:** My name is Aiyanna. And you, what is your *(ms)* name?

**Merlin:** My name is Merlin.

**Aiyanna:** Good! Take care!

**Merlin:** We'll *(d)* see each other!

---

**Merlin:** Chris, what's her name?

**Chris:** Her name is Aiyanna.

**Merlin:** Her name is Aiyanna? Good.

**Chris:** Good.

**Merlin** *to Aiyanna:* Your name is Aiyanna?

**Aiyanna:** Yes. My name is Aiyanna. Yours *(ms)*?

**Merlin:** My name is Merlin.

**Merlin:** Hello! How are you *(md/p)*?

**Alice and Augustin:** Good, and you *(ms)*?

**Merlin:** Good thank you. What are your *(md)* names?

**Alice:** My name is Alice. Him, his name is Augustin.

**Augustin:** Y'all two, you're named Alice and Albert?

**Merlin:** No, my name is Merlin.

**Augustin:** OK. We'll *(p)* see each other!

**Merlin:** How are you *(fs)*?

**Alice:** Good. Thanks!

**Merlin:** He is my friend. His name is Chris.

**Alice:** His name is Chris.

**Merlin:** Yes. What is your name?

**Alice:** My name is Alice.

**Merlin:** Great! Take care!

**Alice:** We'll *(p)* see each other!

---

**Alice:** Hello! How are you *(fd/p)*?

**Aiyanna and Naomi:** Good, and you *(fs)*?

**Alice:** Good thank you. The man, what is his name?

**Naomi:** His name is Dave. The women, what are their *(fd/p)* names?

**Alice:** Their *(fd)* names are Summer and Rose.

**Naomi:** Thank you.

**Augustin:** The men, what are their *(mp)* names?

**Chris:** Their names are Merlin, Nathan, and Winston. The women, what are their *(fp)* names?

**Augustin:** Their names are Alice, Rose, and Diamond.

**Chris:** Good thank you.

**Alice:** Naomi, the two people, what are their *(md)* names?

**Naomi:** The two people on their part, their names are Merlin and Alfred.

**Alice:** Good. And hers? The woman, what is her name?

**Naomi:** The woman on her part, her name is Cyndi.

# Chapter 2

**Aiyanna:** What are you *(fs)* doing?

**Alice:** I am dancing. What are you *(fs)* doing?

**Aiyanna:** I am singing.

**Alice:** You *(fs)* are singing?

**Aiyanna:** Yes, I am singing.

**Alice:** It is a good thing.

**Merlin:** What are you *(ms)* doing?

**Chris:** I am walking. What are you *(ms)* doing?

**Merlin:** I am running.

**Chris:** You *(ms)* are running?

**Merlin:** Yes, I am running.

**Chris:** It is a good thing.

**Merlin:** What is Chris doing?

**Aiyanna:** He is jumping. What is Alice doing?

**Merlin:** She is running. What are you *(fs)* doing?

**Aiyanna:** I am singing. What are you *(ms)* doing?

**Merlin:** I am sleeping.

**Aiyanna:** It is a good thing.

**Aiyanna:** What are Chris, Merlin, and Dave doing?

**Alice:** They *(mp)* are eating.

**Aiyanna:** What are Augustin, Henry, and Clyde doing?

**Alice:** They *(mp)* are swimming.

**Aiyanna:** It is a good thing.

**Merlin, Chris, Dave:** What are you *(fp)* doing?

**Aiyanna, Alice, Rose:** We are laughing. What are you *(mp)* doing?

**Merlin, Chris, Dave:** We are playing.

**Aiyanna, Alice, Rose:** You *(mp)* are playing?

**Merlin, Chris, Dave:** Yes, we are playing.

**Aiyanna, Alice, Rose:** It is a good thing.

**Merlin:** What are Alice, Aiyanna, and Rose doing?

**Chris:** They *(fp)* are swimming.

**Merlin:** Are they *(fp)* laughing?

**Chris:** No, they *(fp)* are swimming.

**Merlin:** It is a good thing.

---

**Naomi:** What are you *(md)* doing?

**Chris, Augustin:** We *(md)* are thinking.

**Naomi:** You *(md)* are writing?

**Chris, Augustin:** No, we *(md)* are thinking. What are you *(fs)* doing?

**Naomi:** I am bathing.

**Chris, Augustin:** It is a good thing.

**Merlin, Naomi:** What are you *(fd)* doing?

**Alice, Rose:** We are fighting. What are you *(md)* doing?

**Merlin, Naomi:** We are writing.

**Alice, Rose:** You *(md)* are writing?

**Merlin, Naomi:** Yes we are writing.

**Alice, Rose:** It is a good thing.

**Merlin:** What are Chris and Henry doing?

**Aiyanna:** They *(md)* are eating. What are Rose and Alice doing?

**Merlin:** They *(fd)* are thinking. What are Dave and Anna doing?

**Aiyanna:** They *(md)* are crying.

**Merlin:** They *(md)* are crying?

**Aiyanna:** Yes, they *(md)* are crying.

**Merlin:** That's not good.

# Chapter 3

**Aiyanna:** What did Chris do?

**Merlin:** He drank. What did Diamond do?

**Aiyanna:** She prayed.

**Merlin:** She prayed?

**Aiyanna:** Yes, she prayed.

**Merlin:** It is a good thing.

**Merlin:** What did you *(fs)* do yesterday?

**Naomi:** I walked. What did you *(ms)* do yesterday?

**Merlin:** I fell yesterday.

**Naomi:** You fell?! Not good.

**Augustin:** Dave, are you departing? You arrived yesterday!

**Dave:** Yes, sorry. I slept well!

**Augustin:** It is a good thing. For my part, I slept well yesterday.

**Dave:** Thank you. I am going!

---

**Aiyanna:** What did you *(mp)* do day before yesterday?

**Chris, Merlin, Augustin:** We got lost day before yesterday.

**Aiyanna:** You *(mp)* got lost? Sorry. I went back to our house the day before yesterday.

**Chris, Merlin, Augustin:** What did Diamond, Summer, and Genesis do the day before yesterday?

**Aiyanna:** They talked, they combed their hair. It is a good thing.

**Rose, Naomi, Aiyanna:** What did Chris, Merlin, and Henry do?

**Alice, Diamond, Lisa:** They *(mp)* talked. What did you *(fp)* do?

**Rose, Naomi, Aiyanna:** We got lost. We did not enter our home. Did you *(fp)* drink yesterday?

**Alice, Diamond, Lisa:** No, we *(p)* prayed.

**Rose, Naomi, Aiyanna:** It is a good thing.

---

**Aiyanna, Rose:** Did you *(md)* work yesterday?

**Merlin, Chris:** Yes, we *(d)* worked yesterday. What did you *(fd)* do yesterday?

**Aiyanna, Rose:** We *(d)* studied yesterday.

**Merlin, Chris:** It is a good thing. Did you *(fd)* finish?

**Aiyanna, Rose:** No. Did you *(md)* finish?

**Merlin, Chris:** Yes, it is a good thing.

**Augustin:** What did Aiyanna and Alice do day before yesterday?

**Rose:** They *(fd)* left. They stopped, and they didn't work.

**Augustin:** Did Chris and Dave leave?

**Rose:** No Chris and Dave remained.

**Augustin:** It is a good thing.

# Chapter 4

**Bill:** How old are you *(fs)*?

**Aiyanna:** I am 13 years old. And you *(ms)*, how old are you?

**Bill:** I am 99 years old.

**Aiyanna:** Many years! It is a good thing!

**Alice:** How old are you *(ms)*?

**Dave:** I am 47 years old. And you *(fs)*, how old are you?

**Alice:** I am 38 years old!

**Dave:** It is a good thing! Summer, on her part, how old is she?

**Alice:** She is 26 years old. James, on his part, how old is he?

**Dave:** He is 25 years old.

**Naomi:** Augustin, how much is three plus five?

**Augustin:** Eight.

**Naomi:** Yes. Eight. Rose, how much is ten minus one?

**Rose:** Nine.

**Naomi:** Yes. Nine. Merlin, how many is four times four?

**Merlin:** Fourteen.

**Naomi:** No. Not fourteen. Alice, how many?

**Alice:** Four times four equals sixteen.

**Naomi:** Yes. It equals sixteen. Merlin, how many is fifteen divided by three?

**Merlin:** It equals five.

**Naomi:** Yes. It equals five.

---

**Merlin:** What was the name of the first Tunica-Biloxi chief?

**Rose:** I think it was Chief Paul.

**Merlin:** Aaaaa. Was Brides les Boeufs the second chief?

**Rose:** No. Brides les Boeufs was the third chief.

**Merlin:** Which chief was second?

**Rose:** Cahura Joligo was the second chief.

**Merlin:** We *(d/p)* have many Tunica chiefs!

---

**Naomi:** During what month do we *(p)* dance?

**Alice:** We *(p)* dance during May.

**Naomi:** What months do we *(p)* swim?

**Alice:** We *(p)* swim in June, July, and August.

**Chris:** How old are you *(ms)*? In what month is your *(ms)* birthday?

**Augustin:** I'm 99 years old. My birthday is August 24. And you *(ms)*?

**Chris:** I'm 11 years old. My birthday is in December.

**Aiyanna:** What month has twenty-eight days?

**Merlin:** February has twenty-eight days.

**Aiyanna:** What months have thirty-one days?

**Merlin:** January, March, May, July, August, October, and December have thirty-one days.

**Chris:** How many days does a week have?

**Augustin:** It has seven days.

**Chris:** What is the first day of the week called?

**Augustin:** It is called Sunday.

# Chapter 5

**Dave:** What are you looking at, Naomi?

**Naomi:** I found a cat.

**Dave:** I don't see a cat.

**Naomi:** I'm pointing at the cat.

**Dave:** I see the cat!

*Dave grabs a branch, and he brings it over. When the cat grabs the branch, Dave grabs the cat.*

*Naomi grabs the cat.*

**Naomi:** Thank you, Dave!

**Rose:** Hi, Augustin! What are you doing?

**Augustin:** I'm eating food. I'm drinking water. What are you doing? Are you reading?

**Rose:** No, I'm writing a story.

**Augustin:** Great!

**Rose:** In the story a man and a dog are playing. The man grabs a ball and he throws it. The dog sees a cat, he doesn't watch the ball. The man points at the ball. The dog didn't find the ball.

**Augustin:** That's a good story!

**Rose:** Thank you.

## Chapter 6

**Alice:** Let's go!

**Merlin:** Yes! Henry, watch the dog!

**Henry:** I am watching the dog.

**Merlin:** Study!

**Henry:** Yes, I am studying.

**Merlin:** Good. When you finish, sleep well!

**Henry:** Yes. Leave!

**Merlin:** We are leaving. Alice, look for a book!

**Alice:** I found a book.

**Merlin:** Good, bring the book! Let's leave!

**Dave:** Enter! Open the door!

**Chris, Naomi:** Thank you. Let's play!

**Dave:** No, I am working today. Come back tomorrow!

**Chris, Naomi:** Awww, that's not good.

**Dave:** When you leave, close the door! Let's play tomorrow!

---

**Teacher:** Grab some paper! Students, write the words, please: Practice, Work, Book…

*The students write. They finish.*

**Teacher:** Great! Aiyanna, grab the papers please.

**Aiyanna:** Yes. I am doing it.

**Teacher:** Thank you!

**Naomi:** Chris, open the door, please.

**Chris:** Say it again, please?

**Naomi:** Open the door!

**Chris:** I am coming.

**Naomi:** Now!

---

**Robber:** Don't move! I'm taking the money.

**Teller:** No! Don't take the money!

**Robber:** Open it!

**Teller:** I am not moving! Leave the bank! Men are on their way.

*The men enter the bank.*

**Robber:** I am leaving!

**Alice:** Chris, what are you doing?

**Chris:** I am throwing food.

**Alice:** Don't do that! Eat the food!

**Chris:** I am not eating it!

*Chris throws food. Then Henry and Chris fight.*

**Alice:** This is not good! Don't fight! Stop!

**Henry:** Chris did it.

**Alice:** Chris, say "sorry!"

**Chris:** Sorry, Henry.

**Alice:** Good.

# Chapter 7

**Teacher:** What will you do in the summer, Alice?

**Alice:** In the summer I will read every day.

**Teacher:** How many books will you read?

**Alice:** Thirty-five.

**Teacher:** What will you read first?

**Alice:** First I will read *Harry Potter*.

**Teacher:** It is a good thing. And you, Dave, what will you do in the summer?

**Dave:** For my part, I will swim every day.

**Teacher:** Where will you swim?

**Dave:** I will swim in the pond.

**Teacher:** It is a good thing. Aiyanna, what will you?

**Aiyanna:** I will go to the powwow. I will dance and I will sing.

**Teacher:** It is a good thing. And you, Rose, what will you do?

**Rose:** I will play ball.

**Teacher:** And you, Chris, what will you do?

**Chris:** For my part, I will sleep.

**Naomi:** What will Alice, Aiyanna, Chris, and Dave do tonight?

**Augustin:** Tonight they will play ball.

**Naomi:** Will Rose and Lisa play ball?

**Augustin:** No, Rose and Lisa will not play ball. Tonight they will stay at home. And you, will you play ball tonight?

**Naomi:** No! Tonight Merlin and I will dance at the powwow. And you?

**Augustin:** As for me, I will not dance. I will sing at the powwow.

**Naomi:** It is a good thing!

---

**Augustin:** Naomi, Rose, what will you be doing for New Year's?

**Naomi, Rose:** We are going to Times Square. We will be dancing!

**Augustin:** I am also going to Times Square!

**Naomi, Rose:** Great! Let's meet up! We will all dance!

**Augustin:** It is a good thing!

**Aiyanna:** What will we be doing tonight?

**Alice:** First we will eat. Second we will read. Third we will play in the woods.

**Aiyanna:** As for Chris, what will he be doing?

**Alice:** He will be playing ball.

**Aiyanna:** Yes, he brought stickball sticks.

*Aiyanna, Alice, Dave, and Chris meet.*

**Alice:** What will you two be doing tonight?

**Dave, Chris:** We will be playing ball. And you two?

**Alice:** We will eat. Then we will read, and we will play.

**Chris:** Will you two not play ball also?

**Aiyanna:** It is a good thing. Let us all play each other!

**Chris:** Great! We will play each other. Come on!

## Chapter 8

**Alice:** Aiyanna, what are they doing?

**Aiyanna:** They are playing ball.

**Alice:** Who is winning?

**Aiyanna:** We for our part are winning!

**Alice:** How many points?

**Aiyanna:** Six.

**Alice:** And the others? How many points?

**Aiyanna:** Four. The players are playing ball well.

**Alice:** Very good. Let's win!

**Rose:** Where are you going?

**Chris:** I am going to the powwow.

**Rose:** Why?

**Chris:** I am dancing today!

**Rose:** Good! How will you go?

**Chris:** Merlin and I will walk.

**Rose:** When will you go?

**Chris:** We will go tonight.

**Rose:** Go quickly! Merlin walks slowly.

**Chris:** Yes. We will go quickly.

---

**Naomi:** Dave, how are you?

**Dave:** Not good. I'm angry.

**Naomi:** Why are you angry?

**Dave:** Henry and Aiyanna left. I'm lonely.

**Naomi:** You are not pitiable. Come on! Let's play!

**Dave:** I don't want to. I'm tired.

**Naomi:** Now I'm sad.

**Dave:** That's not good. Let's play!

**Alice:** Aiyanna! I have a sweetheart! His name is Samuel. He's smart, he's respectful. I'm happy and I'm in love.

**Aiyanna:** Great!

**Alice:** And you?

**Aiyanna:** I don't have a sweetheart. Yesterday I met up with Fred. He's rude. I don't like him.

**Alice:** Sorry, that's not good.

**Naomi:** Aiyanna, you're very cold. I'm curious; why are you cold?

**Aiyanna:** I'm in poor health.

**Naomi:** Why are you in poor health?

**Aiyanna:** I slept in the woods last night.

**Naomi:** You poor thing.

---

**Aiyanna:** Do you know him?

**Chris:** Yes, I know him.

**Aiyanna:** What is his name?

**Chris:** His name is Samuel. He is widowed.

**Aiyanna:** Sorry. Do you know where he resides?

**Chris:** He owns a house in the village.

**Aiyanna:** Ah, I know him. He is old.

**Chris:** Yes. He is 90 years old.

**Aiyanna:** It is a good thing.

**Augustin:** I am hungry. Let's eat!

**Naomi:** Yes, I'm hungry too. And I'm thirsty.

**Augustin:** Come on! Are you clothed?

**Naomi:** No, I'm not clothed!

**Augustin:** Why are you not clothed?

**Naomi:** I forget. Just a second!

**Augustin:** I am going, I don't have time. When you are clothed, we will eat.

**Naomi:** I'm ashamed...I will find my clothes.

## Chapter 9

**Rose:** I'm studying.

**Alice:** Me too. I'm writing many pages.

**Rose:** I'm not. I am studying on this computer.

**Alice:** I want a computer.

**Rose:** The school has many computers.

*The teacher enters the classroom. She turns on the lights. The students enter. They sit down.*

**Teacher:** Today we will make paper dolls. Grab the paper, pens, crayons, glue and scissors!

*The students run to the table. They make paper dolls.*

**Teacher:** Henry, do you want stickers?

**Henry:** Yes. I want lots of stickers.

*The teacher looks for the stickers.*

**Henry:** That sticker over there fell.

**Teacher:** This sticker?

**Henry:** Yes.

*The teacher grabs the sticker.*

**Henry:** Thank you!

**Augustin:** What time is it?

**Merlin:** I don't know.

*Merlin looks at the clock above the whiteboard. He points.*

**Merlin:** Look! It's 5 o'clock.

**Augustin:** That clock isn't correct. Look at this clock!

**Merlin:** Hmm, it's 7 o'clock on that clock.

**Augustin:** Yes, that's correct.

---

**Augustin:** Who is that way over there?

**Naomi:** That over there is the teacher.

**Augustin:** Who are those people?

**Naomi:** Those are the students. They are sitting in chairs, and writing in notebooks on the desks.

**Augustin:** Those (kids) are laughing. It is a good thing.

**Aiyanna:** Those two, what are they doing?

**Merlin:** Those two are watching TV.

**Aiyanna:** These two, are they watching TV?

**Merlin:** No, these two are talking on the phone.

**Aiyanna:** Why? Are they working?

**Merlin:** Yes.

---

**Teacher:** What is this called?

**Students:** That is a laptop.

**Teacher:** Yes. Those (things) on the desk, what are they called?

**Students:** They are called tablets.

**Teacher:** That over there above the door, what's that called?

**Students:** That is called a picture.

**Teacher:** Good!

*The students are playing in the classroom. The teacher comes in.*

**Teacher:** Sit on that bench!

*The students sit.*

**Teacher:** Grab pencils, erasers, and calculators! Aiyanna, write on the board!

*Aiyanna goes to the board.*

**Teacher:** Grab these notebooks! Clyde, please read the first story. Aiyanna, write the story in Tunica!

**Aiyanna, Clyde:** Great!

# Chapter 10

**Merlin:** What color is this crawfish?

**Chris:** That crawfish is red.

**Merlin:** Is this black?

**Chris:** No. The crawfish is red.

**Merlin:** It is a good thing. I will eat the crawfish!

**Chris:** Look! That bird there is red, like the crawfish.

**Merlin:** Yes. Like the crawfish.

**Aiyanna:** What color is this banana?

**Alice:** This banana is yellow.

**Aiyanna:** Thank you. That cat, what color is it?

**Alice:** That cat is gray.

**Aiyanna:** Which cat is sleeping?

**Alice:** That black cat is sleeping.

**Aiyanna:** Thank you.

**Aiyanna:** That blue jay is singing. What color is it?

**Alice:** The blue jay is blue. What color is that cow?

**Aiyanna:** That cow is spotted. Are blue jays striped?

**Alice:** Yes. Are cats multi-colored?

**Aiyanna:** Yes, cats are multi-colored.

**Merlin:** What color is the tree?

**Chris:** The tree is green, and its bark is brown.

**Merlin:** Thank you. What color is the mushroom?

**Chris:** That is brown!

**Merlin:** Thank you.

**Merlin:** I built a fire. Look! What color is it?

**Chris:** It is red.

**Merlin:** Yes. The smoke, on its part, is it red?

**Chris:** No. The smoke is gray.

**Merlin:** What are you eating?

**Aiyanna:** I am eating an orange.

**Merlin:** What color are oranges?

**Aiyanna:** Oranges are orange.

**Merlin:** It is a good thing.

---

**Augustin:** What are their names?

**Alice:** Their names are Merlin and Henry.

**Augustin:** Which is the tall one?

**Alice:** Merlin is tall.

**Augustin:** Henry is the short one?

**Alice:** Yes. Henry is short.

**Chris:** Is that desk heavy?

**Merlin:** No. This desk is light.

**Chris:** But the desk is big!

**Merlin:** The desk is empty.

**Naomi:** Those two, what are they called?

**Aiyanna:** This is a computer, and that is a laptop.

**Naomi:** Is the computer small?

**Aiyanna:** No, the laptop is small.

**Naomi:** Is this laptop new?

**Aiyanna:** Yes.

**Naomi:** As for that computer, is it new?

**Aiyanna:** No, this computer is old.

**Alice:** That cow is beautiful!

**Merlin:** Yes. That cow is beautiful, black, and soft.

**Alice:** This bench is hard and flat.

**Marlin:** And ugly! It's brown-colored.

**Alice:** Yep. Not good.

## Chapter 11

**Diamond:** Aiyanna, your dress is beautiful! I like your headband. Where did you buy your headband?

**Aiyanna:** I bought my headband at the store. Where did you buy your sunglasses?

**Diamond:** I found these sunglasses in the village.

**Aiyanna:** It is a good thing!

**Naomi:** James! Why are you not clothed?

**James:** I don't know.

**Naomi:** Put on clothes quickly! First grab your underwear, your pants, and your belt, second grab your glasses, your hat, and your coat!

**James:** I don't want to.

**Naomi:** Then I'm leaving.

**Merlin:** Why do you have shorts and a coat?

**James:** I'm cold. But I like my shorts.

**Merlin:** Take my overcoat! I'm not cold.

**James:** Thank you!

---

**Teacher:** Long ago, people had other clothes. Women had their bonnets, gloves, stockings, skirts, and shawls. Men had their hats, boots, and gloves.

**Student:** Did the men have breechcloths?

**Teacher:** Yes. Our people had breechcloths long ago.

**Student:** I have a shawl. I bring it to powwows.

**Teacher:** That is a good thing.

**Rose:** Let's go to the store!

**Chris:** What will you buy?

**Rose:** I will buy rings and earrings. Will you buy things?

**Chris:** Yes, I will buy a shirt and socks. When I've found my shoes, we will go.

**Rose:** Good.

## Chapter 12

**Frankenstein:** I am making a person. I am looking for his heart, his belly, his arm, his leg, his head, and his chest.

**Igor:** Yes Frankenstein.

**Frankenstein:** First, his head. Find his eyes, his ears, his nose, and his mouth!

**Igor:** Great! This is his face and his tongue. Are you looking for his hair?

**Frankenstein:** Yes. Let us make his body! Grab his legs and feet!

**Igor:** I am grabbing his big toe!

**Frankenstein:** Good. Do you see his teeth?

**Igor:** No. But I found his lungs!

**Frankenstein:** Good. Bring his lungs!

**Igor:** What is this?

**Frankenstein:** That is his brain.

**Igor:** Where does it go?

**Frankenstein:** His brain goes in his head.

**Frankenstein, Igor:** We are finished!

**Jay:** Are you good?

**Kay:** No, not good. I fell.

**Jay:** Not good! Did you cry?

**Kay:** No. But my back, my shoulder, my arm and my knee hurt.

**Jay:** I'm sorry. My hand hurts. Night before last I fell when I was playing ball.

**Kay:** I'm sorry.

---

**Alice:** Greetings Dave! Come in! Take off your overcoat!

**Dave:** Thank you. I am taking off my hat.

**Alice:** Greetings Aiyanna! Come in! Take off your shoes!

**Aiyanna:** OK! I am wearing socks. When I leave, I will put my shoes on.

**Chris:** What are you wearing around your head Rose?

**Rose:** I am wearing my headband.

**Chris:** Did you put on glasses?

**Rose:** Yes.

**Chris:** When you sleep, do you put on your glasses?

**Rose:** No! When I sleep, I take off my headband and I take off my glasses.

**Chris:** It is a good thing.

**Aiyanna:** The powwow is Saturday. How will you dress up?

**Alice:** I'm going to wear my new dress!

**Aiyanna:** What color is your new dress?

**Alice:** Blue. And you, how are you going to dress up?

**Aiyanna:** I'm going to wear my white skirt.

**Alice:** Very pretty!

**Merlin:** I am wearing a hat.

**Chris:** Which hat?

**Merlin:** I am wearing my big hat.

**Chris:** When you pray, do you take it off?

**Merlin:** Yes! When I pray, I take it off.

**Chris:** It is a good thing.

**Aiyanna:** My belly is very big! I am taking off my belt.

**Alice:** Did you eat a lot of food?

**Aiyanna:** Yes! Last night I ate a lot. I put on my belt, but now I'm taking it off.

**Alice:** It is a good thing.

**Naomi:** Dave, Genesis, what are you two wearing?

**Dave, Genesis:** We are wearing shorts.

**Naomi:** No. Put on long pants! Are you putting your shoes on?

**Dave, Genesis:** No…

**Naomi:** Put on your shoes!

**Dave, Genesis:** Yes, sorry…

## Chapter 13

*Aiyanna came over to Chris's house. His family was gathered there.*

**Aiyanna:** What is his name?

**Chris:** His name is Anthony. He's my grandfather.

**Aiyanna:** Is he your mother's father?

**Chris:** Yes.

**Aiyanna:** You're his grandson?

**Chris:** Yes.

**Aiyanna:** And her, what is her name?

**Chris:** That is my grandmother. Her name is Claudia.

**Aiyanna:** Is she Anthony's wife?

**Chris:** Yes. Anthony is her husband. Aiyanna, this is my maternal uncle, Dave.

**Aiyanna:** Hello! How are you?

**Dave:** Good, thank you. It's good that you came!

**Aiyanna:** Thank you!

**Chris:** Mother, Father, this is my friend, her name is Aiyanna.

**His mother:** Hello! You're my son's friend?

**Aiyanna:** Yes, we are friends.

**Rose:** My paternal aunt wants a baby.

**Alice:** When she has a child it will be a good thing. Our children will play!

**Rose:** Look at the children over there! They are happy. Our families are beautiful!

---

**Rose:** Are you Jeremy's sister?

**Aiyanna:** Yes.

**Rose:** Do you have a younger sister?

**Aiyanna:** Yes. Her name is Silvia.

**Rose:** Silvia is my friend! You're her older sister.

**Aiyanna:** Yes! We are siblings (of the same gender).

**Merlin:** Do you know who Jim is?

**Chris:** Yes, Jim is my father's younger brother.

**Merlin:** Ahh. His son's name is Bobby. So Bobby is your cousin?

**Chris:** Yes. Bobby's younger brother's name is Juston. Juston is also my cousin.

**Merlin:** Do you have a female cousin?

**Chris:** Yes, her name is Emma. Her mother is my mother's older sister.

**Merlin:** Thanks.

**Augustin:** Is your dad's older brother coming to our house?

**Alice:** Yes! Is your mom's younger sister living at y'all's house?

**Augustin:** No, she left. Now she is living at my (male) cousin's house.

**Alice:** It is a good thing.

## Chapter 14

**Aiyanna:** Hi! Welcome! Did Rose (on her part) arrive?

**Chris:** Yes. Rose is sitting over there. Where is your bathroom?

**Aiyanna:** The bathroom is there.

**Chris:** Thanks.

**Rose:** Hi! I am hungry. Do you have food?

**Aiyanna:** Hon. Welcome! Come on! The kitchen is over there. Take anything! Eat!

**Rose:** Thank you!

*Augustin arrives.*

**Augustin:** Hello! I didn't find your garage. Where do I leave my car?

**Aiyanna:** My garage is over there. Please, leave your car there inside the garage.

**Augustin:** Okay.

**Dave:** Alice! You came back to town. How many days are you staying here?

**Alice:** I am staying here for seven days. I sleep over there at that hotel.

**Dave:** Do you like the hotel?

**Alice:** Yes. Over there the bed is soft and the window is big. It has a restaurant and a coffee shop.

**Dave:** Does it have a pool, too?

**Alice:** No. However, I swim in the bayou there. Where is the library?

**Dave:** Take this long road. You will see the library next to the police station.

**Alice:** Thanks!

---

**Chris:** My cat got lost!

**Alice:** Did you look under your house?

**Chris:** Yes. I did not find my cat there.

**Alice:** Did you look behind your T.V.?

**Chris:** Yes. I did not find my cat there.

**Alice:** Did you look to the right of/in front of the window? Did you look on the other side of the bed? Did you look in the bathroom?

**Chris:** I looked everywhere. My cat is lost!

**Alice:** Look! I see your cat way over there. He is sleeping near the road.

**Chris:** Great! My cat isn't lost!

**Naomi:** Merlin, go outside! Today is a beautiful day.

**Merlin:** Yes, I'm going. I will run around the village. After that, I'll sit beneath a tree.

**Naomi:** It is a good thing. I am also going outside. I will do work behind our house.

**Merlin:** It's good when the two of us work outside of the house.

**Naomi:** Yes. Let's go!

---

*The first day at school.*

**Teacher:** Good morning, everyone!

**Students:** Good morning, teacher!

**Teacher:** Everyone, sit down!

*Two students are fighting.*

**Teacher:** Stop! Why are you fighting?

**Chris:** I am not sitting next to Genesis.

**Samuel:** Me too, I am not sitting next to Genesis.

**Teacher:** Chris, sit here! Samuel, sit there! Genesis, sit between where Chris and Samuel are sitting, please.

**Genesis:** No. I don't want to. As for me, I will sit between where Diamond and Summer are sitting.

**Lisa:** Teacher, as for me, I will sit between where Chris and Samuel are sitting.

**Teacher:** Great! Thanks, Lisa. Sit between Chris and Samuel. Genesis, you will sit between Diamond and Summer.

*Everyone sat down.*

**Alice:** This store is really big! How will I find my stuff?

**Chris:** What are you looking for?

**Alice:** I am looking for pens.

**Chris:** Pens are along side notebooks.

**Alice:** Where are notebooks?

**Chris:** Where the stickers are, you will find notebooks between them.

**Alice:** Thank you. Where will I find a chair?

**Chris:** You will find the chairs around the table.

**Alice:** Is the table in front of a white board?

**Chris:** No. The table is to the left of the whiteboard.

**Alice:** I still don't see the table.

**Chris:** Where you see the TVs and computers, the table is between them.

**Alice:** Thank you. Now I see the table.

---

*Augustin arrives at the Tunica-Biloxi reservation. But he gets lost.*

**Augustin:** Is the library here?

**Naomi:** No. This is the casino. The library is close to here.

**Augustin:** Is the library south of the museum?

**Naomi:** No. The library is in the Cultural and Educational Resources Center (CERC). The museum is also in the CERC.

**Augustin:** How do I get to the CERC?

**Naomi:** Walk north on the nature trail.

**Augustin:** When I came here, I saw a cemetery.

**Naomi:** Yes. There is a small cemetery near the health center. The powwow grounds lie east of the cemetery. The big road is to the west.

# Chapter 15

**Alice:** Merlin, I am looking for my daughters. Did you come across them today?

**Merlin:** No. I have not come across them today. Did you look for them in the woods? They play there.

**Alice:** No. I did not look for them in the woods. I will go there. Thank you.

**Merlin:** When you find them, tell me!

**Alice:** I will tell you. Thanks.

*The next day:*

**Merlin:** Did you find your daughters?

**Alice:** Yes. I found my daughters.

**Merlin:** Where?

**Alice:** They were playing in the woods.

**Merlin:** You found them. I'm glad. Take care of your daughters!

**Jay:** Kay, do you remember when we met?

**Kay:** Yes, I remember. When we met, I greeted you. We talked all night long. Then, when it got to be morning, we watched the sun.

**Jay:** Yes. When I'm with you, I'm happy. Kay, will you marry me?

**Kay:** Yes, Jay! I will marry you. I am also happy. Kiss me!

*He kisses her.*

**Jay:** We will be together all our days.

---

**Henry:** Where are you going?

**Alice:** I'm going to the store.

**Henry:** What will you bring me?

**Alice:** What do you want?

**Henry:** Bring me a puppy!

**Alice:** They don't have puppies at that store.

**Henry:** Oh, then bring me a younger brother.

**Alice:** We don't buy people.

**Henry:** Do they have candy? Bring me candy!

**Alice:** Yes. I will bring you candy.

**Chris:** What are you doing?

**Rose:** Christmas is coming. I am wrapping presents.

**Chris:** It is a good thing. What will you give your mother?

**Rose:** I bought her a shawl.

**Chris:** As for your brother, what will you buy him?

**Rose:** Nothing. I made him a necklace.

**Chris:** Great! What will you give your dad?

**Rose:** I will give him a ball. His ball is old. Everyday, he throws the ball to the dog.

**Chris:** What's that?

**Rose:** My uncle's gift. Tomorrow I will send it to him. He gave me beautiful dance moccasins.

**Chris:** And me, what will you give me?

**Rose:** I won't tell you. Christmas morning you will see. What will you give me?

**Chris:** My heart.

## Chapter 16

---

**Merlin:** What do you want to do?

**Aiyanna:** I want to weave a basket.

**Merlin:** Do you have cane?

**Aiyanna:** No. I have pine needles. Do you want to weave baskets?

**Merlin:** No. I want to go fishing. Do you want to go?

**Aiyanna:** Yes. Thanks. I will weave baskets while I sit on the bank.

**Merlin:** Do you want to bring a chair?

**Aiyanna:** No. I like to sit on the bank.

**Merlin:** Me, too. Let's go!

*They went to the river. Merlin is catching fish.*

**Merlin:** Take this fish! Scale it!

**Aiyanna:** No, I don't want to scale it. You do it!

**Merlin:** Do you want to eat fish?

**Aiyanna:** Yes. I like to eat fish.

**Merlin:** Then scale it!

**Rose:** Mom, I want to see my friends!

**Her mother:** Did you finish your work?

**Rose:** Yes!

**Her mother:** Where will y'all go?

**Rose:** We will go to the store. We want to buy new dresses.

**Her mother:** It is a good thing. Your friends also like to see you.

**Rose:** Thank you!

---

**Merlin:** Where are you going?

**Chris:** I'm going to gather food.

**Merlin:** What will you gather?

**Chris:** I will gather mulberries, elderberries, and blackberries in order to prepare food.

**Merlin:** Great! I like mulberries. I will arrive at your house to eat your food.

**Chris:** Come on!

**Aiyanna:** Why do we study the Tunica language?

**Naomi:** Why do we study the Spanish language?

**Aiyanna:** We study in order to speak it.

**Naomi:** We also study the Tunica language in order to speak it. In order to speak Tunica, we study every day. We are Tunica, we will speak our language.

**Aiyanna:** It is a good thing.

---

**Rose:** Today I saw two mice in my house.

**Naomi:** Were you afraid?

**Rose:** No. I saw them, but I wasn't afraid. But mice are living in my house. It is not a good thing.

**Naomi:** Why?

**Rose:** They steal my food.

**Naomi:** What will you do? Will you kill them?

**Rose:** I don't like mice, but I don't want to kill them.

**Naomi:** You will catch them.

**Rose:** And then…?

**Naomi:** You will leave them near Naomi's house. She has cats.

**Rose:** But her cats will kill the mice!

**Chrisku:** While the Tunica lived at Quizquiz, who was our chief?

**Naomihchi:** Cahura Joligo was our chief.

**Chrisku:** Why did we leave Quizquiz?

**Naomihchi:** Long ago, the Natchez wanted to meet with Cahura Joligo. Cahura Joligo gave them food and beds. But at night the Natchez came back. They killed Cahura Joligo. They killed our chief, but they didn't kill his wife and son. The Natchez killed many of our people. But the rest left. When we abandoned Quizquiz, we went south. We left our homes, but we made new ones. Nowadays, the Tunica and the Biloxi live together.

# Chapter 17

**Augustin:** I'm cooking supper.

**Naomi:** Great! What are you making?

**Augustin:** I am roasting venison. What else do we want to eat?

**Naomi:** Do you want corn, potatoes, and vegetables?

**Augustin:** Yes. Are you shucking the corn?

**Naomi:** Yes. I will also mash the potatoes. I am also steaming the vegetables. What do you want to drink?

**Augustin:** Just water. I am filling a pitcher.

**Naomi:** Great! I'm hungry.

**Merlin:** Today I am teaching my daughters to trap.

**Naomi:** What will you trap?

**Merlin:** We will trap rabbits, squirrels, and possums. My daughters also hunt deer, turkey, and ducks.

**Naomi:** It is a good thing.

**Merlin:** What are you doing today?

**Naomi:** Today I am teaching my children to weave baskets.

**Merlin:** Do your children listen to you?

**Naomi:** Yes, they listen to me. They are always asking me questions.

**Merlin:** It is a good thing. When we finish, let's eat together!

**Naomi:** Good! I will build a fire.

---

**Chris:** Merlin, what did you eat last night?

**Merlin:** Last night Anna and I cooked meat.

**Chris:** Meat? Was it chicken? Was it pork?

**Merlin:** It was chicken.

**Chris:** Ah. What else did you two cook?

**Merlin:** We also cooked corn. We ate a lot!

**Rose:** Mother, I want some tea.

**Alice:** Good, I boiled some water.

**Rose:** Please fill my cup.

*Alice fills her cup.*

**Rose:** Did you sweeten the tea?

**Alice:** No. But I will sweeten it.

**Rose:** Thank you.

**Dave:** Are you baking bread?

**Augustin:** Yes.

**Dave:** Did leave the bread dough to rise?

**Augustin:** No. I am still mixing the dough.

**Dave:** I want to see how you make bread dough.

**Augustin:** First, I sifted the flour. Then, I stirred in salt, lard, yeast, and milk. Then I will leave it to rise.

**Dave:** Great! You taught me something new.

---

**Chris:** My friends and I are going outside to play stickball.

**Naomi:** Eat breakfast first! Don't exert yourself!

**Chris:** I will eat breakfast. I will not exert myself.

**Naomi:** Are you lying to me? Answer me!

**Chris:** No! I always listen to you.

**Naomi:** It is a good thing.

**Rose:** I want to hear a story. Tell me a story, please.

**Alice:** One day, a Tunica chief turned into an eagle, it is said. Now he whoops above. When you listen well, you know where he is circling.

**Rose:** Great! Again! Tell me another story!

**Alice:** I want to bake a cake.

**Merlin:** Great! I will help you.

**Alice:** I want berries and pecans.

**Merlin:** I will drive to the store to buy them. They sell berries and pecans there.

*Merlin drove to the store and returned.*

**Alice:** Did you find pecans and berries? Which berries did they have?

**Merlin:** Yes. I bought strawberries.

**Alice:** Good, thank you.

## Chapter 18

**Rose:** I want to play! Let's play outside! It's a good day, the sky is blue.

**Dave:** I can't play outside. I am working.

**Rose:** When can we play?

**Dave:** First I must finish doing my work.

**Rose:** Okay. When you are finished doing your work, we can play.

**Dave:** It is a good thing. We will play.

**Chris:** I can't eat ice cream.

**Augustin:** What? I like ice cream a lot! Why can't you eat it?

**Chris:** There is milk in ice cream. I can't consume milk.

**Augustin:** I forgot. I can consume milk, but you must not consume it. There isn't milk in this biscuit. We can both eat it. I'm hungry! Let's eat!

**Chris:** Yes! Let's eat biscuits!

**Rose:** Do you see that young man? He has a cute puppy.

**Aiyanna:** Yes I see him. His dog is sleeping on the ground.

**Rose:** The young man is also cute. Let's talk to him!

**Aiyanna:** We must not do it. We don't want to wake up the puppy.

**Rose:** Yes. We must not talk to him.

---

**Alice:** Henry, what are you doing?

**Henry:** I am trying to climb this tree. Can you help me?

**Alice:** Yes, I'll try to help you.

*When Henry has climbed the tree, he descends.*

**Henry:** Thanks! You saved me.

**Alice:** It was nothing. You aren't heavy.

**Naomi:** I am about to go to the store. Do you want anything?

**Aiyanna:** Can you buy me new strings? I need to re-string my fiddle.

**Naomi:** Are you about to write a new song?

**Aiyanna:** Yes. I will tell the story of "When the Tunica and the Biloxi become friends".

**Naomi:** Okay, I am going now.

**Aiyanna:** Thanks. Take care!

**Rose:** I'm hungry. What do we want to eat?

**Naomi:** Chicken?

**Merlin:** No. I already ate chicken yesterday.

**Naomi:** Beef stew?

**Rose:** No. We already ate beef stew on Monday.

**Naomi:** Rice?

**Merlin:** No. I am trying to eat a lot of vegetables.

**Naomi:** Rice with vegetables?

**Merlin:** Yeah, okay.

**Rose:** Let's eat!

# Chapter 19

**Aiyanna:** I'm hungry.

**Chris:** Do you want to eat outside?

**Aiyanna:** No, it's not sunny.

**Chris:** But when it gets to be midday, it will clear up.

**Aiyanna:** Yes, you speak the truth. Let's eat outside!

**Henry:** Father, look! It's a full moon!

**His father:** Yes, it was waxing the day before yesterday.

**Henry:** How many weeks does the moon wax?

**His father:** It waxes for two weeks. Then the moon is full for three days. Then it wanes for two weeks.

**Henry:** Ah, now I get it.

**Rose:** My friends and I are going off to study.

**Alice:** But it is already nighttime!

**Rose:** I know, but we must read lots of books.

**Alice:** Yes. But when morning comes, you have to go to school.

**Rose:** I know mom. I will return before long.

**Alice:** It is a good thing.

---

**Aiyanna:** Henry, look out the window!

**Henry:** Look at the ground! It's frosted!

**Aiyanna:** Yes. The wind is blowing, and it's about to snow.

**Henry:** Must we go to school today?

**Aiyanna:** I don't know. When it hails, we won't go to school.

**Henry:** It is a good thing.

**Chris:** Why did you stop playing stickball?

**Rose:** It was raining. Now it's beating down (rain).

**Chris:** It is thundering. It was flashing in the sky.

**Rose:** When it's drizzling, and when the wind is blowing gently, we can return to our homes.

**Chris:** Yes. Let's stay in the house!

*Merlin and Naomi are driving to the cemetery.*

**Merlin:** I can't drive.

**Naomi:** Why?

**Merlin:** I can't see well. It is sleeting.

**Naomi:** It's not sleeting. It's foggy.

**Merlin:** Can you hear that? Its pattering on the car.

**Naomi:** Yes. However, it is not sleeting. The wind is blowing in circles.

**Merlin:** In that case, you should drive.

## Chapter 20

**Chris:** What are you doing?

**Alice:** I am planting.

**Chris:** What are you planting?

**Alice:** I am planting the “three sisters”: corn, beans, and squash.

**Chris:** Are you a farmer? Do you own a farm?

**Alice:** No. I plant behind my house, I plant in order to eat well.

**Chris:** It is a good thing.

**Aiyanna:** Merlin, what is your occupation (what work are you doing)?

**Merlin:** I am a musician.

**Aiyanna:** What (instrument) do you play?

**Merlin:** I play fiddle, drum, and flute. Do you want to hear a song?

**Aiyanna:** Yes! Great!

**Henry:** Are you my commander?

**Dave:** Yes! I am your commander. Greetings, soldier!

**Henry:** Are we fighting a war today?

**Dave:** No, we are not fighting today. We thank the Creator!

**Henry:** Yes. What are your orders?

**Dave:** I am giving you orders to scrub the bathroom and the lobby.

**Henry:** Yes, commander!

---

*Chris is playing with his toy.*

**Henry:** Give me your toy!

**Chris:** No!

*Henry tries to take the toy.*

**Henry's mother:** Henry! Stop! Do you want his toy? First you must ask him. You have to talk to Chris.

**Henry:** Chris, I want to play. Please lend me your toy.

**Chris:** Do you want to play together?

**Henry:** Yes!

**Henry's mother:** Good! Shake hands!

*Henry and Chris shake hands.*

**Aiyanna:** Alice, did you dream the night before last?

**Alice:** Yes! In my dream, I examined a hole.

**Aiyanna:** What did you see?

**Alice:** Crawfish were swimming in the hole. I tried to catch them.

**Aiyanna:** I also dreamed two nights ago. In my dream, I tanned (hide) in order to make myself moccasins.

**Alice:** Great!

# Appendix B: Selected answer key

## TOPICS:

# Chapter 1

## Hinu 1

1.1.1.1. **Merlinku:** Eti hɛma lapun?
**Aiyannahchi:** Lapu, **mahat** ?
**Merlinku:** Lapu, tikahch. Kanahku **hetisa** ?
**Aiyannahchi:** Aiyanna etisa. Kanahku **wetisa** ?
**Merlinku:** Merlin **etisa** .
**Aiyannahchi:** Lapu.

1.1.2.4. Mahat, kanahku wetisa? **c. Chris etisa.**

## Hinu 2

1.2.1.4. Hinimat Alice, Aiyanna, Naomi **hentisan** ?

1.2.1.7. Sinimat Naomihchi, Aiyannahchi, Alicehchi **sentisan** ?

1.2.2.3. What are their names? *(3 boys)* **Kanahku setisa?**

## Hinu 3

1.3.1.3. Merlinku, Chrisku **on'unima** .

1.3.2.1. Ima **etisa** .

# Chapter 2

## Hinu 1

2.1.1.2. Kanahku yaka/yaki? **d. Pitakani.**

2.1.2.3. Wachihkwitin? **Wachihkwinan?**

2.1.3.4. Kanahku yahkhina/yahkwina? **Pitahkina.**
*Answers may vary but should end with -hkina.*

## Hinu 2

2.2.1.5. Kanahku yahkiti? *(if males)* **a. Shimihkwiti.**

2.2.2.2. We are walking. **Pitahkiti.**

2.2.3.5. Woyuhkwiti. **You all *(mp)* are swimming.**

## Hinu 3

2.3.1.2. Kanahku yahkuna? **e. Hinahkuna.**

2.3.2.1. Huwahkiti. **Huwahkina.**

2.3.3.3. Kanahku yahkuna? **Niyuhkuna.**
(for example)

# Chapter 3

## Hinu 1

3.1.1.5. Ma sak' **i**. (saku)

3.1.2.1. lɔt'a **lɔta** **-a** **hɛma** **Hɛma lɔt'a.**
3.1.2.6. shim'i **shimi** **-i** **ma** **Ma shim'i.**

3.1.3.3. Sarani. **I prayed.**

3.1.4.2. He drank. **Kɔrawi.**

## Hinu 2

3.2.1.2. Kanahku ya'iti? *(if mixed)* **d. Rahawiti.**

3.2.2.5. Yanit'ɛhɛ. **You all *(fp)* didn't speak.**

3.2.3.4. They *(mixed group)* didn't enter. **Akat'aha.**

## Hinu 3

3.3.1.3. Kanahku yasina? **b. Worusina.**

3.3.2.3. Rahahk'ɛhɛ. **Rah'it'ɛhɛ.**

3.3.3.4. Yakani. **Yak'iti.**

# Chapter 4

## Hinu 1

4.1.1.4. Tihika kashku uhkyuk'aki? (79)
Tihika **michu tayihkutɛya tohkusahku** uhkyuk'aki.

4.1.2.7. 29 + 6 = **michu enihkutɛya sinku.**
4.1.2.10. 80 ÷ 8 = **michu sahku.**

4.1.3.3. ili yahki manku **tisihku** sinkshku.
4.1.3.7. tohkusahku ahomu enihku **enihku** sinkshku.

## Hinu 2

4.2.1.3. tayihku **tayihkuhta**

4.2.1.6. manku **mankuhta**

4.2.2.5. michu ilihta **michu ili**

## Hinu 3

4.3.1.2. Tihika sahku tahch'a kashku tihkara? **Michu sahkutɛya ili.**

4.3.1.8. Ashutayi tihkashuhki sinkuhta kanahku tetisa? **Rapumanku.**

4.3.2.1. Tahch'awɛka **h. New Year's Day**

4.3.2.11. Tahch'asap'aratohku **e. Thanksgiving**

4.3.3.4. Tahch'atapa **michu enihku.**

4.3.3.9. Tahch'aruwina Tehukuma **michu enihku.**

# Chapter 5

## Hinu 1

5.1.1.3. Taminu weniwiti. **c. You *(mp)* found the cat.**

5.1.2.4. A man read it. **b. Oni rohina powi.**

5.1.3.4. We *(p)* grab a dog. **Sa tapihkiti.**

5.1.4.4. Saku yata. **They *(mp)* made food.**

# Chapter 6

## Hinu 1

| | VERB | TO A GIRL | TO A BOY | TO MANY GIRLS | TO MANY BOYS/ MIXED GROUP |
|---|---|---|---|---|---|
| 6.1.1.3. | me | **me'ɛki** | **me'iki** | **mehitiki** | **mewitiki** |
| 6.1.1.6. | hotu | **hot'ɔki** | **hot'iki** | **hotitiki** | **hotuwitiki** |

6.1.2.4. Let's read! **Rohina po'itiki!**

6.1.2.8. Find the book! *(to a girl)* **Tarowina wen'ɛki!**

## Hinu 2

6.2.1.2. Arhilani hininatan. **Arhilani hin'atan.**

6.2.2.3. Rowina lehpiwitiki! **Rowina lehp'iki!**

6.2.3.2. Ɛp'atan! **Ɛp'aki!**

6.2.3.8. Lapuya rapitiki! **Lapuya rapititan.**

## Hinu 3

6.3.1.5. leyu **ley'ɔhɔtan!**

6.3.1.10. ɛpa **ɛp'ahatan!**

6.3.2.2. Find the money! (to many boys) **Talaspi weniwitiki!**

6.3.2.9. Don't read the story! **Tarhila rohina po'ɔhɔtan!**

# Chapter 7

## Hinu 1

7.1.1.1. hot'iti **hot'itik'ahcha**

7.1.1.6. chuhksiti **chusitik'ahcha**

7.1.2.7. mewin'aha **mewinak'ahch'aha** **You *(md)* will not find it.**

7.1.2.8. po'it'ɛhɛ **po'itik'ahch'aha** **We will not watch.**

## Hinu 2

7.2.1.3. ima uwi + ama **ima uw'ɛma**

7.2.1.7. sa + hat **sahat**

7.2.2.4. Augustin slept as well. **Rapuwi Augustinkupa.**

7.2.2.8. You *(ms)* and I will meet up. **Ma im'ama akuhp'inak'ahcha.**

# Chapter 8

## Hinu 1

8.1.1.3. romantohku **kana**

8.1.2.3. Kaku lapuya rahpakata? **Tarahpanisɛma lapuya rahpakata.**

## Hinu 2

8.2.1.2. I am respectful. **a. Ihkshtamari.**

8.2.2.2. **Tihk** sh'ɛpa. She's happy.

8.2.2.10. **Wihk** yaru. You *(ms)* are curious.

8.2.3.3. Sinkshtamari. **They *(fd/p)* are respectful.**

8.2.4.3. I am tired. **Ihktohkuni.**

### Hinu 3

8.3.1.1. hi + -eht'ira → **heht'ira**
8.3.1.6. sink + -elu → **sinkelu**
8.3.1.12. wi + -etisa → **wetisa**

8.3.2.1. **ihk** yahpa
8.3.2.9. **sink** sipi
8.3.2.12. **ihk** elu
8.3.2.20. **hi-** esahku

8.3.3.2. u + -eht'ira → **oht'ira**
8.3.3.10. in + -ehtini → **entini**

## Chapter 9

### Hinu 1

9.1.1.1. that clock **hi'ɛshuhkitawirani**
9.1.1.6. those four scissors over there **mitakahpuni manku**

9.1.2.3. hɛrihkɔra **this table**
9.1.2.8. mirowinarasinima **those whiteboards over there**

### Hinu 2

9.2.1.5. **Hεku** uhkshpitu.

9.2.1.9. **Hisεma** serusa.

9.2.2.2. Kanahku hεsinima? (*women*): **Hεsinima nuhchisinima.**

9.2.2.7. Kanahku misinima? (*ball players*): **Misinima tarahpanisinima.**

### Hinu 3

9.3.1.2. Hisinima ukitamashu. **Those are benches.**

9.3.2.5. Those over there are tablets. **Misinima pahitaniyu εsa.**

9.3.3.4. Misinima halani. **c. Those over there are pictures.**

## Chapter 10

### Hinu 1

10.1.1.4. Taminu risa lɔtaku. **The multi-colored cat is running.**

10.1.2.5. The bark is striped. **Tahkishi wosu.**

### Hinu 2

10.2.1.1. Tarihku tika patawi. **The big tree fell.**

10.2.2.2. The table is new like the chair. **Tarihkɔra nisa tachehkininahku.**

10.2.3.3. kosuhki **hεntohku** yanishi **tika**

10.2.4.1. rukasa **e. tashle**

# Chapter 11

## Hinu 1

11.1.1.3. our *(p)* dresses **inktira**

11.1.1.10. his underwear **uhktirahalu**

11.1.2.2. wihktirahalu **a. your *(ms)* underwear**

## Hinu 2

11.2.1.2. sɛnshkalahpit'ɛ **their *(fd/p)* boots**

11.2.1.8. sehtiwahkuni **their *(mp)* breechcloths**

11.2.2.4. your *(fs)* stockings **hɛshkarahpuni**

11.2.2.7. your *(mp)* boots **wɛnshkalahpit'ɛ**

| | | | | |
|---|---|---|---|---|
| 11.2.3.1. | *skirt* | -astayitira | ɛstayitira | **my skirt** |
| 11.2.3.6. | *belt* | **tiratasaru** | **sihktiratasaru** | their *(mp)* belts |

# Chapter 12

## Hinu 1

12.1.1.4. his hair **ɔlakashi**

12.1.1.12. their *(fp)* big toes **sɛnshkat'ɛ**

12.1.2.5. irishi **my nose**

12.1.2.9. sichihki **their *(mp)* bellies**

## Hinu 2

12.2.1.1. Ihktawohku wohkuni. Ihktawohku **kowuni.**

12.2.1.10. Kaydenku uhktiratasaru saruwi. Kaydenku uhktiratasaru **rasuwi.**

12.2.2.1. kowuni **e. ihktawohku**

12.2.3.2. Henryku lapuya pok'ɔhɔ. **Henry, wihktapo pahch'iki!**

# Chapter 13

## Hinu 1

13.1.1.3. **i** hchi **sinima**

13.1.1.8. **hin** cha **hchi**

13.1.2.2. win- + eti + -hchi **wentihchi** **your *(md/p)* friend *(f)***

13.1.2.7. sin- + shayi + -sɛma **sinshayisɛma** **their *(fd/p)* husbands**

13.1.3.4. Your *(fs)* mom is pretty. **Higachihchi tashle.**

13.1.3.10. Their *(md)* 3 sons play. **Unmila enihkusɛma shimikata.** or **Unmilasɛma enihku shimikata.**

## Hinu 2

13.2.2.3. What does Gwen call Carla? **ihtat'ɛ**

13.2.3.5. What does Tom call Suki? **ɛhɛyahchi**

13.2.4.8. your maternal uncle *(said to a girl)* **hikiku**

13.2.5.4. sintat'ɛhchi **their *(fd/p)* older sister**

# Chapter 14

## Hinu 1

14.1.1.1. I swim in the pool here. **Hɛhchi woyushi kichu woyukani.**

14.1.2.3. Mihchi po'ɔki! **Look *(fs)* way over there!**

## Hinu 2

14.2.1.3. Tasa (taritasaku **ahkishi** ) sakuku. **Tasa sakuku.**

14.2.2.4. Wetiku uhktawohku haluhta ɔlakashi uhkaran?
**Does your friend have hair under his hat?**

14.2.3.3. The children are playing outside the school.
**Tɔkasinima taritaworu hɔwashi shimikata.**

## Hinu 3

14.3.1.2. Buddyku, Samuelku wachihkuna. Unkminu wahaku.
**Kata Buddyku, Samuelku wachihkunahch, unkminu atɛhkala wahaku.**

14.3.2.4. Kata inima rapuhkitihch, inksapa atɛhkala rapuku.
**Our dog sleeps between us.**

14.3.3.5. He and I are working; you (fs) are playing between us
**Uwi im'ama yoyani yahkinahch, hɛma atɛhkala shimika.**

## Hinu 4

14.4.1.3. Tahch'i lekatishtihki hilakati. **The sun moves to the west.**

14.4.2.4. The CERC is west of the powwow grounds.
**Taritetimili tahali hipu lekatishi kal'ura.**

14.4.3.1. Baton Rouge **a. Tasapashi**

# Chapter 15

## Hinu 1

15.1.1.4. Ɛhɛli sihktamakani. **I am living with my family.**
15.1.1.7. Uhchatohkusɛma sihkchuhpawi. **He kissed his grandchildren.**

15.1.2.2. I married my husband. **Ihkshayiku uhkkipani.**
15.1.2.10. Do you *(ms)* remember me? **Ihkniyupokin?**

15.1.3. Sehitihch, ɛsiku igachihchi **tihk** heniku, **tihk** chuhpaku.

## Hinu 2

15.2.1.4. **Ingras'ashuhki sehitihch, Daveku ɔnchayhchi takayuwa tihkyuwawik'ahcha.**

15.2.2.3. Naomihchi Merlinku uhkkahati. **Naomi met with Merlin.**

15.2.3.5. The teacher gave her students many gifts.
**Taworunihchi tihktaworusɛma takayuwa namu sihkyuwati.**

# Chapter 16

## Hinu 1

16.1.1.2. Alicehchi **wila** tihksh'ɛpa.

16.1.2.4. *(Many answers, for example)* Takuwatohkusinima **woyu** sinkwana.

## Hinu 2

16.2.1.1. I prepare food in order to eat. **Sakuwan yukikani.**

16.2.2.5. Kaya rahpuntira rahpuka? (hɔwashi ami)
**Rahpuntira hɔwashi amiwan rahpukani.**

16.2.2.7. Kaya tahina lapuwi? (hina) **Tahina hinawan lapuwi.**

## Hinu 3

16.3.1.3. Sakunik'ahcha. Ihkyahp'aha. **Sakunik'ahcha. Hinahkushkan ihkyahp'aha.**

16.3.2.3. Sakunik'ahcha. Hinahkushkan ihkyahp'aha.
**Sakunik'ahchashkan, ihkyahp'aha.**

# Chapter 17

## Hinu 1

17.1.1.6. Winima wishita'eri **moluhkwinta**.

17.1.1.8. Ima igachihchi **tihkwirahkatani**.

17.1.2.2. -hkiti **d. -hkinta**

17.1.2.8. -kata **k. -hkanta**

## Hinu 2

17.2.1.1. She cooked the deer meat. **Ya uhktishuma sam'ata.**

17.2.2.2. Iyut'ɛ wɛrɛta. **You *(fs)* hunted pig.**

17.2.3.5. Daveku, Augustinku tatishuma pɔht'unta. → **pɔhtahkunta**
17.2.3.9. Rosehchi, Alicehchi, Lisahchi hahkamuchi suhpihksinta. → **suhpisinta**

## Hinu 3

17.3.1.2. Ima **pakan'ɛhɛ** tan!
17.3.1.6. Ma **teshuni** wihksh'ɛpan?

17.3.2.4. Hichut'ɛsinima tehini sinksh'ɛpa. **Eagles like to circle.**

17.3.3.5. How do you *(fs)* tame a chicken? **Kana kapashi wistahkhɛta?**

# Chapter 18

## Hinu 1

18.1.1.5. Tɛwali lɔt'ashtukun/lɔt'ishtukun?
**Hon, tɛwali lɔtanishtuku.** / **Aha, tɛwali lɔtanishtuk'ɔhɔ.**

18.1.2.1. Taworusɛma - wi (-hchan) **Taworusɛma wi'ɛntahchan.**

18.1.3.3. Sihkhiy'intashtuku. → **Sihkhiy'intashtuk'ɔhɔ.**

18.1.4.4. tihklɔhka + -tohku **tihklɔhkatohku** **her little basket**

### Hinu 2

18.2.1.3. tahi + -po- + -ata **tahipo'ɔta**

18.2.2.4. Tayɛhtat'ɛ palilawi. **c. He almost trapped the turkey.**

18.2.3.3. We already sold our car. **b. Inkkɔra palɔp'inta.**

## Chapter 19

### Hinu 1

19.1.1.3. There is quite a bit of light outside, even though it's nighttime. **b. tahch'a tolu**

19.1.2.4. Tahch'i, tahch'a nuhchisiniman? **Hon. Tahch'i, tahch'a nuhchisinima.**

### Hinu 2

19.2.1.1. wɛka **Tahch'a**
19.2.1.10. mɔcha **Rahihta**

19.2.2.5. Rahihkut'ahahch, **b. woyukani.**

## Chapter 20

### Hinu 1

20.1.1.1. niyu **niyu** **a thought**

20.1.2.4. A mixer (device) **tahekuni**
20.1.2.8. A trap **tapala**

20.1.2.15. A dressing room **irashi**

20.1.3.2. tahɛra **guard (one who guards)**
20.1.3.5. taworunishi **teacher's lounge (a place of teachers)**
20.1.3.10. tawini **hearing aid (a listener, an instrument of hearing)**

## Hinu 2

20.2.1.2. Ashuki Tikahchyuwa 'Thanksgiving day'
**ashuhki 'day' + tikahch 'thanks' + yuwa 'give'**
20.2.1.7. ritaworutohku 'classroom'
**ri 'house, building' + ta '-er' + -woru 'study' + tohku 'little'**

*(answers will vary)*
20.2.2.3. cucumber **elu ɔshta yuru 'long green fruit'**
20.2.2.10. sundress **tahch'i tira 'sundress'**

# Appendix C: List of terms

**1st person** The person speaking, or groups that include the person speaking, e.g., **ima** 'I', **inima** 'we'. *p. 11*

**2nd person** The person or people being spoken to, e.g., **ma** 'you *(ms)*', **hɛma** 'you *(fs)*', etc. *p. 11*

**3rd person** The person, people, or things being spoken about, e.g., **uwi** 'he', **tihchi** 'she'. *p. 11*

**adjective** A word that modifies a noun, e.g., **kosuhki *mili*** 'a *red* crawfish'. Called a **taka halani** in Tunica. *p. 149*

**agent** The person or thing that does the action in a sentence. The agent is also most often the subject in both English and Tunica. For example, ***Henryku* puna wiy'i.** '*Henry* threw a ball.' ***Buddyku* Alicehchi kosutahini tihkyuw'i.** '*Buddy* gave Alice a colored pencil.' *p. 232*

**agentive noun** A word that means the doer of some verb/action, e.g., ***ta*woruni** 'teach*er*', ***ta*hara** 'sing*er*'. *pp. 299, 300*

**alienable** Describes nouns that are optionally possessed. This means that alienable nouns may or may not have possessive prefixes attached to them, e.g., ***hihk*taharani** ('*her* fiddle'), **taharani** ('fiddle'). *p. 157*

**cardinal directions** Principal points of the compass. These are **tasapashi** 'north', **tihikashi** 'south', **pikatishi** 'east', and **lekatishi** 'west'. *p. 220*

**cardinal numbers** Counting numbers, e.g., **sahku** 'one', **ili** 'two', etc. In Tunica, these are called **wirakashi**. *p. 64*

**Class I verbs** Called **taya korini sahku** in Tunica. These verbs take a different set of endings than Class II verbs (**taya korini ili**). Class I habitual endings can be found on page 36 and the completive endings can be found on page 50. *p. 254*

**Class II verbs** Called **taya korini ili** in Tunica and causative verbs by Haas. These verbs take a different set of endings than Class I verbs (**taya korini sahku**). Class II habitual endings can be found on page 254 and completive endings can be found on page 259. *p. 254*

**command** An order, e.g., **lɔt'aki!** 'run *(to a woman)*!'. Called **taya waka** in Tunica. *p. 85*

**completive** Verb endings for actions that are over. *p. 41*

**compounding** Putting two or more words together to make a new word. For example, **ɔndetishitɔrahki** 'ice cream', from **ɔndetishi** 'milk' + **tɔrahki** 'ice'. *p. 304*

**direct object** In English, the person or thing that usually comes right after a transitive verb. In English, the direct object is usually the patient of the sentence and undergoes the action in the sentence, e.g., **Johnku *elu kayi yuru* sakuwi.** 'John ate *a banana*.' *p. 232*

**dual** Refers to two people or things. *p. 12*

**feminine** One of the two grammatical genders in Tunica. Feminine is the default gender for the plural for non-humans. *p. 11*

**future** An event that hasn't yet occurred. Verbs that describe events that takes place in the future use the completive endings followed by **-k'ahcha**. e.g., **Ritalapush *aminik'ahcha*** 'I *will go* to the store', **Hiputak'ahcha** 'They *will dance*'. Called a **tayak'ahcha** in Tunica. *p. 99*

**gender-number ending** An ending for nouns that indicates the gender and number of the noun, e.g., **kuw'*unima*** 'two ducks' < **kuwa** 'duck' + **unima** 'masculine dual'; **kuwa*sinima*** 'three or more ducks' < **kuwa** 'duck' + **sinima** 'feminine plural'. *p. 20*

**glottal stop** A sound created by closing the vocal cords. Written as **'** in Tunica, e.g., **hichut'ɛ** 'eagle'. Can be heard in English between the two words of 'uh oh'. *p. 3*

**grammatical gender** In Tunica, this means that every noun or pronoun is either masculine or feminine. In duals and plurals, mixed groups of men and women take the masculine marking. *p. 11*

**habitual** Verb endings for actions that are happening now or happen regularly. *p. 27*

**inalienable** A noun that cannot be used without a possessive prefix. Most are family members, body parts, or clothing words that are associated with body parts, e.g., ***wi*gachihchi** 'his mother', ***e*hniyu** 'my heart', ***he*hniyutamihku** 'your *(fs)* shirt'. They are marked with inalienable possessive prefixes. *pp. 69, 157, 162*

**inanimate** Non-living. *p. 158*

**indirect object** A grammatical role for the noun that is usually the recipient in a sentence, e.g., **Tihchi elu kayi yuru *ihk*yuwati.** 'She gave *me* a banana.' *p. 232*

**instrumental** An object used to accommplish an action, e.g., **tahina** 'pen' (literally 'instrument of writing'). *p. 299*

**intransitive verb** A type of verb that has a subject (someone who is doing the action) but no object (someone or something that the action is done to). e.g., **pita** 'to walk', **wɛsa** 'to jump'. Called an **taya oni sahku** in Tunica. *p. 27*

**masculine** One of the two grammatical genders in Tunica. Masculine is the default gender for people whose gender is unknown, as well as the default for inanimate objects and animals in the singular and dual. *p. 11*

**mixed group** A group of people that contains both men and women. *p. 12*

**neologism** A word that has been deliberately created to describe a new thing, idea, or concept *p. 297*

**object** The person or thing that an action in a sentence is done to. In Tunica, transitive verbs can mark the object with a prefix on the verb, e.g., ***wihk*henikani** 'I greet you'. *p. 77*

**ordinal numbers** The set of numbers that are used to put things in order, e.g., **sahkuhta** 'first', **masahkihta** 'sixth'. Known as **wirakashihta** in Tunica. *p. 64*

**patient** The person or thing on which an action is carried out or that undergoes a change due to the action. In English, the patient is usually in the direct object position in the sentence. In Tunica, it comes after any agent and recipient in the sentence, and before the verb. For example, **Buddyku *puna* lapuwi.** 'Buddy bought *a ball.*' *p. 232*

**plural** Refers to three or more people or things. *p. 12*

**possession** When someone or something has ownership of a noun, e.g., **toniku *u*shtosu** 'the man's eyes', **tanuhchihchi *tihk*ri** 'the woman's house'. Tunica has two types of possession, alienable possession for things that are optionally possessed, and inalienable possession, for things that are always possessed, like family members and parts of the body. *p. 157*

**possessive prefixes** Prefixes on nouns that tell who the owner of the noun is, e.g., ***tihk**sa* 'her dog'. There two sets of prefixes: those for alienable possession (e.g., **ihk-**, **hihk-**, **wihk-**, **tihk-**, **uhk-**) and those for inalienable possession (e.g., **i-**, **hi-**, **wi-**, **ti-**, **u-**). *p. 70*

**postposition** A word that indicates the place of a person or thing, e.g., **kotitayuki *kichu*** '*in* the kitchen', **titihki *rɔhpant*** '*by* the bayou'. Notice that in Tunica, this locating word comes after the noun whose position it specifies. In English, we put these locating words *before* the noun. In Tunica, this is called an **ahkihtaku** *p. 210*

**prefix** A word building block that must be attached to the front of another word, e.g., *pre-* 'before' in *prefix* or **wihk-** 'his' in **wihkpuna** 'his ball'. *pp. 7, 70*

**pronoun** A word that replaces a noun, e.g., **ima** 'I', **ma** 'you', **uwi** 'he', **tihchi** 'she'. *p. 11*

**recipient** The person or thing that receives the patient (the thing undergoing the action) in the sentence. In English, the recipient often occupies the indirect object position. In Tunica, the recipient comes after the agent, and before the patient and the verb. For example: **Daveku *Diamondhchi* puna tihkyuw'i.** 'Dave gave *Diamond* a ball.' *p. 232*

**singular** Refers to only one person or thing. *p. 12*

**stative verb** Verbs that express different states of being. Sometimes these verbs express ideas that would be conveyed using adjectives in English, e.g., **-hniyulapu** ('to be smart'), **-yashi** ('to be angry'), **-elu** ('to like something'). Called static verbs in Haas. *p. 115*

**subject** Often the person or thing doing an action or being described. In Tunica, transitive verbs and intransitive verbs mark the subject with endings on the verb, e.g., **pita*kani*** 'I walk'; **wihkheni*kani*** 'I greet you'; **sama*hkinta*** 'we *(p)* cook'. Stative verbs mark the subject with prefixes on the verb. ***ihk*sh'ɛpa** 'I am happy'. *p. 27*

**suffix** A word building block that must be attached to the end of another word, e.g., **-wi** in **wɛsa*wi*** 'he jumped' *p. 7*

**syllable** Word parts that are pronounced as a unit. In Tunica, syllables consist of a vowel and one or more consonants and form a unit. In the following words, the syllables are separated by periods: **a.pa.ru** 'sky'; **pɛl.ka** 'flat'; **hin.ya.tihch** 'then'. *p. 42*

**taka halani** A word that describes a noun, e.g., **rowina *ɔshta*** 'the *blue* book'. Called an adjective in English. *p. 149*

**taya korini ili** Class II verbs, or what Haas called causative verbs. These verbs take a different set of endings than **taya korini sahku** (Class I verbs). **taya korini ili** habitual endings can be found on page 254 and completive endings can be found on page 259. *p. 254*

**taya korini sahku** Class I verbs. These verbs take a different set of endings than **taya korini ili** (Class II verbs). **taya korini sahku** habitual endings can be found on page 36 and the completive endings can be found on page 50. *p. 254*

**taya nahchu** A verb that has both a subject (someone who is doing the action) and an object (someone or something that the action is done to), e.g., **Tihchi ɔndetishi laputi.** 'She bought milk.' Called a transitive verb in English. *p. 77*

**taya oni sahku** A type of verb that has a subject (someone who is doing the action) but no object (someone or something that the action is done to). e.g., **pita** 'to walk', **wɛsa** 'to jump'. Called an intransitive verb in English. *p. 27*

**Taya Rahihta** These are weather verbs that describe the actions of the Thunder Being. Since the Thunder Being is responsible for these weather conditions, the verb always takes a third person masculine singular ending, e.g., **miraku** 'he is lightning-ing; he is causing lightning to flash'. For weather verbs describing Sun Woman's actions, see **Taya Tahch'i** *p. 289*

**Taya Tahch'i** These are weather verbs that describe the actions of Sun Woman. Since Sun Woman is responsible for these weather conditions, the verb always takes a third person feminine singular ending, e.g., **mirakati** 'she is clearing off the sky, lighting up the sky'. For weather verbs describing Thunder Being's actions, see **Taya Rahihta** *p. 285*

**taya waka** An order or a command, e.g., **lɔt'aki!** 'run *(to a woman)*!' Tunica has both strong and polite commands. *p. 85*

**taya wana** Verbs that express different states of being. Sometimes these verbs express ideas that would be conveyed using adjectives in English, e.g., **-yahpa** 'to be hungry', **-shniyu** 'to be lonely', **-sipi** 'to be cold'. Called stative verbs in English. *p. 115*

**tayak'ahcha** A verb describing an event that takes place in the future. Formed by taking the completive form of the verb and adding **-k'ahcha**, e.g., **Johnku hipuwik'ahcha.** 'John will dance.' Known as the future in English. *p. 99*

**transitive verb** A type of verb that has a subject (someone who is doing the action) and an object (someone or something that the action is done to). e.g., **tapi** 'to catch', **wiya** 'to throw'. Called a **taya nahchu** in Tunica. *p. 77*

**unaspirated** Not accompanied by a strong burst of breath. In Tunica, /p/, /t/, and /k/ are unaspirated when they come before a glottal stop, e.g., the **t** in **hichut'ɛ**. In English, /p/, /t/, and /k/ are aspirated at the beginning of words (e.g., /t/ in *top*), but usually not elsewhere (e.g., /t/ in *stop*). *p. 4*

**voiceless** Refers to a sound that is made without vibration of the vocal cords. For example, /p/, /t/, and /k/ are voiceless, while /b/, /d/, and /g/ are their voiced counterparts. *p. 2*

**vowel blending** When two vowels occur next to each other within words of more than one syllable, they combine to form a single vowel, which will be preceded by a glottal stop. If the vowel of a one-syllable word touches another vowel, the second vowel may change to be more like the first vowel (assimilation), but the first vowel will remain. Vowel blending can also spread across **h**, as in **woyuw'ɛhɛ** 'he didn't swim', from **woyu** + **wi** + **aha**. *p. 42*

**wh-word** In English, wh-words are words that indicate questions, like **kanahku** 'what', **kaku** 'who', **kata** 'where', etc. In Tunica, they are known as **yoluyana-*ka***, because they all start with **ka**. *p. 111*

**wirakashi** The set of numbers that are used to count, e.g., **sahku** 'one', **masahki** 'six'. Known as cardinal numbers in English. *p. 64*

**wirakashihta** The set of numbers that are used to put things in order, e.g., **sahkuhta** 'first', **masahkihta** 'sixth'. Known as ordinal numbers in English. *p. 64*

**yoluyana-*ka*** In Tunica, words that indicate questions, e.g., **kanahku** 'what', **kaku** 'who', **kata** 'where'. The English equivalent is wh-words. *p. 111*

# Appendix D: List of vocabulary

This glossary is an exhaustive list of all of the Tunica terminology from the vocabulary boxes in this textbook. For a more complete dictionary of Tunica (and English-to-Tunica), see the Tunica Webonary site, the Tunica language app, or Mary Haas's *Tunica Dictionary*.

This glossary is organized alphabetically, based on the English alphabet. While this is hopefully quite logical and straightforward, it means that even though 'sh' and 'ch' are separate sounds in Tunica (and in English), you can find words starting with 'sh' under **S**, rather than in its own separate section. Because **C** isn't used on its own in Tunica, **Ch** has a section of its own. Tunica does however have several characters that are not part of the English alphabet: **ɛ**, **ɔ**, and **'** (IPA **ʔ**). We have alphabetized **Ɛ** following **E**, and **Ɔ** following **O**. We do not write words beginning with **'** in Tunica, so **'** does not have its own section. When **'** appears in the middle of a word, it is alphabetized as though it is not present (so **-eht'ira** can be found between **-ehtini** and **-ehtiwakuni**).

As you learn in this textbook, most words in Tunica cannot stand alone. Words that cannot stand alone are indicated by putting a dash either before the word (like **-ahali** 'family'), to indicate that it requires an element before it, or after the word (like **a-** 'together; each other') which indicates it requires an element after it. These dashes do not affect alphabetization.

Finally, verbs in Tunica belong to three classes: **taya wana** 'stative', **taya korini sahku** 'Class I', and **taya korini ili** 'Class II'. **taya wana** cannot appear without a prefix and therefore are indicated by a dash (e.g., **-shruka** 'to be afraid'). **Taya korini ili** are indicated by (II) following the verb in Tunica (e.g., **arhila (II)** 'to tell a story'). Because **taya korini sahku** are the most numerous type of verb, they are not accompanied by any special marking.

**A**

**-a** you *(fs)* _____ed *p. 41*
**a-** together; each other *p. 102*
**-aha** not *p. 45*
**-aha** to not have *(stative verb)* *p. 114*
**aha** no; nothing; nowhere *pp. 15, 98*
**-ahali** family *p. 186*
**-ahatan** negative command *p. 91*
**-ahaya** opposite-gender sibling *p. 192*
**-ahayasahu** opposite-gender cousin *p. 192*
**ahkalayihtatahinu** train *p. 298*
**ahkihta** in back of; behind *p. 209*
**ahkishi** in back of; behind *p. 209*

**ahkishisɛma** the rest; remainder (of people) *p. 244*
**ahomu** divided by *p. 58*
**aka** to enter; to go in *p. 45*
**akuhpani** together *p. 244*
**akurani** around; surrounding *p. 214*
**ala** cane *p. 238*
**ala kayi** brown thrasher *p. 145*
**ala kichu** canebrake *p. 248*
**-alakashi** hair *p. 170*
**-alawɛcha** ear *p. 170*
**-alawɛcha mayisahu** left ear *p. 217*
**-alawɛcha tirishi** right ear *p. 217*
**-alawɛchatapahchu** earring *p. 161*
**-ama** and; along with *p. 98*
**ami** to go; to depart *p. 40*
**am'ilta** both *p. 270*
**-anchayi** wife *p. 186*
**-ani** it is said *p. 263*
**-anta** they *(mp)* _____ed (II) *p. 259*
**aparu** sky *p. 270*
**aparu muchu** to skydive *p. 298*
**apo'inan** we *(d)* will see each other *p. 10*
**apo'itin** we *(p)* will see each other *p. 15*
**-ara** to have *p. 114*
**arhila (II)** to tell a story *p. 263*
**arhilani** story *p. 76*
**arupo** to dream; a dream *p. 303*
**-ashka** foot; toe *p. 170*
**-ashka mayisahu** left foot *p. 217*
**-ashka tirishi** right foot *p. 217*
**-ashkalahpi** shoes *p. 161*
**-ashkalahpi chɛra** dance moccasins *p. 231*
**-ashkalahpit'ɛ** boots *p. 161*
**-ashkarahpuni** stockings *p. 161*
**-ashkarahpuni kochu** socks *p. 161*
**-ashkat'ɛ** big toe *p. 170*
**-ashkatɛrashki** leg *p. 170*
**-ashkatɛrashki mayisahu** left leg *p. 217*
**-ashkatɛrashki tirishi** right leg *p. 217*
**ashuhki** day *p. 66*
**ashuhkitawirani** clock *p. 128*
**ashuhkitɛpan** every day *p. 98*
**ashutayi** week *p. 66*
**Ashut'ɛ** Sunday *p. 69*
**Ashut'ɛ Tehukuma** Saturday *p. 69*
**-astayi** body *p. 170*
**-astayitira** skirt *p. 161*
**-ata** she _____ed (II) *p. 259*
**atehini** about; around *p. 209*
**atehpi** together; joined together; side-by-side *p. 214*
**atɛhkala** in the middle; in between *p. 214*
**awɛhɛ** nothing *p. 231*
**ay'ɛhɛp'aha** before long; a short while; not long after *p. 284*
**ayi** fire *p. 142*

**Ch**

**chapu** to take off jewelry, glasses *p. 176*
**chehkini** chair *p. 132*
**chihchiru** wren *p. 107*
**-chihki** belly *p. 170*
**-china** knee *p. 170*
**-china mayisahu** left knee *p. 217*
**-china tirishi** right knee *p. 217*
**chiya** squirrel *pp. 167, 252*
**chomu** wildcat *p. 167*
**chɔha** chief *p. 64*
**chu** to take *p. 91*
**chuchuhina** redheaded woodpecker *p. 183*
**chuhki ɔshta** live oak ('evergreen oak') *p. 145*
**chuhpa** to kiss *p. 226*

**chushi** owl *p. 223*
**chuyaka** to bring *p. 76*

E

**-ehku** child (kin or animals) *pp. 186,* see also *ɔka*
**-ehniyu** heart *p. 170*
**-ehniyutamihku** shirt *p. 161*
**-ehniyutirishi** chest *p. 170*
**ehniyuwista** my sweetheart *p. 114*
**-ehp'ira** shoulder *p. 170*
**-ehp'ira mayisahu** left shoulder *p. 217*
**-ehp'ira tirishi** right shoulder *p. 217*
**-ehtini** to own *p. 119*
**-eht'ira** to be clothed *p. 119*
**eht'ira** my clothes *p. 119*
**-ehtiwahkuni** breechcloth *p. 161*
**-ehukuma** younger same-gender sibling *p. 192*
**eksha tɛrashki** pine needles *p. 238*
**-elu** to like something *p. 114*
**elu kayi yuru** banana *p. 142*
**enihku** three *p. 60*
**enti** our friend *p. 15*
**-epushka** lungs *p. 170*
**eru** to laugh *p. 30*
**-eruhkitapahchu** necklace *p. 231*
**-eruhtamihku** shawl *p. 161*
**erunasa** we *(d/p)* know *p. 121*
**-erusa** to know *p. 119*
**erusa** I know *p. 121*
**-esahku** to be widowed *p. 119*
**-esi** father *p. 186*
**-esini** head *p. 170*
**-esintalu** brain *p. 170*
**-esintamihku** bonnet *p. 161*
**-esit'ɛ** father's older brother (older paternal uncle) *p. 192*
**-esitohku** father's younger brother (younger paternal uncle) *p. 192*
**-eti** friend; family *p. 186*
**eti** my friend *p. 10*
**-etisa** to be named *p. 10*
**etisa** I am named *p. 10*
**-eyu** arm *p. 170*
**-eyu mayisahu** left arm *p. 217*
**-eyu tirishi** right arm *p. 217*

Ɛ

**ɛpa** to open *p. 84*
**ɛsha** willow *p. 96*
**ɛstamili** red-tailed hawk *p. 223*

G

**-gachi** mother *p. 186*
**-gachit'ɛ** mother's older sister (older maternal aunt) *p. 192*
**-gachitohku** mother's younger sister (younger maternal aunt) *p. 192*

H

**ha (II)** to borrow; to lend *p. 303*
**hahchi** now *p. 88*
**hahchu** salt *p. 257*
**hahka** corn *pp. 201, 252*
**hahka kayi** yellow corn *p. 145*
**hahka ɔshta** blue corn *p. 145*
**Hahka Ɔshta** Green Corn ceremony *p. 268*
**hahkamuchi** bread *p. 257*
**hahkamuchitohku** biscuit *p. 270*
**hahkamuchitohkutaya** bread dough *p. 257*
**hahkamuchitohkuwista** cake; baked sweets *p. 263*

**hahkatomu** flour *p. 257*
**hahkatomuyasha** yeast *p. 257*
**hahpari (II)** to tell a lie *p. 263*
**halani** picture *p. 136*
**halanipahi** television *p. 132*
**Halayihku** Biloxi person; Biloxi people; Biloxi tribe *p. 244*
**hali** earth; ground; land *p. 270*
**hali** to send *p. 231*
**hali hipu** powwow grounds *p. 219*
**haliwɛka** cemetery *p. 219*
**haluhta** beneath; under; at the bottom *p. 209*
**hal'ukini** village *p. 119*
**halushi** below; down; underneath *p. 209*
**hapa** to stop *p. 49*
**-hapa-** already; finished *p. 276*
**hara** to sing; song *pp. 26, 276*
**hara (II)** to play a musical instrument *p. 296*
**hashita** light *p. 148*
**-hat** on (one's) part *p. 10*
**hatika** again *p. 88*
**-hayi** to be old *p. 119*
**hayi** old *p. 148*
**hayihta** on *p. 132*
**hayishi** above *p. 128*
**-hch** when; during; while *p. 66*
**-hcha** grandparent *p. 186*
**-hchan** must; have to *p. 270*
**-hchat'ɛ** great-grandparent *p. 248*
**-hchatohku** grandchild *p. 186*
**-hchi** father's sister (paternal aunt) *p. 186*
**-hchi** gender-number ending *(fs)* *pp. 10, 20*
**heku (II)** to mix in; to stir up *p. 257*
**hemu** (the moon) to wax *p. 284*
**heni** hello!; greetings!; to greet *pp. 10, 226*
**henishi** lobby; reception area *p. 296*
**heru (II)** to steam *p. 252*
**herunasa** you *(fd/p)* know *p. 121*
**herusa** you *(fs)* know *p. 121*
**hetisa** you *(fs)* are named *p. 10*
**hɛ-** here, this, these *p. 128*
**hɛ'ɛsh** today *p. 84*
**hɛhchi** here *p. 204*
**hɛku** this *p. 137*
**hɛlawu** tonight *p. 98*
**hɛma** you *(fs)* *pp. 10, 12*
**hɛmat** you *(fs)*, on your part *p. 10*
**-hɛnta** you *(fd/p)* _____ed (II) *p. 259*
**hɛntohku** small *p. 148*
**hɛra** to watch *p. 226*
**hɛsinima** these *(3+)* *p. 137*
**-hɛta** you *(fs)* _____ed (II) *p. 259*
**hɛ'unima** these two *p. 137*
**hi-** you *(fs stative)*; your *(fs inalienable)* *pp. 120, 162*
**hi-** there, that, those *p. 128*
**hichut'ɛ** eagle *p. 263*
**hihchi** there *p. 204*
**hihk-** you *(fs stative)*; your *(fs alienable)*; you *(fs object)* *pp. 116, 158, 227*
**hihkutohku** mouse *p. 244*
**hihkyuk'aki** you *(fs)* are (_____ years old) *p. 58*
**Hiki Hipu** Quail Dance *p. 268*
**hiku** that *p. 137*
**hikuwa** panther *pp. 96, 167*
**hila** to move *p. 91*
**-hila-** about to; almost; nearly; fixin' to *p. 276*
**hin-** you *(fd/p stative)*; your *(fd/p inalienable)* *pp. 120, 162*

**-hina** you _____ed *(fd)* *p. 50*
**hina** to write *p. 34*
**hinahkushkan** but; nevertheless; however *p. 148*
**hinahkutan** maybe *p. 244*
**hinatamurini** eraser *p. 136*
**hinima** you *(fd/p)* *p. 12*
**hink-** you *(fd/p stative)*; your *(fd/p alienable)*; you *(fd/p object)* *pp. 116, 158, 227*
**hinto!** come on! *p. 102*
**hinu** practice *pp. viii, 88*
**hinyatihch** then; now; so; after that *p. 91*
**hipirashu** your *(fs)* birthday *p. 66*
**hipu** to dance *p. 26*
**hisawa** bloodroot *p. 248*
**hishi (II)** to sift *p. 257*
**hishtahahki** still; always *p. 214*
**hisinima** those *(3+)* *p. 137*
**hita** take care! *p. 10*
**-hiti** you _____ed *(fp)* *p. 46*
**hiyu (II)** to wake (someone) up *p. 270*
**hi'unima** those two *p. 137*
**-hkanta** they *(mp)* are _____ing (II) *p. 254*
**-hkata** she is _____ing (II) *p. 254*
**-hkatani** I am _____ing (II) *p. 254*
**-hkeni** hand; finger *p. 170*
**-hkeni mayisahu** left hand *p. 217*
**-hkeni tirishi** right hand *p. 217*
**-hkenirahpuni** glove *p. 161*
**-hkenitamuri** ring *p. 161*
**-hkhɛnta** you *(fd/p)* are _____ing (II) *p. 254*
**-hkhɛta** you *(fs)* are _____ing (II) *p. 254*
**-hkhina** you *(fd)* are _____ing *p. 35*
**-hkhiti** you *(fp)* are _____ing *p. 31*
**-hkina** we *(d)* are _____ing *p. 35*
**-hkinta** we are _____ing (II) *p. 254*
**-hkiti** we are _____ing *p. 31*
**-hksina** they *(fd)* are _____ing *p. 35*
**-hksinta** they *(fd/p)* are _____ing (II) *p. 254*
**-hksiti** they *(fp)* are _____ing *p. 31*
**-hkuna** they *(md)* are _____ing *p. 35*
**-hkunta** they *(md)* are _____ing (II) *p. 254*
**-hkuta** he is _____ing (II) *p. 254*
**-hkwina** you *(md)* are _____ing *p. 35*
**-hkwinta** you *(md/p)* are _____ing (II) *p. 254*
**-hkwita** you *(ms)* are _____ing (II) *p. 254*
**-hkwiti** you *(mp)* are _____ing *p. 31*
**hokokura** elderberry *p. 241*
**hon** yes *p. 15*
**honu** to descend; to come down (from); to recede *p. 276*
**hotu** all; every; everyone *p. 102*
**hotu** to finish *p. 49*
**hɔhkaheluni** a hole; a depression *p. 303*
**hɔwahta** outside of *p. 209*
**hɔwashi** outdoors; outside of; outside *p. 209*
**-hta** on; with *p. 128*
**-hta** -st, -rd, -th (ordinal) *p. 64*
**-hta** same-gender sibling *p. 192*
**-htani** I _____ed (II) *p. 259*
**-htasahu** same-gender cousin *p. 192*
**-htat'ɛ** older same-gender sibling *p. 192*
**huchilami** to tan (hides) *p. 303*
**huma** berry *p. 263*
**humameli** blackberry *p. 241*
**humamili** strawberry *p. 263*
**huri** to blow (wind); wind *p. 288*
**hurikorini** whirlwind *p. 293*

**huwa** to wash oneself; to scrub *pp. 34, 296*

## I

**-i** you _____ed *(ms)* *p. 41*
**i-** I *(stative)*; my *(inalienable)* *pp. 120, 162*
**ihk-** I *(stative)*; my *(alienable)*; me *pp. 116, 158, 227*
**ihkyuk'aki** I'm (_____ years old) *p. 58*
**ili** two *p. 60*
**ima** I *p. 12*
**in-** we *(stative)*; our *(d/p inalienable)* *pp. 120, 162*
**-ina** we _____ed *(d)* *p. 50*
**Ingras'ashuhki** Christmas *p. 231*
**inima** we *(d/p)* *p. 12*
**ink-** we *(d/p stative)*; our *(d/p alienable)*; us *(d/p)* *pp. 116, 158, 227*
**inkara** we have *p. 64*
**inkrish** to our house *p. 45*
**-inta** we _____ed (II) *p. 259*
**ipirashu** my birthday *p. 66*
**ira** to wear; to dress *p. 176*
**ishu (II)** to shuck (corn); to strip (cane) *p. 252*
**Ispani** Spanish; Spanish person; Spanish people *p. 241*
**-iti** we _____ed *(p)* *p. 46*
**iyushɛla** possum *pp. 107, 252*
**iyut'ɛ** pig *p. 257*

## K

**-ka** you are _____ing *(fs)* *p. 27*
**ka'ash** when *p. 110*
**kafi** coffee *p. 204*
**kaha** to meet; to come upon; to come across *pp. 102, 226*
**-k'ahcha** will (future) *p. 98*
**kaku** who; which *pp. 64, 110*
**kali** to stand *p. 236*
**kal'ura** it is (standing) *p. 204*
**kana** how *p. 110*
**kanahku** what *pp. 10, 110*
**-kani** I am _____ing *p. 27*
**kapashi** chicken *p. 257*
**Kapashi Hipu** Chicken Dance *p. 268*
**kashi** truth; true; original; real *p. 284*
**kashku** how many; how much *pp. 58, 110*
**-kata** they are _____ing *(mp)* *p. 31*
**kata** where; somewhere; anywhere *pp. 98, 110*
**-kati** she is _____ing *p. 27*
**katotu** everywhere *p. 209*
**kaya** why *p. 110*
**kayi** yellow; gold; brown; orange *p. 142*
**kɛra** speckled; spotted; mottled *p. 142*
**kɛrashi** a farm *p. 296*
**-ki** command suffix *p. 84*
**-ki** you are _____ing *(ms)* *p. 27*
**-ki** mother's brother (maternal uncle) *p. 186*
**kichu** in; inside *p. 76*
**kimu** to take off a headwrapping (bandana, headdress, headband) *p. 176*
**kipa** to marry *p. 226*
**kiwa** beaver *p. 167*
**kochu** short *p. 148*
**kohina** cup *p. 257*
**kohku** turtle; terrapin *p. 107*
**kolu** minus *p. 58*
**Komelitahch'a** March *p. 68*
**ko'o** great! *p. 10*
**kosu** color *p. 142*

**Kosuhk'ariya** Crawfish Shaman *p. 293*
**kosuhki** crawfish *p. 142*
**kosutahina** crayon; marker; colored pencil *p. 128*
**kosuyuwishi** rainbow *p. 293*
**kotitapa** vegetables *p. 252*
**kotitayuki** kitchen *p. 204*
**kowu** to take off a hat *p. 176*
**kɔra** car *p. 204*
**kɔra** to drink *p. 40*
**kɔrahaluni** tractor *p. 298*
**kɔrashi** garage *p. 204*
**kɔsa** to scrape (scales or hide) *p. 238*
**kɔta** gray *p. 142*
**-ku** gender-number ending *(ms)* *pp. 10, 20*
**-ku** he is _____ing *p. 27*
**kuhpa** to meet; to come together *p. 186*
**kunkuri** drum *p. 296*
**kuwa** duck *p. 252*
**kuwatohku** bird *p. 142*

L

**la** to set; to get to be night *p. 284*
**lahpi** to put on or wear shoes *p. 176*
**laka** to frost *p. 288*
**laka** to live *(3fp/3mp)* *p. 244*
**lalahkihihkut'ɛ** muskrat *p. 167*
**lamihta** soft *p. 148*
**lap'ɔhɔ** not good; bad *p. 34*
**lapu** to buy *p. 156*
**lapu** good; thoroughly; well; correct *p. 10*
**lapuhch** it is a good thing *p. 26*
**lapuya** well *p. 40*
**lapuya aka** welcome (verb) *p. 204*
**laspi** metal; money *p. 91*
**laspi ri** bank *p. 91*
**laspi tapahchu** metal ornament *p. 167*
**laspikayi** gold ('yellow metal') *p. 145*
**Lawu Ahara Hipu** Daybreak Dance *p. 268*
**lawu yuru** all night long *p. 226*
**lawumihta** day before yesterday *p. 45*
**lawushi** yesterday; the day before; at night *p. 40*
**Lawutɛhkala Hipu** Midnight Dance *p. 268*
**le** to get lost *p. 45*
**lehpi** to close *p. 84*
**lekatishi** west *p. 219*
**leyu** to point at something *p. 76*
**lɔhka** basket *p. 238*
**lɔpatɛra** unidentified vine that deer like to eat *p. 236*
**lɔta** to run *p. 26*
**-lu** tongue; language *p. 170*
**luhchi** language *p. 241*
**luhchi Yoroni** the Tunica language *p. 136*
**lutamashu** grammar *p. viii*

M

**ma** you *(ms)* *pp. 10, 12*
**mahat** you *(ms)*, on your part *p. 10*
**-mahka** to love *p. 114*
**maka** lard; grease; oil; fat *p. 257*
**manku** four *p. 60*
**mari** to gather (things) *p. 241*
**maru** to return *p. 263*
**masahki** six *p. 60*
**mashu** to make; to build *p. 128*
**mayihta** on the other side of *p. 209*
**mayisahu** left side; on the left *p. 214*
**me** to search for; to look for *p. 84*
**meli** black *p. 142*

**mi-** way over there, that one way over there, those way over there *p. 128*
**michu enihku** thirty *p. 60*
**michu enihkutɛya enihku** thirty-three *p. 60*
**michu enihkutɛya ili** thirty-two *p. 60*
**michu enihkutɛya manku** thirty-four *p. 60*
**michu enihkutɛya masahki** thirty-six *p. 60*
**michu enihkutɛya sahku** thirty-one *p. 60*
**michu enihkutɛya sinku** thirty-five *p. 60*
**michu enihkutɛya tayihku** thirty-seven *p. 60*
**michu enihkutɛya tisihku** thirty-eight *p. 60*
**michu enihkutɛya tohkusahku** thirty-nine *p. 60*
**michu ili** twenty *p. 60*
**michu ilitɛya enihku** twenty-three *p. 60*
**michu ilitɛya ili** twenty-two *p. 60*
**michu ilitɛya manku** twenty-four *p. 60*
**michu ilitɛya masahki** twenty-six *p. 60*
**michu ilitɛya sahku** twenty-one *p. 60*
**michu ilitɛya sinku** twenty-five *p. 60*
**michu ilitɛya tayihku** twenty-seven *p. 60*
**michu ilitɛya tisihku** twenty-eight *p. 60*
**michu ilitɛya tohkusahku** twenty-nine *p. 60*
**michu manku** forty *p. 60*
**michu masahki** sixty *p. 60*
**michu sahku** ten *p. 60*
**michu sahkutɛya enihku** thirteen *p. 60*
**michu sahkutɛya ili** twelve *p. 60*
**michu sahkutɛya manku** fourteen *p. 60*
**michu sahkutɛya masahki** sixteen *p. 60*
**michu sahkutɛya sahku** eleven *p. 60*
**michu sahkutɛya sinku** fifteen *p. 60*
**michu sahkutɛya tayihku** seventeen *p. 60*
**michu sahkutɛya tisihku** eighteen *p. 60*
**michu sahkutɛya tohkusahku** nineteen *p. 60*
**michu sinku** fifty *p. 60*
**michu tayihku** seventy *p. 60*
**michu tisihku** eighty *p. 60*
**michu tohkusahku** ninety *p. 60*
**mihchi** over there *p. 204*
**mihku** to wear a headwrapping (bandana, headdress, headband); to wear on the head *p. 176*
**miku** that way over there *p. 137*
**-mila** daughter; son *p. 186*
**mili** red *p. 142*
**minu** cat *p. 76*
**mira** to lighten up; to clear up (weather) *p. 284*
**mira (II)** to flash *p. 288*
**misinima** those *(3+)* way over there *p. 137*
**mi'unima** those two way over there *p. 137*
**mohti (II)** to snow *p. 288*
**mohtu** to wrap *p. 231*
**molu (II)** to fill *p. 252*
**mɔcha (II)** to drizzle *p. 288*
**muhkini** smoke *p. 142*

**N**

**-n** yes/no question *p. 10*
**nahka** butterfly *p. 309*
**-nahku** like; similar to *p. 142*
**nahtali** bank (of a river); shore *p. 238*
**naka** war; battle; warrior; soldier *p. 296*
**nalu (II)** to hail *p. 288*

**namu** many; much *p. 58*
**nɛhtali** bed *p. 204*
**nɛra** spirit; ghost *p. 223*
**-ni** I _____ed *p. 41*
**ni** to tell; to say *p. 226*
**-ni** tooth; teeth *p. 170*
**nihkirhipu** powwow *p. 98*
**nini** fish *p. 238*
**nira** to steal *p. 244*
**nisa** new *p. 148*
**nisara** young person *p. 270*
**niyu** to think; to consider *p. 34*
**-niyulapu** to be smart *p. 114*
**niyupo** to remember *p. 226*
**nokushi** bear *p. 167*
**nuhchi** woman *p. 19*
**nuhki** otter *p. 167*

**O**

**oni** person; man *p. 19*
**oni laspi ri** bank teller *p. 91*
**onimahoni** American Indian; Native American *p. 219*
**onrɔwahka** rice *pp. 276, 298*
**orunasa** they *(md)* know *p. 121*
**orusa** he knows *p. 121*
**Osin'ili Hipu** Double-Head Dance *p. 268*
**otisa** his name is *p. 15*

**Ɔ**

**ɔka** child (general) *pp. 186,* see also *-ehku*
**ɔkatɛkaha** they _____ed *(md) p. 55*
**ɔmahka** alligator *p. 309*
**ɔmaka** sorcerer; sorceress *p. 183*
**ɔndetishi** milk *p. 257*
**ɔndetishitɔrahki** ice cream *p. 270*
**ɔshkachehkini** iron pot *p. 248*
**ɔshta** blue; green; purple *p. 142*

**P**

**-pa** too; also; even *p. 102*
**pahchu** to put on jewelry, glasses *p. 176*
**pahita** lightning *p. 183*
**pahitaniyu** computer *p. 128*
**pahitaniyu ɛsa** tablet *p. 136*
**pahitaniyutohku** laptop *p. 136*
**pahitawali** phone *p. 132*
**pahitawirani** calculator *p. 136*
**paka (II)** to reply; to answer *p. 263*
**pala** to trap *p. 252*
**pala** to win *pp. 38, 110*
**palatohku** goal; point; score *pp. 38, 110*
**pali** to take off shoes *p. 176*
**palu (II)** to sell *p. 263*
**panu** very *p. 110*
**paru** to take off coats, stockings *p. 176*
**pata** to fall *p. 40*
**pɛlka** flat *p. 148*
**-p'ɛsha** to be sad; to be unhappy *p. 114*
**pikatishi** east *p. 219*
**pira (II)** to become; to turn into *p. 263*
**pita** to walk *p. 26*
**po** to look at; to watch; to see; to read *p. 76*
**-po-** to try *p. 276*
**polun sahku** one hundred *p. 60*
**polunt'ɛ hayi** million *p. 298*
**pɔhta (II)** to boil (something) *p. 257*
**puhti** to be foggy *p. 288*
**puna** ball *pp. 38, 76*
**punatarahpani** stickball (game); ball sticks *pp. 38, 102*

**R**

**ra** hard *p. 148*
**raha** to comb one's hair *p. 45*
**rahi (II)** to thunder *p. 288*

**Rahihta** the Thunder Being *p. 288*
**rahpa** to play ball *pp. 38, 98*
**rahpa (II)** to play (stick)ball *p. 263*
**rahpu** to put on (coat, stockings, etc.) *pp. 156, 176*
**rahpuntira** coat *p. 156*
**rahpuntira yuru** overcoat *p. 156*
**rapa** to kill *p. 244*
**Rap'ili** Tuesday *p. 69*
**Rap'onihku** Wednesday *p. 69*
**rapu** to sleep *p. 26*
**Rapumanku** Thursday *p. 69*
**Rapusahku** Monday *p. 69*
**Rapusinku** Friday *p. 69*
**rasu** to unbelt *p. 176*
**rayi** mulberry *p. 241*
**ri** house; home; building *p. 98*
**rihkɔra** table *p. 128*
**rihkɔratahina** desk *p. 132*
**rihk'ɔsht'elutohku** yaupon holly *p. 281*
**rihku** tree *p. 142*
**rihkuyahoni** tree branch *p. 76*
**rikafi** café; coffee shop *p. 204*
**rikini** too (much) *p. 201*
**risa** multi-colored; variegated; dappled *p. 142*
**risep'ɛhɛ** health center *p. 219*
**-rishi** nose *p. 170*
**ritahɛra** police station *p. 204*
**ritalapu** store; market *p. 156*
**ritarapu** hotel *p. 204*
**ritarohinapo** library *p. 204*
**ritasaku** restaurant *p. 204*
**ritaworu** school *p. 128*
**ritaworutohku** classroom *p. 128*
**Ritetimili** Cultural & Educational Resources Center (CERC) *p. 219*
**riwantaha** museum *p. 219*
**rohina** letters; alphabet *p. 76*
**romana** heavy *p. 148*
**romantohku** slow; slowly *p. 110*
**roptini** cotton *p. 201*
**rowina** book; paper *p. 84*
**rowinahina** notebook *p. 132*
**rowinara** whiteboard *p. 128*
**rɔhpa (II)** to roast *p. 252*
**rɔhpant** beside; next to; near; close by *p. 204*
**rɔwa** white *p. 142*
**ruhkini** in front *p. 214*
**rukasa** ugly *p. 148*
**rurɔwa** white hickory *p. 281*
**rushta** rabbit *pp. 153, 252*
**rut'ɛ elu** walnut *p. 248*

## S

**sa** dog *p. 76*
**sachi** to rain *p. 288*
**sahku** one *p. 60*
**sahu** other *p. 110*
**saku** to eat *p. 30*
**saku** food *p. 76*
**sama (II)** to cook; to bake *p. 252*
**Samdi** Saturday *p. 69*
**sapi** to beat down (rain) *p. 288*
**sara** to pray; sorry *p. 40*
**saru** to belt *p. 176*
**satohku** puppy *p. 231*
**say'ɔhta** bead *p. 167*
**sehi** to rise (of the sun); morning; dawn *p. 284*
**sehi lapu** good morning *p. 214*
**sehinta** tomorrow *p. 84*
**sehitihch** at dawn; when the sun rises/rose *p. 226*
**-sepi** to be in poor health *p. 114*

**serunasa** they *(fd/p)* know *p. 121*
**serusa** they *(mp)* know *p. 121*
**sɛhapo** to examine *p. 303*
**sɛkana** pecan *p. 263*
**-sɛma** gender-number ending *(mp)* *pp. 19, 20*
**sɛma** they *(mp)* *p. 12*
**-sh** to; toward *p. 98*
**shahu** to patter *p. 288*
**-shari** to have time *p. 119*
**-shayi** husband *p. 186*
**-sh'ɛlama** to be pitiable *p. 114*
**-sh'ɛpa** to be happy; to like to; to enjoy *pp. 114, 238*
**-shi** at; location of *p. 98*
**shihka (II)** to help; to assist; to aid *p. 263*
**Shihkalpalkaku** Natchez person; Natchez people; Natchez tribe *p. 244*
**shihpari** beans *p. 296*
**shihpi (II)** to drive (a vehicle) *p. 263*
**shimi** to play *p. 30*
**shimila** blue jay *p. 142*
**-shira** back *p. 170*
**shira (II)** to strain; to exert oneself *p. 263*
**-shkan** but; nevertheless; however *p. 244*
**-shniyu** to be lonely *p. 114*
**-shohu** mouth *p. 170*
**-shpitu** to forget *p. 119*
**-shruka** to be afraid *p. 244*
**-shtahahki** only *p. 119*
**-shtahpu** face *p. 170*
**-shtamar'ɛhɛ** to be rude; to be disrespectful *p. 114*
**-shtamari** to be respectful; to be polite *p. 114*
**-shtihki** toward *p. 219*
**-shtosu** eye *p. 170*
**-shtosu mayisahu** left eye *p. 217*
**-shtosu tirishi** right eye *p. 217*
**-shtuku** can; able to *p. 270*
**shuchi** to shoot (with a bow and arrow) *p. 55*
**shuhpa (II)** to suck (something) up *p. 293*
**shuhpali** pants *p. 156*
**shuhpali kochu** shorts *p. 156*
**shulihkitohku** squash *p. 296*
**si-** they *(mp stative)*; their *(mp inalienable)* *pp. 120, 162*
**sihina** clean *p. 268*
**sihk-** they *(mp stative)*; their *(mp alienable)*; them *(mp)* *pp. 116, 158, 227*
**sihkpih'ɔta** she hid them *p. 96*
**-sihu** to be thirsty *p. 119*
**sin-** they *(fd/p stative)*; their *(fd/p inalienable)* *pp. 120, 162*
**-sina** they _____ed *(fd)* *p. 50*
**-sinima** gender-number ending *(fd/p)* *pp. 19, 20*
**sinima** they *(fd/p)* *p. 12*
**sink-** they *(fd/p stative)*; their *(fd/p alienable)*; them *(fd/p)* *pp. 116, 158, 227*
**sinkara** they *(f)* have *p. 66*
**sinkshku** equals *p. 58*
**sinku** five *p. 60*
**-sinta** they *(fd/p)* _____ed (II) *p. 259*
**-sipi** to be cold (person) *p. 114*
**-siti** they _____ed *(fp)* *p. 46*
**suhpi** supper *p. 252*
**suhpi (II)** to leave (bread) to rise; to soak *p. 257*

**T**

**-ta** they _____ed *(mp)* *p. 46*

**ta-** the; some *p. 19*
**ta-** -er (agentive/instrumental) *p. 296*
**taharani** fiddle; musician; singer *p. 276*
**taharanishuru** flute *p. 296*
**tahch'a** moon; month *p. 66*
**Tahch'ahipu** May *p. 68*
**Tahch'aruwina** August *p. 68*
**Tahch'aruwina Tehukuma** September *p. 68*
**Tahch'atapa** April *p. 68*
**Tahch'awɛka** January *p. 68*
**Tahch'awɛka Tehukuma** February *p. 68*
**Tahch'awɛra** October *p. 68*
**tahch'i** sun *p. 156*
**tahch'i tapo** sunglasses *p. 156*
**Tahch'asap'ara** December *p. 68*
**Tahch'asap'aratohku** November *p. 68*
**taheni** greetings *p. 10*
**tahi (II)** to string an instrument *p. 276*
**tahina** pen; pencil; marker *p. 128*
**tahka** bat (animal) *p. 309*
**-tahki** only; nothing but *p. 252*
**tahkishi** skin; hide; bark; shell *p. 142*
**taka** thing *p. 161*
**takahpuni** scissors *p. 128*
**takashimi** toy *p. 303*
**takayuwa** gift *p. 231*
**tama** to be with; to live with; to accompany *p. 226*
**tamarɔha** mountain cave *p. 309*
**-tan** polite command *p. 88*
**tanahchuni** stickers *p. 128*
**tanira** thief *p. 91*
**tapa** to plant; to farm; a farm *pp. 201, 296*
**tapi** to grab; to catch *p. 76*
**tapiheni** to shake hands *p. 303*
**tapo** glasses *p. 156*
**tarahpani** ballplayer *p. 38*
**tarku** the woods; the forest *p. 102*
**tarukɔsa** hickory sticks stripped of bark *p. 281*
**tasahchuni** glue *p. 128*
**tasapashi** north *p. 219*
**tashle** beautiful *p. 148*
**Tasiwa** Owl-mammoth *p. 55*
**tatapa** farmer *p. 296*
**Ta'uchɛhkatonayi** Old Toad Woman *p. 55*
**Tawatoruwishipɛta** Coulée de Grues *p. 223*
**tawɛhani** light *p. 128*
**tawɛhani yuru** laser *p. 298*
**tawista** candy; sweets *p. 231*
**tawohku** hat *p. 156*
**taworu** student *p. 88*
**taworuni** teacher *p. 58*
**taya korini ili** class II verb *p. 252*
**taya korini sahku** class I verb *p. 252*
**taya waka** command *p. 84*
**tayihku** seven *p. 60*
**Tayoroni nuhchi** Tunica woman *p. 153*
**Tayoroniku** the Tunica person/people; the Tunica tribe *p. 244*
**Tayoroniku-Halayihku** Tunica-Biloxi *p. 64*
**Tayoronishi** Tunica man *p. 153*
**tehi (II)** to go around; to circle *p. 263*
**tehk'elukayi** orange (fruit) *pp. 142, 145*
**teliy'oni** doll *p. 128*
**terusa** she knows *p. 121*
**teshu (II)** to eat breakfast *p. 263*
**teti** road; path; trail; way *p. 204*
**tetimili** culture *p. viii*
**tetirihku** nature trail *p. 219*
**tetisa** her name is *p. 15*

**tewali** fast *p. 110*
**-t'ɛ** big *p. 66*
**tɛnakɔlakuwatohku** hummingbird *p. 183*
**tɛnayi** ember *p. 268*
**tɛrashki** page *p. 128*
**(-)tɛya** plus *p. 58*
**-ti** she _____ed *p. 41*
**ti-** she *(stative)*; her *(inalienable)* *pp. 120, 162*
**tihchɛt** she, on her part *p. 15*
**tihchi** she *p. 12*
**tihika** year; summer *p. 58*
**tihikashi** south *p. 219*
**Tihikatahch'a** June *p. 68*
**Tihikatahch'a Tehukuma** July *p. 68*
**tihk-** she *(stative)*; her *(alienable)*; her *(object)* *pp. 116, 158, 227*
**tihkara** she (it) has *p. 66*
**tihkashuhki** her (its) day *p. 66*
**tihkyuk'aki** she is (_____ years old) *p. 58*
**tika** big *p. 148*
**tikahch** thank you *p. 10*
**tipirashu** her birthday *p. 66*
**tira** dress *p. 156*
**tirahalu** underwear *p. 156*
**tiratamihku** headband *p. 156*
**tiratasaru** belt *p. 156*
**tirishi** right side; on the right; in front of *p. 209*
**Tirishichɔha Hipu** Chief-Ahead Dance *p. 268*
**tishi** to sleet *p. 288*
**tishki** broth; soup; stew *p. 276*
**tishuhki** door *p. 84*
**tishuhɔhka** window *p. 204*
**tishuma** meat *p. 252*
**tisihku** eight *p. 60*
**titihki** bayou; canal; stream *p. 204*
**titiht'ɛ** river *p. 238*
**-tohku** small; little; young *p. 270*
**tohkuhch** please *p. 88*
**-tohkuni** to be tired *p. 114*
**tohkusahku** nine *p. 60*
**tolu** full (moon); round *p. 284*
**tomu** to pound; to mash *p. 252*
**tonimahoni hal'ukini** reservation; Native American village *p. 219*
**tostohku** baby *p. 186*
**tɔha (II)** (the sun) to pass the meridian *p. 284*
**tɔhashi** casino *p. 219*
**Tuwatasiwat'ɛ** Owl-Mammoth *p. 55*

## U

**u-** he *(stative)*; his *(inalienable)* *pp. 120, 162*
**Uhayishiku** The One Above *p. 296*
**uhk-** he *(stative)*; his *(alienable)*; him *pp. 116, 158, 227*
**uhkkosu** its color *p. 142*
**uhkyuk'aki** he is (_____ years old) *p. 58*
**uki** to sit; to dwell; to remain *p. 49*
**ukitamashu** bench *p. 136*
**un-** they *(md stative)*; their *(md inalienable)* *pp. 120, 162*
**-una** they _____ed *(md)* *p. 50*
**-unima** gender-number ending *(md)* *pp. 19, 20*
**unima** they *(md)* *p. 12*
**unk-** they *(md stative)*; their *(md alienable)*; them *(md)* *pp. 116, 158, 227*
**-unta** they *(md)* _____ed (II) *p. 259*
**upirashu** his birthday *p. 66*

**ura** it is (lying down) *p. 214*
**uru (II)** to whoop; to yell; to shout *p. 263*
**-uta** he _____ed (II) *p. 259*
**uwɛt** he, on his part *p. 15*
**uwi** he *p. 12*

## W

**wachi** to fight *p. 34*
**waha** to cry *p. 34*
**waka** to command; an order *p. 296*
**-wan** in order to *p. 241*
**-wana** to want *p. 114*
**wantaha** a long time ago *p. 161*
**weht'ira** your *(ms)* clothes *p. 156*
**weni** to find; to discover *p. 76*
**wentisa** your *(md/p)* names are *p. 15*
**werunasa** you *(md/p)* know *p. 121*
**werusa** you *(ms)* know *p. 121*
**wetisa** you *(ms)* are named *p. 10*
**wɛha** to be sunny *p. 284*
**wɛka** (the moon) to wane *p. 284*
**wɛra (II)** to hunt *p. 252*
**wɛsa** to jump *p. 26*
**-wi** he _____ed *p. 41*
**wi (II)** to listen *p. 252*
**wi-** you *(ms stative)*; your *(ms inalienable)* *pp. 120, 162*
**wichi** to climb; to mount *p. 276*
**wihk-** you *(ms stative)*; your *(ms alienable)*; you *(ms object)* *pp. 116, 158, 227*
**wihkyuk'aki** you *(ms)* are (_____ years old) *p. 58*
**wihu** to blow gently (wind) *p. 288*
**wila** to braid; to weave *p. 238*
**win-** you *(md/p stative)*; your *(md/p inalienable)* *pp. 120, 162*
**-wina** you _____ed *(md)* *p. 50*
**winima** you *(md/p)* *p. 12*
**winimat** you *(md/p)*, on your part *p. 15*
**wink-** you *(md/p stative)*; your *(md/p alienable)*; you *(md/p object)* *pp. 116, 158, 227*
**-winta** you *(md/p)* _____ed (II) *p. 259*
**wipirashu** your *(ms)* birthday *p. 66*
**wira (II)** to ask a question; to count *p. 252*
**wirakashi** numbers *p. 58*
**wirakashihta** ordinal numbers *p. 64*
**wiralepi (II)** to ask a question *p. 303*
**wirani** minute; time *p. 128*
**tiranit'ɛ** hour *p. 128*
**wiranitohku** second (unit of time) *p. 119*
**wishi** water *p. 76*
**wishipɛta** pond *p. 98*
**wishita'eri** pitcher; water jug *p. 252*
**wishiyimohku** tea *p. 257*
**wista (II)** to sweeten; to tame *p. 257*
**-wita** you *(ms)* _____ed (II) *p. 259*
**-witi** you _____ed *(mp)* *p. 46*
**wiya** to throw *p. 76*
**wo** to build (a fire); to turn (something) on *pp. 128, 142*
**wohku** to go fishing; to catch fish *p. 238*
**wohku** to put on a hat *p. 176*
**wolushi** restroom *p. 204*
**woru** to learn; to study *p. 49*
**woru (II)** to teach *p. 252*
**wosu** striped *p. 142*
**woyu** to swim *p. 30*
**woyushi** pool *p. 204*

## Y

**ya** deer *pp. 167, 252*
**ya** to do; to make *p. 26*
**yahki** times (multiplied by) *p. 58*
**-yahpa** to be hungry *p. 119*

**yaka** to come back *p. 45*
**yaka ɔshta** little blue heron *p. 145*
**yaluhki** mushroom *pp. 96, 142*
**yama** to dress in finery; to put on regalia *p. 176*
**yana** to talk; to speak; word *pp. 45, 88*
**yanalepi (II)** to speak; to talk *p. 303*
**yanalepini** dialogue *p. viii*
**yanishi** bull; bovine *p. 142*
**yanishi nuhchi** cow *p. 142*
**yanishikashi** buffalo *p. 167*
**-yari** to be ashamed *p. 119*
**-yaru** to be curious *p. 114*
**yasha ihkyakati** it hurts (me) *p. 170*
**-yashi** to be angry *p. 114*
**yayi** to take care of; to save; to be saved *pp. 226, 276*
**yɛhtat'ɛ** turkey *pp. 167, 252*
**yimohku** plant; herb *p. 281*
**yishi** raccoon *p. 167*
**Yishi Hipu** Raccoon Dance *p. 268*
**yit'ɛ** potato *p. 252*
**yoluyana** vocabulary *p. viii*
**yoluyana-*ka*** question word *p. 110*
**Yoroni** Tunica person; Tunica people *p. 241*
**yorum'aha** wild animal *p. 107*
**yowi (II)** to blow circularly (wind) *p. 288*
**yoyani** work *pp. 88, 238*
**yoyani ya** to work *p. 49*
**yɔla** to leave *p. 49*
**yɔla** empty *p. 148*
**yuhtari** feather *p. 167*
**yuka** to arrive *p. 40*
**yuki** to prepare food *p. 241*
**yunka taharani** fiddle strings *p. 276*
**yuru** tall; long *p. 148*
**yusawa** southern sugar maple *p. 248*
**yuwa** to give *p. 231*

# Appendix E: Common phrases

**Heni!** Hi!

**Sehi lapu!** Good morning!

**Tɔha lapu!** Good afternoon!

**Lati lapu!** Good evening!

**Lawu lapu!** Good night!

**Kanahku hayihta?** What's up?

**Lapuya akawitiki!** Welcome! *(said to a group)*

**Lapuya ak'aki!** Welcome! *(said to one woman)*

**Lapuya ak'iki!** Welcome! *(said to one man)*

**Eti hɛma lapun?** How are you? *(said to a woman)*

**Eti ma lapun?** How are you? *(said to a man)*

**Kanahku hetisa?** What's your name? *(said to a woman)*

**Kanahku wetisa?** What's your name? *(said to a man)*

**Kata hɛna?** Where are you from? *(said to a woman)*

**Kata wina?** Where are you from? *(said to a man)*

**Hita!** Take care! *(used as a farewell)*

**Apo'inan!** See you! *(said to one person)*

**Apo'itin!** See you! *(said to more than one person)*

**Lapuhch!** (That) would be a good thing! *(Often said when making a request, i.e., "if you X, that would be a good thing." **Lapuhch** is also sometimes used to end a conversation.)*

**Tikahch** Thank you

**"Tikahch" ninishtuk'ɔhɔ amari.** I can't thank you enough.

**Tohkuhch** Please

**Sara** (I'm) sorry

**Wayitohku!** (Be) careful!

**Moyutohku!** (Be) careful! (Be) quiet!

**Romantohku!** Quietly! Softly!

**Dan?** Ready?

**Hinto!** Come on!

**Ko'o!** Great!

**Ko!** Wow!

**Wo'o!** Nice! Great!

**Kashi!** True!

**Kashilehe!** Of course!

**Erusa.** I know.

**Erus'aha.** I don't know.

**Erunasa.** We know/understand.

**Herusan?** Do you understand? *(said to a woman)*

**Werusan?** Do you understand? *(said to a man)*

**Hap'aki!** Stop! *(said to a woman)*

**Hap'iki!** Stop! *(said to a man)*

**Hipirashu lapu!** Happy birthday! *(said to a woman)*

**Wipirashu lapu!** Happy birthday! *(said to a man)*

## Cultural Phrases

*Stickball phrases*

**puna tarahpani** Stickball stick

**puna** ball, stickball game

**rihkuchahka** goalpost

**palatohku** goal/score

**Ihkwiy'aki!** Throw it to me! *(said to a woman)*

**Ihkwiy'iki!** Throw it to me! *(said to a man)*

**Lɔt'aki!** Run! *(said to a woman)*

**Lɔt'iki!** Run! *(said to a man)*

*Powwow phrases*

**Heht'irayama tashle!** Your regalia is beautiful! *(said to a woman)*

**Weht'irayama tashle!** Your regalia is beautiful! *(said to a man)*

**Kunkuri tapɛkasɛma hapata.** The drummers stopped.

**Tahipusɛma akakata.** The dancers are entering.

**Tahipusɛma hali hipu akurani tehihkanta.**
The dancers are circling the powwow grounds.

## Holiday phrases and wishes

Holidays below are listed in order, starting with the Green Corn Ceremony, which traditionally marked the new year.

| Date | Holiday | Phrase |
|---|---|---|
| July 1[1] | Green Corn festival | **Hahka Ɔshta mari inksh'ɛpa.**<br>We are happy to gather the Green Corn. |
| July 4 | Fourth of July | **Ashuhki Manku hilahta!**<br>Happy Fourth of July! |
| Sep 4 | Labor Day | **Tayoyani Sihkashuna lapu!**<br>Have a good Labor Day! |
| Sep 22 | Native American Day | **Hɛ'ɛsh Ashuhki Onimahoni.**<br>Today is Native American Day. |
| Sep 25 | Tunica-Biloxi Federal Acknowledgment Day | **Hɛ'ɛsh inkonisɛma inktakashini erunasa.**<br>Today, we remember the Federal Acknowledgment of our Tribe. |
| | Indigenous People's Day | **Hɛ'ɛsh Onimahoni Inkashuhki.**<br>Today is Indigenous People's Day. |
| Oct 31 | Halloween | **Lawu Nɛra lapu!**<br>Happy Halloween! |
| Nov 1 | All Saints Day | **Hɛ'ɛsh Nɛra Hotu Hal'ukini Atɛhkala Kichusɛma Sihkashuhki.**<br>Today is the Day of All Saints. |
| Nov 11 | Veteran's Day | **Nakasɛma hotu henihkiti.**<br>We salute all soldiers. |
| | Thanksgiving Day | **Ashuhki Tikahchyuwa hilahta!**<br>Happy Thanksgiving Day! |
| Dec 25 | Christmas | **Ingras'ashuhki lapu!**<br>Merry Christmas! |
| Jan 1 | New Year's Day | **Tihika Nisa lapu!**<br>Happy New Year! |

[1] The Green Corn festival was traditionally celebrated at the summer solstice; it is now celebrated July 1st.

| | | |
|---|---|---|
| | Martin Luther King Day | **Hɛ'ɛsh Martin Luther King Juniorku erunasa.**<br>Today we remember Martin Luther King Jr. |
| | Lundi Gras | **Rapusahku Maka hilahta!**<br>Happy Lundi Gras! |
| | Mardi Gras | **Rapili Maka hilahta!**<br>Happy Mardi Gras! |
| Feb 14 | Valentine's Day | **Ash'ohniyu hilahta!**<br>Happy Valentine's Day! |
| | Ash Wednesday | **Hɛ'ɛsh Raponihku Ayihahpushi.**<br>Today is Ash Wednesday. |
| | President's Day | **Hɛ'ɛsh chɔhasɛma hotu erunasa.**<br>Today we remember all presidents. |
| Mar 17 | St. Patrick's Day | **Ash'oshta hilahta!**<br>Happy St. Patrick's Day! |
| | Good Friday | **Hɛ'ɛsh Rapusinku Uhayishiku.**<br>Today is Good Friday. |
| | Easter Sunday | **Ashuhkimeli hilahta!**<br>Happy Easter! |
| | Mother's Day | **Ashuhki Ingachisinima hilahta!**<br>Happy Mother's Day! |
| | Memorial Day | **Hɛ'ɛsh nakasɛma hotu erunasa.**<br>Today we remember all soldiers. |
| | Father's Day | **Ashuhki Ensisɛma hilahta!**<br>Happy Father's Day! |

# Tunica at a Glance

## Word Order

The basic order of words in Tunica is

**Subject + Object + Verb**

and adjectives come after the noun they describe.

## Gender-Number Endings

| | Singular | Dual | Plural |
|---|---|---|---|
| *f* | -hchi | -sinima | -sinima |
| *m* | -ku | -unima | -sɛma |

For inanimate objects and most animals, groups of one or two will use the masculine endings, while plurals and collectives will use the feminine endings. These are also used for people in the 3rd person.

## Yoluyana Ka-

| | |
|---|---|
| Kaku? | Who? |
| Kanahku? | What? |
| Ka'ash? | When? |
| Kata? | Where? |
| Kaya? | Why? |
| Kana? | How? |
| Kashku? | How many/much? |

## Subject Pronouns

| | Singular | Dual | Plural |
|---|---|---|---|
| 1st | ima | inima | inima |
| 2nd *f* | hɛma | hinima | hinima |
| 2nd *m* | ma | winima | winima |
| 3rd *f* | tihchi | sinima | sinima |
| 3rd *m* | uwi | unima | sɛma |

## Vowel Blending

When an ending beginning with h follows a word with more than one syllable, the **h goes away** and the vowels that are together blend. This includes when you use taya korini ili endings. When 2 vowels come together, a **glottal stop** goes before the blended vowel.

## Forming a Question

For yes/no questions, add **-n** to the end of the normal sentence:

Harakati. →Harakati**n**?

For all other questions, use a question word from the table above:

**Kanahku** harakati?

## Vowel Blending Patterns

| | | | | | | |
|---|---|---|---|---|---|---|
| a + a → a | e + a → ɛ | ɛ + a → ɛ | i + a → ɛ | o + a → ɔ | ɔ + a → ɔ | u + a → ɔ |
| a + e → e | e + e → e | ɛ + e → ɛ | i + e → e | | | u + e → o |
| a + ɛ → ɛ | | ɛ + ɛ → ɛ | i + ɛ → ɛ | o + ɛ → ɔ | | u + ɛ → ɔ |
| a + i → i | | ɛ + i → ɛ | i + i → i | | | u + i → i |
| a + o → o | | ɛ + o → ɛ | I + o → o | o + o → o | | |
| a + ɔ → ɔ | | ɛ + ɔ → ɛ | I + ɔ → ɔ | | ɔ + ɔ → ɔ | |
| a + u → u | | ɛ + u → ɛ | i + u → u | | | u + u → u |

## This and That

**Singular**

| | |
|---|---|
| hɛku | this |
| hiku | that |
| miku | that over |

**Dual**

| | |
|---|---|
| hɛ'unima | these two |
| hi'unima | those two |
| mi'unima | those two over there |

**Plural**

| | |
|---|---|
| hɛsinima | these |
| hisinima | those |
| misinima | those over there |

**Places**

| | |
|---|---|
| hɛhchi | here |
| hihchi | there |
| mihchi | over there |

These can also be used for indicating any noun. The prefixes **hɛ-** 'this,' **hi-** 'that,' and **mi-** 'that over there' are added to the beginning of a noun like **minu** to make **hɛminu**, **himinu**, and **miminu**.

## Completive Endings

**Taya korini sahku**

| | Singular | Dual | Plural |
|---|---|---|---|
| 1st | -ni | -ina | -iti |
| 2nd *f* | -a | -(h)ina | -(h)iti |
| 2nd *m* | -i | -wina | -witi |
| 3rd *f* | -ti | -sina | -siti |
| 3rd *m* | -wi | -una | -ta |

| Example | Singular | Dual | Plural |
|---|---|---|---|
| 1st | hipuni | hip'ina | hip'iti |
| 2nd *f* | hip'ɔ | hipina | hipiti |
| 2nd *m* | hip'i | hipuwina | hipuwiti |
| 3rd *f* | hiputi | hipusina | hipusiti |
| 3rd *m* | hipuwi | hip'una | hiputa |

**Taya korini ili**

| | Singular | Dual | Plural |
|---|---|---|---|
| 1st | -htani | -inta | -inta |
| 2nd *f* | -(h)ɛta | -(h)ɛnta | -(h)ɛnta |
| 2nd *m* | -wita | -winta | -winta |
| 3rd *f* | -ata | -sinta | -sinta |
| 3rd *m* | -uta | -unta | -anta |

| Example | Singular | Dual | Plural |
|---|---|---|---|
| 1st | uruhtani | ur'inta | ur'inta |
| 2nd *f* | urɔta | urɔnta | urɔnta |
| 2nd *m* | uruwita | uruwinta | uruwinta |
| 3rd *f* | ur'ɔta | urusinta | urusinta |
| 3rd *m* | ur'uta | ur'unta | ur'ɔnta |

## Habitual Endings

**Taya korini sahku**

| | Singular | Dual | Plural |
|---|---|---|---|
| 1st | -kani | -hkina | -hkiti |
| 2nd *f* | -ka | -hkhina | -hkhiti |
| 2nd *m* | -ki | -hkwina | -hkwiti |
| 3rd *f* | -kati | -hksina | -hksiti |
| 3rd *m* | -ku | -hkuna | -kata |

| Example | Singular | Dual | Plural |
|---|---|---|---|
| 1st | hipukani | hipuhkina | hipuhkiti |
| 2nd *f* | hipuka | hipuhkhina | hipuhkhiti |
| 2nd *m* | hipuki | hipuhkwina | hipuhkwiti |
| 3rd *f* | hipukati | hipuhksina | hipuhksiti |
| 3rd *m* | hipuku | hipuhkuna | hipukata |

**Taya korini ili**

| | Singular | Dual | Plural |
|---|---|---|---|
| 1st | -hkatani | -hkinta | -hkinta |
| 2nd *f* | -hkhɛta | -hkhɛnta | -hkhɛnta |
| 2nd *m* | -hkwita | -hkwinta | -hkwinta |
| 3rd *f* | -hkata | -hksinta | -hksinta |
| 3rd *m* | -hkuta | -hkunta | -hkanta |

| Example | Singular | Dual | Plural |
|---|---|---|---|
| 1st | uruhkatani | uruhkinta | uruhkinta |
| 2nd *f* | uruhkhɛta | uruhkhɛnta | uruhkhɛnta |
| 2nd *m* | uruhkwita | uruhkwinta | uruhkwinta |
| 3rd *f* | uruhkata | uruhksinta | uruhksinta |
| 3rd *m* | uruhkuta | uruhkunta | uruhkanta |

## Taya Waka

When telling someone to do something, you use the verb root + the completive ending + one of three endings: **-tan** (polite), **-ki** (informal), or **-hchan** (strong)

| Polite | Singular | Plural |
|---|---|---|
| 1st | --- | hap'ititan |
| 2nd *f* | hap'atan | hapititan |
| 2nd *m* | hap'itan | hapawititan |

| Informal | Singular | Plural |
|---|---|---|
| 1st | --- | hap'itiki |
| 2nd *f* | hap'aki | hapitiki |
| 2nd *m* | hap'iki | hapawitiki |

| Strong | Singular | Plural |
|---|---|---|
| 1st | --- | hap'itihchan |
| 2nd *f* | hap'ahchan | hapithchan |
| 2nd *m* | hap'ihchan | hapawitihchan |

## Negative Taya Waka

To say "Don't **X**!" add **-ahatan** to the verb root with no other endings:

Hap'**ahatan**!

## Possessives and Taya Wana

Don't forget: Stative verbs take the same prefixes as alienable nouns, except for some vowel-initial taya wana that take the inalienable set.

**Alienable Prefixes**

| | Singular | Dual | Plural |
|---|---|---|---|
| 1st | ihk- | ink- | ink- |
| 2nd *f* | hihk- | hink- | hink- |
| 2nd *m* | wihk- | wink- | wink- |
| 3rd *f* | tihk- | sink- | sink- |
| 3rd *m* | uhk- | unk- | sihk- |

| Example | Singular | Dual | Plural |
|---|---|---|---|
| 1st | ihkminu | inkminu | inkminu |
| 2nd *f* | hihkminu | hinkminu | hinkminu |
| 2nd *m* | wihkminu | winkminu | winkminu |
| 3rd *f* | tihkminu | sinkminu | sinkminu |
| 3rd *m* | uhkminu | unkminu | sihkminu |

**Inalienable Prefixes**

| | Singular | Dual | Plural |
|---|---|---|---|
| 1st | i- | in- | in- |
| 2nd *f* | hi- | hin- | hin- |
| 2nd *m* | wi- | win- | win- |
| 3rd *f* | ti- | sin- | sin- |
| 3rd *m* | u- | un- | si- |

| Example | Singular | Dual | Plural |
|---|---|---|---|
| 1st | irishi | inrishi | inrishi |
| 2nd *f* | hirishi | hinrishi | hinrishi |
| 2nd *m* | wirishi | winrishi | winrishi |
| 3rd *f* | tirishi | sinrishi | sinrishi |
| 3rd *m* | urishi | unrishi | sirishi |

# For Indiana University Press

Emily Baugh, Editorial Assistant
Tony Brewer, Artist and Book Designer
Brian Carroll, Rights Manager
Gary Dunham, Acquisitions Editor and Director
Brenna Hosman, Production Coordinator
Katie Huggins, Production Manager
Darja Malcolm-Clarke, Project Manager/Editor
Dan Pyle, Online Publishing Manager
Pam Rude, Senior Artist and Book Designer
Stephen Williams, Marketing and Publicity Manager